FAITH
ALONE

STUDIES IN HEBREWS 11

PAUL YOUNG

FAITH ALONE: STUDIES IN HEBREWS 11
By: Paul Young
Copyright © 2016
GOSPEL FOLIO PRESS
All Rights Reserved

Published by Gospel Folio Press
304 Killaly St. West Port Colborne, ON L3K 6A6

ISBN: 9781927521861

Cover design by Danielle Robins

Printed in Canada

PREFACE

These brief biographical studies of the great men and women of God who are found in the triumphant eleventh chapter of Hebrews were first produced for the programme "Truth for Today" which was aired on Trans World Radio. They are now given a more permanent format and we trust that they will be read with prayerful interest.

The desire is that in our generation there will be men and women raised up by God with faith, vision, loyalty and commitment who will follow in the footsteps of these mighty saints of God from a previous age. We serve the same God and have the wonderful resources of prayer, the Bible and the Holy Spirit. Therefore, we have no excuse for not fulfilling our calling and potential in the service of the Lord.

My thanks to all who made this book possible.

Paul Young

CONTENTS

CHAPTER 1

FAITH

"Faith sees God and God sees faith."

Anonymous

Now faith is being sure of what we hope for and certain of what we do not see. This is what the ancients were commended for. By faith we understand that the universe was formed at God's command, so that what is seen was not made out of what was visible.

Hebrews 11:1-3

This fascinating chapter, namely Hebrews 11, is a great gallery of Old Testament men and women who achieved something successful and special. They did not succeed because of their outstanding brain power or great physical strength but the recurring theme is their faith. They trusted the Lord and as a result they achieved what they did *"by faith"*. Through total dependence upon Almighty God they succeeded and won great and notable victories. Indeed we are told *"But without faith it is impossible to please* [God]*..."* (11:6). Thus faith is vitally important and yet there is a great deal of confusion on the part of many people today as to what constitutes faith.

BELIEVING WHAT ISN'T TRUE!

I well remember being in the dentist's chair and had my gum injected by the dentist ready for the drill and a filling. After I had waited for the usual length of time the dentist asked whether the anaesthetic was working and I said, "I hope so". He replied that it was a scientific fact and mentioned something about how the anaesthetic worked. Then he said, "I thought in your profession that you were supposed to encourage faith?" To which I replied that it had to be faith in the right thing. When he had my mouth open at full stretch and had filled it with instruments and fingers he then made a really provocative statement. He said, "I heard a definition of faith which is believing what isn't true!" I could not reply with any coherence because I was unable to speak. However, there may be many people who think that Christian faith is simply about believing in something that isn't true. Yet when one studies the evidence about Christianity we are left with the certainty that it is based upon truth, rock solid evidence and indisputable historical facts. Christian faith is not a jump into the dark but a decision made upon clear and powerful evidence. One writer has made this abundantly clear in his book, *Evidence that Demands a Verdict* (Josh McDowell). Thus if anyone is willing to look at Christianity with an open mind they will come face to face with overwhelming factual, historical evidence for its truthfulness.

BELIEVING ONLY WHAT I CAN SEE!

Some years ago I spoke at a lunchtime Christian Union meeting in a school and at the end I asked for questions. Usually this is greeted by silence or with so many questions that one couldn't begin to answer them all. This meeting was different as on the back row was one boy with a question or at least a statement. Looking at his friends he seemed to give the impression that what he had to say would demolish Christianity for all time. He stated that he only believed what he could see. He could see the desk and the walls and so could accept them as real but he couldn't see God or Jesus and so couldn't believe in them.

I suppose he felt rather intellectual and in response I said, "When I was young I used to play cricket and rugby, but whenever I kicked or threw the ball into the air it always returned to earth. What a miracle that was!" He rather scornfully told me of Isaac Newton who sat under a tree and an apple fell on his head and he asked why the apple came down and didn't go up. The result was that he discovered the law of gravity and that is why a ball falls to earth. So I said, "Show me gravity." The obvious point is that gravity, like the wind or magnetism, is invisible. So the questioner did believe in things he couldn't see. However he should then have said and maybe he wasn't wise enough for this yet, that you can't see gravity but you can see what it does. You can't see magnetism but you can see the effects of magnetism. Similarly I would have answered, "You can't see God but you can see the effects of God's presence in a human life when someone places their faith and trust in the Lord Jesus." When we exercise faith in the Lord and receive Him as our Saviour a wonderful transformation takes place. God indwells us by His Spirit and we are made good enough for heaven. The drunkard becomes sober, the thief becomes honest, the adulterer becomes faithful and people are totally transformed. We may not see God with our physical eyes but we can see what He does in a person who is committed in faith to Christ.

ONLY THE WEAK BELIEVE

Some people have concluded that Christian faith is a crutch for the weak, namely those who are psychologically or emotionally unable to stand on their own two feet. These may be the very young who don't understand fully the issues of life, or the elderly who feel a deep sense of their own mortality. However, we must point out that some of the toughest and strong minded of people have been Christians. The early disciples were so committed to Christ that they were willing to endure torture, persecution and even martyrdom rather than give up their faith. They were tough people. Throughout the ages there have been some very strong people who have been people of faith. They have stood for truth, justice, equality and fairness often against overwhelming odds, but they had strength to endure.

It can also be said that in the final analysis we are all weak, because we all die. I remember being on a plane going to Ireland and the man next to me entered into conversation. He asked, "Why do people in church always talk about death?" Well firstly we don't always talk about death but it is an important subject. Once we have settled the death question and know with certainty that heaven is our final destination then we can truly live our lives on earth with confident assurance. The point is that we must all stand before God's great tribunal and it will be a dreadful day of condemnation if we are not prepared. However it will be a day of great joy if we are prepared and that preparation only comes through faith in Jesus Christ. In that day we will all be weak unless we have come to the Saviour in faith. I do hope that you know Jesus personally in your life through faith.

FAITH IS HYPOCRISY

I well remember being told by a coal miner when I was in my teens that all those who go to church and chapel are hypocrites. He said it with very real anger in his voice and so I wonder what bad experience he may have had in the past. However, I began to think and ask whether his statement was true. Do all Christians masquerade as being something which they are not? Or that they pretend to be good when really they are bad. The more one thinks about this the more that man's statement stands out as foolishness. If someone claims to be a Christian then they are in effect saying that they are a sinner. The act of becoming a Christian is first of all an act of confession and admitting to the Lord that we need to be forgiven. Thus it is not an attempt to hide personal sinfulness but of openly admitting it. In becoming a Christian we recognize the simple fact that we have broken God's laws and can never reach the standards of perfection that God expects from those who indwell heaven. Therefore we admit that we could never be good enough for the glory of heaven. Thus we admit our failure, sin and disobedience and then place our faith in the one who can bring forgiveness to us. We exercise faith in Christ and trust Him as our Saviour. Thus in admitting that I am a Christian then I am simply saying that I am a sinner who has been forgiven and saved by Christ in whom I have exercised faith.

FAITH IS ONLY SINCERITY

I have heard it said that it doesn't matter what you believe as long as you believe it sincerely. This is patently absurd and should never be taken seriously by anyone. When we were first married we lived in a small house in Wales which was furnished. We had a three piece suite in the lounge but one of the chairs in the suite did not have the springs that held up the cushion. It had legs, a back, the usual two arms but the cushion was balanced with nothing to really hold it up. So to every visitor who came to the house we always said that they were not to sit on that chair unless they wanted to sit on the floor jammed in the frame of a chair! Yet wherever we put that chair in the room visitors always seemed to make a beeline for it. It was absolutely uncanny.

I well remember my uncle and aunt coming to stay over-night and as we were distracted talking to my auntie, my uncle went to sit in "the chair" and as we turned he seemed to be in mid air and was clearly looking forward to a comfortable sit down. We both said "No" but it was too late and we had to pull him out of the chair frame. Thankfully he had a good sense of humour and saw the funny side of the situation. However, I remember seeing his face just before he landed on the cushion and it was a face of absolute sincerity. He truly believed that he would have a comfortable sit down, but no amount of sincere faith could alter the fact that the chair wasn't worth believing in. His faith could not change the chair and it was a useless chair even though it looked fine.

The point is that it is not the **quality** of our faith which is important but the **object** of our faith that is vitally important. If the object is not worth believing in then no amount of faith can alter that fact. In the religious or spiritual realm the truth is that no one has died for sins and risen from the dead except the Lord Jesus and so that makes Him worthy of our faith and capable of saving us from our sins when we trust Him. When He is the object of our faith, then even if our faith is small, as small as a grain of mustard seed as the Bible says, then God can bring His blessing to us and enable that faith to grow.

So the sincerity of faith is not enough but the object of our faith is of great importance.

FAITH IS COMMITMENT

Sometimes when I take a high school assembly I make the point about faith by asking one of the pupils to come to the front. I then place a chair next to him and announce that this is a chair. That is obvious and then I point out what the chair is made of, namely strong materials and that it is put together in a proper manner and that people in the room who are heavier than him are sitting comfortably on similar chairs. I then ask him, "Do you believe that this chair will take your weight?" He stands there and says, "Yes". I then point out that he does not believe and sometimes this starts a sort of light-hearted disagreement. I say. "You don't believe" and he tells me, "I do believe!"

The point of the exercise is to draw the distinction between knowledge and faith. The boy knew that the chair would take his weight as all the evidence said so. Yet to know that the chair would take his weight was not the same as believing that the chair would take his weight. He had knowledge but not faith. Faith is commitment to a course of action and only when the boy committed his weight to the chair did he exercise faith.

There may be many people who know a lot of facts about Jesus. They know that He loves them very deeply and that to prove that love He died on the cross at Calvary for their sins. They know that Christ died for their sins, was buried and rose again but to simply know that these facts are real does not make anyone a true Christian. There needs to be a step of faith. There must be a commitment of the life to the Lord Jesus. It is letting go of control, letting go of the reins of life and letting Jesus take control and take up the reins. It is the surrender of the will to the Lord Jesus Christ.

FAITH

Here we are at the crux of the truth of Christianity. Here we are at the main reason why people do not follow Christ. There are ultimately no intellectual questions that prevent people coming to Christ, because all questions are capable of answers. The real reason that most people stay away from Christ is the question of the will. They want to remain in charge of their own lives but the act of faith that pleases God is when we give up that charge and let Jesus be Lord of our lives. Thus faith is an act of absolute commitment.

My wife and I don't have children and therefore don't have any grandchildren but there is a family in our church who have four children. They are like our honorary grandchildren and it is in many ways privilege without responsibility. Yet I remember that one of them jumped, launched herself might be a better description, off a chair and into my arms. She had absolute confidence that I had the strength and the love to prevent her falling to the floor and hurting herself. She was totally sure that I would catch her. She exercised true faith in my willingness to catch her. Is that not like our faith in Christ? We launch ourselves totally into His safekeeping, knowing that He will hold us and protect us for all eternity. This is because He is powerful and has the ability to protect us and also He is all-loving and has the compassion to protect us. It is wonderful to exercise such faith in the One who showed His love by dying for our sins on the cross.

ONLY A CERTAIN TYPE BELIEVES

Someone once told me that he was not the "believing type" and he did not qualify it by saying "the religious believing type". Clearly he hardly knew what he was talking about because we all exercise faith in some way or another constantly. When we sit on a chair, cross the road, get in the car and a hundred and one other actions are all based upon faith. We believe that the chair will hold our weight, that we will cross the road safely and that the car will take us where we want to go. The faith is based upon the evidence of our eyes, of our knowledge, of the word of other people, of past experience. This is so true when we think of Christian faith and so everyone or anyone can exercise Christian faith and it is not restricted to certain people from particular types of background. It can be noted that there are Christians in every race and nationality, from every strata of society, from every level of educational attainment, from all kinds of working backgrounds and no one need be excluded. The wonder is that when we exercise faith in Christ our lives are instantly transformed by God, even if we feel nothing. He forgives our sins, cleanses us from unrighteous and makes us fit to dwell in His holy presence in heaven. It is at that point of faith that the Lord grants us eternal life and so we have that new life that is the life of God in us as Christian believers.

Christian faith is not a closed, mystical book but an open book and is available to anyone who truly wants to know God. Indeed the Lord says that anyone who seeks me shall find me if they search for me with all their hearts. I do hope that you have exercised faith in Christ and come to the Son of God as your Lord and Saviour.

> *"Of all graces faith honours Christ most; therefore of all graces Christ honours faith most."*
>
> *Matthew Henry*

CHAPTER 2

FAITH: GOD FOCUSED

"You do not need a great faith, but faith in a great God."

Hudson Taylor

> Now faith is the substance of things hoped for, the
> evidence of things not seen. For by it the elders
> obtained a good report. Through faith we under-
> stand that the worlds were framed by the word of
> God, so that things which are seen were not made
> of things which do appear. By faith Abel offered
> unto God a more excellent sacrifice than Cain, by
> which he obtained witness that he was righteous,
> God testifying of his gifts: and by it he being dead
> yet speaketh. By faith Enoch was translated that he
> should not see death; and was not found, because
> God had translated him: for before his translation
> he had this testimony, that he pleased God. But
> without faith it is impossible to please him: for he
> that cometh to God must believe that he is, and that
> he is a rewarder of them that diligently seek him.
>
> Hebrews 11:1-6

Once again we must note a key truth in this passage from
the book of Hebrews and it is found in the words of verse
six, *"But without faith it is impossible to please* [God].*"* Thus it
is impossible, utterly impossible to please or have personal
dealings with God apart from faith. Indeed we have no relationship with God apart from faith. Our relationship with
God is built upon faith and true communion or fellowship
with God cannot exist without faith. So the reason for faith is
to please God. Ultimately nothing else should be important
to us and as Christians we must always make it the goal of
our lives to please God.

At the end of our lives on earth we will find that this truth
was so important. It will be found that it was not important

that we pleased our parents or our children, our friends or our families, our work colleagues or fellow church members but it was utterly vital that we pleased God. Of course we must not deliberately upset people and we trust and pray that in pleasing God other people will be blessed and appreciate the sort of lives we lead, but this might not always be the case. It may be that some will misunderstand us and others will want to criticize us and certainly many of the people of God have found this to be a painful but true experience. We see in this great chapter of Hebrews 11 that the people mentioned are people who pleased God because they acted in faith and towards the end of the chapter there is reference to the suffering of some who were misunderstood by their contemporaries. So it can be that in our pursuit of pleasing God our efforts may be misunderstood and we might offend those who do not know God personally in their lives.

So we should, as Christians, be aiming to bring pleasure to God and the wonderful and glorious fact is that we can be pleasing to God. Sometimes it is hard to please people and with some it might be an utter impossibility. There may be people in our circle of acquaintances that are never pleased or thankful by anything we do or say. Yet God is so different and we can bring pleasure to His heart by exercising faith. In fact apart from faith there is not a single moment when we are pleasing God. Such activities as church attendance, being religious, doing good and giving to charity do not necessarily of themselves please God. They only please God when they are part of our faith in Him. So we need to know what this faith is all about and the writer of this book of Hebrews gives us the clues in this chapter. The faith that truly pleases God believes two things about God. Firstly that God is **real** and secondly that God is a **rewarder**.

GOD IS REAL

The Authorized Version of the Bible puts verse six this way, *"for he that cometh to God must believe that he is"*, while the NIV translates it as, *"because anyone who comes to him must believe that he exists"*. At face value this seems a very strange and peculiar statement. The writer seems to be saying that the faith that pleases God first of all believes in the existence of God. It really seems to be an exercise in circular reasoning: I believe that God exists and so He is pleased! That seems to be far too shallow an understanding of this verse and too narrowly defines the concept of faith. We sense that surely faith must be more significant than simply believing in God's existence. Undoubtedly there is more significance and we must consider the following to gain real insight into the subject of faith.

Firstly, in the days when Jesus lived on earth His greatest enemies were the religious Pharisees. They actually believed in God's existence but they were soundly condemned by the Lord because their faith did not please God. Indeed the strict Pharisee Saul of Tarsus had a strong faith in God's existence but he persecuted the church of God and hated the very name of Jesus Christ. At that time it is obvious that he did not please God.

Secondly, the Devil believes in God's existence and there can be no doubt that his faith is something far removed from giving any pleasure to the heart of God. To believe in an academic sense does not please God because that is a reflection of knowledge and common sense. Life itself would be utterly meaningless if God did not exist.

Thirdly, it is possible to believe in God's existence but refuse to accept biblical truth or embrace the gospel of the Lord Jesus Christ. This is faith in the existence of God but a refusal to listen to God's message or allow God to influence my life or decisions. Such a faith is clearly impossible to please God.

Fourthly, the writer of Hebrews is writing to Christian believers. A Christian is not someone who simply believes in God's existence but is someone who accepts God's revelation, especially about the Lord Jesus. We can hardly imagine that the writer was saying to committed Christians that faith which pleases God accepts the existence of the Almighty! To say to such people they must believe in God's existence to please Him would be a waste of time because they already fully accepted the presence of God. They were absolutely and totally convinced about the existence of God and were sure that they had a personal relationship with Him through Jesus Christ His Son.

Fifthly, he writes, *"whoever would draw near to God must believe that he exists"* (11:6, ESV). It must be considered a strange idea for someone to come or draw near to God if he didn't believe in God's existence. So the very act of seeking to come to God would presume belief in the existence of God.

Sixthly, we must remember that the Christians of the first century were experiencing severe and intense persecution. The church was under the most terrible pressure as the forces of government and society generally were determined to destroy it. This was state sponsored terrorism against the church. Christians were being hounded and imprisoned, tortured and killed and it was a desperate time to be a believer in Christ. For many believers it must have seemed as though the enemies of the gospel were all-powerful, while the presence of God had all but disappeared. This has also been the experience of many Christians down through the ages as there have been times of terribly intensive persecution against the church. Clearly what the writer to the Hebrews is saying is that in times like this you must believe that God exists. Or in the words of Ron Dunn, "He must believe that God still is, even when it looks like He isn't!"

It is when we experience the tough times that we must believe that God exists. Those are the times when our prayers seem to be unanswered, our troubles and worries seem to multiply and get bigger and all that could go wrong does go wrong. We feel that things couldn't get worse and yet they do. At such times it would be simple to doubt God's existence or His power or His love or His ability to do anything. Yet the answer is to keep coming to Him and drawing near to Him in prayer and obedience. It is when He doesn't seem to be there that we must remember and we must believe that God is real. This is the real test of faith. Faith is never tested in the good times but the bad. As we have come to know God in the times when everything was going well, so we can be sustained when things fall apart by the knowledge of the truth that God is real.

It is Oswald Chambers who once wrote, "God withdraws at times His conscious blessings, in order to teach us to walk by faith." In the Old Testament a man who eventually became a great leader in Israel once asked the question, "Where is God?" At that time it seemed that God no longer existed or at least had utterly abandoned His people Israel. There was no evidence of the presence of God in the land or among the people. The enemies had invaded the land and the Israelite people were terribly oppressed and totally impoverished by the exploiting invading army. Gideon's first lesson was to learn to trust God even when the evidence seemed to suggest that God wasn't there. Has this not been true for a missionary lady lying on the floor of her home in Africa while bullets fly through her house as two sides in a violent dispute attack each other? At such a time one could be forgiven for asking the question, "Where is God?" but at such times there is the absolute necessity to reaffirm confidence in the presence of God and say "God is real".

It is vitally important to remember that to love and serve God does not guarantee a charmed life with no difficulties and problems. At the very least the Christian is still part of the human race and faces the same traumas and troubles as other people. Also because of his faith he can face particular persecution from those who oppose Christ. Clearly there can be times when it would seem as though God wasn't there. In Hebrews 11 we read of those who found strength and power from God to be victorious and who were specially delivered from oppression but in verses 35-39 we have a catalogue of those who suffered. So we read,

> *...others were tortured, not accepting deliverance;*
> *that they might obtain a better resurrection: And*

others had trial of cruel mockings and scourg-ings, yea, moreover of bonds and imprisonment: They were stoned, they were sawn asunder, were tempted, were slain with the sword: they wandered about in sheepskins and goatskins; being destitute, afflicted, tormented; (Of whom the world was not worthy:) they wandered in deserts, and in moun-tains, and in dens and caves of the earth. And these all, having obtained a good report through faith...

Thus the same faith was required to enable some to escape death by the sword and for others to endure death by the sword. Each required faith and it was faith that pleased God.

In the book of Acts we read that the Apostle James was killed by the sword (Acts 12:2) while the Apostle Peter was miraculously delivered from prison and so escaped a violent death by the sword (Acts 12:7-12). They both had faith, deep faith in God and yet one died the martyr's death, while the other was miraculously saved from such a death. It may be that it requires greater faith to endure than to escape. Indeed Ron Dunn writes, "I imagine that it is easier to believe that God is when it looks as though He is, than to believe He is when it looks as though He isn't." We marvel at the miracle but fail sometimes to realize that faith that pleases God can also be the faith that endures martyrdom.

Peter Fleming was a missionary in Ecuador and with four missionary colleagues in 1956 tried to take the gospel to the Auca Indians. All five missionaries were martyred for their efforts as they were speared to death on a sand bank by a river in the interior of Ecuador. Yet Peter's brother Ken has been a missionary for years in South Africa and now serves the Lord back in the United States. One endured a martyr's death, while the other never had to face it. Yet both had to exercise faith in the fact that God is real and that is the faith that pleases God.

God is always at work in our lives whether we know it or not. There is never a time when He is not working in our lives as Christians. Sometimes it is obvious and we know

He is dealing with us, but it may be that in a coming day we will recognize that God did a significant work in us when we could not or did not believe that God was working in us at all. Could Job in the Old Testament really have known what God was doing in his life as he faced the loss of family, wealth, health and credibility in the community? Could he have truly understood that God could trust him with suffering? Could he ever have known what a great and wonderful testimony he was to Satan and to all who read of his experience? Yet Job had to trust God even when it seemed that God had deserted him, as the bottom fell out of his life and his friends and even his wife turned against him.

We must constantly affirm our faith in God and say that God is real, even when the evidence seems to say that He doesn't seem to be there! Yet God is not only **real**, but God is also a **rewarder**.

GOD IS A REWARDER

We read the words, *"…and that he rewards those who earnestly seek him"* (11:6, NIV). Thus the faith that pleases God not only believes that He exists when it seems as though He doesn't but also believes that it is worthwhile and rewarding to seek the Lord, even when it appears that it might be a waste of time to do so. This is the sort of faith that pleases God.

Yet we must note very carefully what is written and it is the words, *"earnestly seek"* and is sometimes translated as *"diligently seeks"* (KJV). This is not a half-hearted search, but a deep, detailed search as if one were trying to uncover treasure. It is like the shepherd in the parable of Jesus who lost one sheep and he kept on searching until he found it. In a similar way the lady who lost a coin in another parable of Jesus searched carefully until she found it. Both parables are found in Luke 15 and are examples of what the writer of Hebrews 11 is saying about seeking. The search is total, with no stone left unturned in the search for God. It is as the prophet Jeremiah says, *"And you will seek Me and find Me, when you search for Me with all your heart"*

(Jer. 29:13, NKJV). This is a whole-hearted search for God and a reaching out to Him with all that we have.

The whole idea has to do with seeking the Lord with the totality of what we are and wanting His will for our lives. It carries the idea of a willingness to obey Him and over and above everything else to know Him personally as our God. The blessing is that He will reward those who seek Him, but the aim of our lives should not be the seeking of the reward but the looking for the Rewarder. This is faith that says that it is God I desire above all, not His gifts. God Himself is my reward and ultimately my eternal blessing. The Old Testament saint who dominates Hebrews 11 is Abraham. He supremely is the man of faith and he heard the voice of God in a vision and God said, *"Fear not, Abram: I am thy shield, and thy exceeding great reward"* (Gen. 15:1). So God Himself would be Abraham's great reward and for those who seek the Almighty He becomes their glad and glorious reward.

Thus the aim of faith is to know God as Real in the present and to anticipate Him as Reward in the future. No wonder we read, *"Now faith is the substance of things hoped for, the evidence of things not seen"* (v. 1). May we exercise this sort of faith and bring pleasure to the heart of God.

"A little knowledge of God is worth more than a great deal of knowledge about Him."

J. I. Packer

CHAPTER 3

THE FAITH OF ABEL

"Faith is the mother of obedience."

Thomas Manton

By faith Abel offered unto God a more excellent sacrifice than Cain, by which he obtained witness that he was righteous, God testifying of his gifts: and by it he being dead yet speaketh.　　　Hebrews 11:4

This great and glorious chapter, Hebrews 11, highlights the incredible faith of men and women who served God in Old Testament times. They achieved great things, became successful and victorious and as a result were pleasing to the Lord because they acted in faith and the key phrase in this chapter is *"by faith"*. The first person to be singled out for specific mention comes from the earliest history of mankind and his name is Abel. The background to the life story of Abel is found in the book of Genesis, the very first book of the Bible, and specifically in chapter four, though his name does appear a number of times in other parts of Scripture. Abel was the second son of Adam and Eve and had an older brother named Cain. Though coming from the same parentage the two brothers were radically different, especially in their approach to worshipping God.

Sadly Abel was the first member of the human race to experience death and tragically he was also the very first person to be murdered. Indeed he was murdered by his own brother as we read in Genesis 4:8, *"when they were in the field, that Cain rose up against Abel his brother, and slew him"*. It was a terrible and reprehensible act and the violence was done in great anger because God had accepted the offering of Abel and had rejected the offering of Cain. The Lord had looked with favour upon Abel and with disfavour upon Cain. It is no wonder that Abel had that particular name. Herbert Lockyer makes the point, "Abel's name, meaning breath or vapour, is associated with the shortness of life." It was cut short because of the violent angry actions of a man who should have cared deeply for him, his older brother Cain. In our verse we read of three things that Abel did *"by faith"*.

BY FAITH ABEL OFFERED GOD A BETTER SACRIFICE THAN CAIN DID

It must be significant that the first person mentioned by name in this chapter is a person who worshipped God by presenting a sacrifice to the Lord. Worship is of very great importance to God and therefore should be to God's people. Indeed it has been said that, "…worship is the number one priority of the church". Jesus' famous statement in John 4:23 that the Father seeks worshippers is unparalleled, for nowhere in the entire corpus of Holy Scripture do we read of God's seeking anything else from a child of God. "God desires sincere heartworship above all else" (R. Kent Hughes). Worship should therefore feature very prominently in the hearts and lives of Christian believers. Yet worship must be according to God's instructions and be in accordance with God's commandments. Indeed Jesus said these words, *"God is a Spirit: and they that worship him must worship him in spirit and in truth"* (John 4:24). Clearly the believer's worship should be inwardly motivated and directed by the Holy Spirit and outwardly conformed to the commands laid down in the Word of God. This is where we see the significance of Abel's sacrifice.

Both brothers, Cain and Abel, came with their sacrifices in worship to God but they had differing views of what was pleasing and acceptable to the Lord. Cain came with the fruit and produce that he had collected and this represented two things. Firstly it was produce from the ground and the Lord had cursed the ground because of the sin of Adam and Eve. Secondly it represented his own efforts and so he was giving to God the works of his hands. He presented to God personal achievement, effort and hard work as an acceptable offering of worship. However, Abel came to the Lord with parts of a dead animal. He brought the best of his flock and offered it as a sacrifice to the Lord.

We must remember that Cain's offering no doubt looked attractive as it was made up with the most beautiful vegetables and fruit. It would have appeared colourful and very attractive and would have been in marked contrast with the blood soaked offering that Abel brought but the verdict of God, and that was the vital matter, was that Abel's sacrifice was better than Cain's. Abel had come to God in the divinely appointed way and not taken his own initiative. He had believed God and obeyed him and brought a sacrifice of an animal as a payment for his own life. It was always true throughout the Old Testament that the Lord demanded the blood of sacrificial animals to be shed on the altars in worship to Jehovah. The picture was one of substitution or atonement where the animal was slain instead of the sinful person. It all pointed to the supreme sacrifice which was to come in the person of the Lord Jesus who died for the sins of the world on Calvary's cross.

So *"by faith"* Abel obeyed God and offered an animal from his flocks in worship to God. He had brought one of his best animals and used it in sacrifice to the Lord. This was the method of approach that God commanded and so his offering was so much better than that of Cain who had come to God with his own efforts and presented the results of his own hard work to the Lord. Essentially this represents the two kinds of religions that are in the world today and that have ever been throughout history. The first says that I must contribute to my salvation by doing something and making an effort to achieve and make myself good enough for God. This approach, like that of Cain's, is doomed to failure. The second approach is to simply trust God and to accept His provision for salvation through the sacrifice of His Son on Calvary. This is the approach of faith that takes the Lord at His Word and does whatever He desires. This was exemplified in Abel.

Abel's first great act of faith was to offer to God a better sacrifice that his brother Cain.

BY FAITH...HE OBTAINED WITNESS THAT HE WAS RIGHTEOUS, GOD TESTIFYING OF HIS GIFTS.

It must be an outstanding epitaph to have upon one's tombstone, *"God spoke well of his offerings"* (11:4, NIV). It was not true for Cain, but for Abel it was true that God spoke well of the sacrifice he offered. God could only speak well about it because in faith Abel had obeyed God and given what God desired. This was certainly the sort of faith that pleased God then and still pleases God today. Indeed it meant that God commended Abel and called him a righteous man (11:4).

To receive the Lord's commendation is a wonderful accolade and it is never for the innate characteristics which we possess, nor for any good deeds that we may do. It is only when we accept the word of the Lord by faith that we can ever be commended and for Abel he was commended as a righteous man. Sadly he was not born righteous because like us all he inherited the sinful nature of Adam which was the result of the fall into disobedience and sin that had led to Abel's parents being driven out of the Garden of Eden. Thus like us all he was therefore by nature a sinner who was prone to do his own thing and to break the laws of God. So he was not born with a righteous nature but with a sinfulness that would manifest itself in behaviour and outlook. Yet still the Lord commends him as righteous.

This point is powerfully rendered in the book of Romans where Paul writes, *"As it is written, There is none righteous, no, not one: There is none that understandeth, there is none that seeketh after God. They are all gone out of the way, they are together become unprofitable; there is none that doeth good, no, not one"* (Rom. 3:10-12). Clearly the Bible emphasizes the universal sinfulness of human nature and there can be no exceptions. All are under the condemnation of sin and are guilty before a holy God who must punish sin and disobedience. So Abel was like us all a sinner who had failed to live up to the standard of absolute righteousness that God demands. Yet he is called by God righteous. One commentator puts it like this, "Abel was a sinning man, and yet a man whose attitude to God was a true one, and whose gift proved his sense of the necessity for forgiveness in order that he might approach. That constituted his right to be spoken of as righteous, 'God bearing witness in respect of his gifts.' So Abel stands forevermore at the head of the long line of worshipping men and women, a revelation of what worship ever ought to be" (G. Campbell Morgan).

To be righteous is to be right in the sight of God. It is to have the right attitude and this is reflected in behaviour and ultimately it is to come to God and seek His cleansing from sin through the means that the Almighty has devised. Thus God says that there must be substitutionary sacrifice for sins and in the Old Testament this took the form of an animal sacrificed in the God-ordained manner for the forgiveness of sins. But those sacrifices were only important because they served as a picture or a pointer to the eternal and effective sacrifice for sin when Christ died on Calvary's cross. So in Abel's sacrifice we have an indicator of the great atoning work of our Saviour on Calvary. Thus Abel was the first person ever to offer an acceptable sacrifice to God and for that he was declared righteous by God and thus good enough to dwell in the glory of heaven.

Today we as Christians must also offer sacrifices to the Lord, but these are not the bodies of dead animals but are described as "living sacrifices". These include our whole beings given in surrender to the authority of Christ upon our lives and also the use we make of our tongues to praise and offer thanksgiving to the Lord. It is a sacrifice of time, energy, discipline and concentration to offer the sacrifice of praise to God continually as Hebrews 13 says we must. If Abel counted the cost of his sacrifice then it was in terms of material or temporal wealth, but we must make our offerings in terms of both the material and the spiritual in order to bring our obedience in line with our worship. Indeed to truly worship the Lord is an act of obedience and it is made effective when it flows from a life of daily obedience and surrender to the will of the Lord.

It may be fairly easy to join in the worship that takes place in a church service. We sing the hymns of praise to God and say 'Amen' to the prayers that are offered. We listen with silent contemplation to the exposition of Scripture and may take part when opportunity is given for free and open praise and worship. In the fellowship of other Christians we can find our hearts strangely warmed so that we give our thanksgiving, praise and worship to the Lord. That reflects the importance of being part of a local church fellowship, where we are encouraged to develop our appreciation of Christ. Yet the times when we meet as a corporate body of Christians is very small and so we must develop a personal, daily attitude of worship to the Lord. This will enhance and enrich the corporate worship for if we have been truly worshipping God at home, with our family and throughout the week, then it will be a blessing to others as we join them in the church services.

Yet the greatest act of worship was when we recognized our sin and gave our lives to the Lord and came to experience His salvation. At that point God pronounced us righteous and we were cleansed from sin by the shed blood of Christ. The result should be that practical righteousness should be seen in our lives as we live in obedience to the will of God. At that point we are walking by faith and following in the footsteps of faithful Abel who worshipped God all those years ago.

BY FAITH... HE STILL SPEAKS, EVEN THOUGH HE IS DEAD.

In Genesis chapter four God spoke to Cain after he had committed the act of murder upon his brother and said, *"... Listen! Your brother's blood cries out to me from the ground"* (Gen. 4:10, NIV). Clearly this was a reminder to Cain that no act of sin escapes the notice of Almighty God. These words have been seen by some as crying out for vengeance upon the perpetrator of the crime and certainly Cain had to face his punishment. Yet really this represents the agonizing cry of humanity as it feels the constant consequences of sinful behaviour. No one is immune and we are all the poorer and weaker for the sin we commit and the sin that is committed against us. It cries out to be dealt with and certainly was dealt with when Jesus shed His own precious blood and died for our sins on the cross.

Indeed the writer of Hebrews goes on to state in 12:24, *"to Jesus the mediator of the new covenant, and to the blood of sprinkling, that speaketh better things than that of Abel."* The blood of Abel spoke and cried out about the injustice and sinfulness of his brother's actions and really spoke more widely of the terrible sinfulness that afflicts the whole of humanity. It could only condemn mankind as it revealed the terrible tragedy that sin had brought and revealed all people as guilty because of their failure to deal with sin in their hearts and lives. So the message of Abel's shed blood was largely negative and revealed mankind under the condemnation of the law of God.

Christ's shed blood speaks of an answer. His work on the cross dealt with the problem of sin. He took our sins and nailed them to His cross and we can rest assured today that He paid the full price for our redemption. The payment and punishment that God demanded from sinful mankind was fully paid by our Saviour on the cross. No wonder a songwriter could pen the following words, "He paid a debt He did not owe; I owed a debt I could not pay; I needed someone to wash my sins away. And now I sing a brand new song, 'Amazing Grace'. Christ Jesus paid a debt that I could never pay" (Ellis J. Crum). Thus we can say in the words of one commentator, "The blood of Jesus declared atonement made. The blood of Abel was the cry of necessity, the cry of need, the anguished cry of humanity excluded from God. The blood of Jesus tells us that there is a way for men to rise, a way of entrance into the Holy Place" (G. Campbell Morgan).

Today Abel still speaks and we note the present tense in our verse. He is still speaking and we can take note of his message. He speaks to us through the pages of Holy Scripture and wherever the Bible is read we can read of the faith of Abel and the blessing of walking by faith. He is a witness to us of how we can please God when we come to Him in worship. Certainly our own ideas and efforts will not do and will never prove to be sufficient for us to gain acceptance with God. It is only through faith in His Son and through the working of the Holy Spirit and in obedience to the revealed will of God that we too can find God being pleased with our offering and accepting it with pleasure. May that be our daily and continuing experience.

"Faith and works are like the light and heat of a candle; they cannot be separated."

Anonymous

CHAPTER 4

THE FAITH OF ENOCH

"Faith is reason at rest in God."

C. H. Spurgeon

> *By faith Enoch was translated that he should not see death; and was not found, because God had translated him: for before his translation he had this testimony, that he pleased God. But without faith it is impossible to please him: for he that cometh to God must believe that he is, and that he is a rewarder of them that diligently seek him.*
>
> Hebrews 11:5-6

We now come to the second Old Testament saint mentioned in this glorious chapter of the faithful. His name is Enoch and of all the people mentioned in Hebrews 11 he is unique. He and he alone did not go through the experience of death. His experience was "translation" and that means "to be transferred to another place." He was taken from time into eternity but not through the gateway of death, which was the experience of everyone else mentioned in the chapter.

HIS BACKGROUND

He is described as *"the seventh from Adam"* (Jude 14) and this distinguishes him from anyone else in the Old Testament with the name Enoch. Also it can hardly be an accident that this outstanding man of God was the **seventh** descendant from Adam. Herbert Lockyer says, "Seven represents spiritual perfection", while John J. Davis wrote, "It is the view of this writer that the only number used symbolically in Scripture to any degree with discernible significance is the number seven. In all cases it seems that the idea conveyed is that of completeness." So here we see the seventh from Adam was someone who was spiritually in tune with his Lord. He was in such a complete and perfect harmony with the Lord, that he was able to walk with God, to please God and to believe God. Do we walk with God? Do we please God? Do we believe God?

The book of Genesis tells us that Enoch was the son of Jared, born when his father was 162 years old. Enoch himself became father of Methuselah, who was born when Enoch was 65 years old. Enoch lived on earth a further 300 years and was translated at the age of 365. Enoch was a prophet because Jude in his epistle tells us, *"Enoch also, the seventh from Adam, prophesied of these, saying, Behold, the Lord cometh with ten thousands of his saints, To execute judgment upon all, and to convince all that are ungodly among them of all their ungodly deeds which they have ungodly committed, and of all their hard speeches which ungodly sinners have spoken against him"* (Jude 14-15). So Enoch was the first person in the Bible to be described as a prophet and his prophecy was so wide ranging that it looked down through the ages, not to the first advent of Christ, as many Old Testament prophets did, but to Christ's second advent and to the awful judgment that God would inflict upon those who are ungodly and who maintained their ungodliness with utter determination.

Enoch is also mentioned in the genealogy of the Lord in Luke 3 and thus through him came the line of descent that led to the glorious, promised Messiah. So this is the background to this outstanding man of God. It lacks detail and we are only given the bare bones of his life and work but we can build up a picture of this man and learn valuable lessons for our own spiritual development, because these things are written for our learning and so can be a rich source of spiritual blessing to us today.

ENOCH WALKED WITH GOD

There is a double reference to this important aspect of his life, as we read in Genesis 5 verse 22. Yet we notice that it says, *"And Enoch walked with God after he begat Methuselah…"*. It would seem that in some way the birth of that child changed the life of Enoch. From then on he walked with God. Certainly he served God before the birth of that son but after the birth that relationship with God was so much deeper. Why did this happen? Well it could simply have been the miracle of birth which changed him. Others have become aware of God in a deeper way as they have witnessed the wonderful phenomenon of new life. However it might be something deeper and more meaningful and could be found in the name of the son, Methuselah. The name means "when he is dead it shall be sent". This is a prophecy wrapped up in a name and means that when his son died then God would send the deluge, namely the flood that would destroy wicked mankind. So every time Enoch mentioned his son's name he was reminded of God's forthcoming judgment.

It is interesting that of all people who ever lived on earth Methuselah's life was the longest. It was as if God was extending the day of grace to enable people to respond to His love and repent of their sins. Today the opportunity of repenting and believing in Christ is still available to you and me and yet it will not remain indefinitely. We need to seize the opportunity while we can. Methuselah had a son named Lamech when he was 187 years old, Lamech had a son named Noah at the age of 182 and when Noah was 600 years old the flood came. If we add up 187 + 182 + 600 it comes to 969, which was the age that Methuselah died. So in the year of his death, the flood came and that fulfilled the prophecy that was bound up in his name. Indeed Jewish tradition states that seven days after Methuselah's death the flood came. Interestingly only one other man is mentioned as walking with God and that was Enoch's great grandson Noah and so one predicted the flood, while the other lived through it.

To walk with God means to be in fellowship with God, to walk in step with God and to go the direction that God is going and that direction is a crusade against sin. Indeed the prophet Amos said, *"Can two walk together, except they be agreed?"* (Amos 3:3). The answer is obviously "No" and so we must agree with God if we are ever to walk with Him. In the

Old Testament we find the prophet Jonah being unwilling to walk with God and he refused to go to Nineveh with the message that warned of divine judgment unless they repented. He lagged far behind God. In the New Testament we find the Apostle Peter cutting off someone's ear with a sword. His eagerness ran ahead of him and he rushed in on behalf of Christ where he should have held back and taken no action. We must be careful neither to lag behind God's will for our lives due to reluctance nor to run ahead of God's desire for us through fleshly enthusiasm. How can we get it right, as it is so easy to get it wrong?

Firstly we must spend a long time in prayer and constantly draw close to the Lord in intercession. Without prayer and it must be true prayer, rather than formal prayers, we will never know the will of God for our lives. Secondly we must study the Word of God and let it impregnate and influence our lives very deeply. As we read the Bible we begin to sense the heart beat of desire that God has for us. Thirdly we must examine carefully our motives and feelings and make sure that they are not false and not for self promotion or self glory. Fourthly we need an openness to hear God's voice and so to know His will and follow His guidance and then to have the blessing of walking with Him in the deepest fellowship.

It would be wonderful for each one of us to know the experience that Enoch had of walking with God. As someone once wrote to me, "May Enoch's companion be yours!" May it be true for all of us.

ENOCH PLEASED GOD

More than anything else I would like as my epitaph the words, "He pleased God". This was the epitaph of Enoch, as Hebrews 11:5 says, *"he was commended as having pleased God"* (ESV). It is not important that we please people, even if those people are our family members or fellow church members but it is vitally important to please God. However we do not want to upset people and certainly don't go out of our way to disturb them and we trust that in pleasing God we will also bring pleasure to people. To please God means a number of things.

1. **Obedience**: this is the first ingredient when it comes to pleasing God. Our obedience to the Lord should be total, unquestioning and instant. There should be no area of our lives where the Saviour does not have direct control. It is just not good enough to have the Lord residing in our lives; He should be presiding in our lives. He should not just be present in our lives but must be pre-eminent. Indeed we must make Christ the number one in our lives as Christian people if we are ever to please God.

2. **Holiness**: the apostle Peter wrote, *"But as he which hath called you is holy, so be ye holy in all manner of conversation; Because it is written, Be ye holy; for I am holy"* (1 Peter 1:15-16). This means a hatred for everything that is sinful, impure and unclean. It is a desire to be totally set apart for God's work and for God's glory. To know in daily experience the reality of a holy life is to bring pleasure to the heart of God.

3. **Love**: it is so important that Christians show this wonderful characteristic and not develop a bitter and hurtful spirit. The local church should be the place where there is the fullness of love and care for people and love needs to be emphasized because it can be weakened and evaporate through a single uncaring remark. This also destroys the unity that can exist amongst the people of God. It is also important to remember that love should be expressed in practical ways and should not just be in words and speech.

4. **Joy**: this is the reality of the Holy Spirit's presence in the heart and life of the Christian. He brings the reality of joy even in the midst of difficulties and problems. This is not to minimize the tragedies of life but to realize that God is in the centre of our being and to rejoice in His presence.

5. **Peace**: this is the freedom from anxieties and cares that can so easily bring the human spirit into despair. It is a freedom from anxiety that is reflected in a deep inner peace and is the result of drawing close to God in prayer. It is so important to learn to cast all our cares upon the Lord, knowing that He cares for us. God takes pleasure in His people being able to trust Him with their cares and burdens.

As God sees these characteristics being worked out in our lives He derives pleasure because it is essentially His work in our lives bearing fruit. I hope it can be said of all of us that we please God.

ENOCH BELIEVED GOD

Here is the great characteristic that truly pleases the heart of God and it is our faith. So we read, *"By faith Enoch...But without faith it is impossible to please* [God]*..."* (11:5-6). We cannot please God apart from believing in God. This is more than the faith that says that God exists or that His Son died for our sins upon the cross. This is faith that says I believe everything that God says is true and that I will act in total obedience upon everything that He tells me to do.

In the book of Acts we read of the Apostle Paul on a ship which was being pounded by the most vicious of storms. The ship had been battered for many days and the cargo and tackle had been jettisoned and the ship was bound together by ropes in an attempt to preserve the lives of those on board. When all seemed lost the Apostle Paul told the assembled passengers and crew about a vision he had received and then he said, *"...I have faith in God..."* (Acts 27:25, ESV). Clearly Paul was not saying that he had just discovered God's existence or that he had just come to faith in Christ as Saviour. He was emphasizing that he utterly trusted the words God had told him and that he had total assurance that what God had said would come to pass. It was the faith that is revealed in the words of C. H. Spurgeon, "Faith sees the invisible, hears the inaudible, touches the intangible and does the impossible." This was the faith that was witnessed in Enoch and indeed in all the people mentioned in Hebrews 11.

William Booth, the founder of the Salvation Army was moved by similar faith. He formed a ragtag army of Christians who went into the impoverished inner cities of Britain and claimed them for God. They went out in faith and prayer and offered help to needy families and proclaimed the gospel of Jesus Christ wherever they went. They were vilified, attacked and abuse was heaped upon their heads but still they kept going and their motive was their utter faith and total dependence upon the Lord. It is a remarkable story of courage exercised through faith in Christ. Surely there is need for similar faith to be exercised by God's people today.

ENOCH WAS TRANSLATED BY GOD

In Genesis 5:24 we read, "...*he was no more, because God took him away*" (NIV). He "...*was taken from this life, so that he did not experience death...*" (11:5, NIV). We can imagine people searching for Enoch and asking the question, "Where is he?" Maybe they sent out search parties as people of another generation were to do when Elijah was taken up into heaven in the most dramatic manner. In both cases the searchers returned empty handed and they failed to find the missing persons. The simple truth was that Enoch had ascended to the presence of God and had gone from glory to glory. He had simply continued walking with his Lord right into the holy presence of heaven.

This reminds us that the day draws ever closer when Christians will also be translated. When they will be drawn from this earthly scene and be presented into the presence of God. It will happen in a moment, in the twinkling of an eye. It will be a momentous occasion as the Apostle Paul makes clear in 1 Thessalonians, "*For the Lord himself shall descend from heaven with a shout, with the voice of the archangel, and with the trump of God: and the dead in Christ shall rise first: Then we which are alive and remain shall be caught up together with them in the clouds, to meet the Lord in the air: and so shall we ever be with the Lord"* (1 Thess. 4:16-17). So Paul makes it abundantly clear that when the Lord returns for His people those believers who will still be alive on earth at that moment will have an Enoch experience and will be translated or transferred to another place without experiencing death. It is a glorious prospect for the Christian.

However, the Apostle John reminds us in his first epistle that in the light of the second coming of Christ we have certain responsibilities. He wrote, *"every man that hath this hope in him purifieth himself, even as he is pure"* (1 John 3:3). Also he wrote, *"And now, little children, abide in him; that, when he shall appear, we may have confidence, and not be ashamed before him at his coming"* (1 John 2:28). When he uses the word "confident" he means the ability to speak freely to the Lord and that will be the wonderful joy for some Christians when the Lord returns. When John uses the word "ashamed", he means to be tongue-tied or have an inability to speak freely with the Lord when He returns. It would be a terrible tragedy for any believer to be unable to speak freely with the Lord when He returns but it will be because they were not living as they ought to be as Christians. How do we live in such a way as to have confidence when the Lord returns? Well Enoch supplies the answer for us. We should live lives that walk with God, that please God and that believe God. That should be our normal manner of living the Christian life and we can then look forward with eager anticipation to the second coming of our Saviour. That blessed day when we shall see our Saviour face to face gets ever closer and gives God's people deep joy and gladness.

"Thus at 365 years of age—a year for every day of our year—God took His servant directly to heaven."

Herbert Lockyer

CHAPTER 5

THE FAITH OF NOAH

"Noah walked with God in spite of surrounding iniquity."

Herbert Lockyer

> By faith Noah, being warned of God of things not
> seen as yet, moved with fear, prepared an ark to the
> saving of his house; by the which he condemned the
> world, and became heir of the righteousness which
> is by faith.   Hebrews 11:7

In the Western world we live in what has often been described as "a sceptical age", where we doubt everything and question anything. We are ready to argue against anything that might be described as spiritual or religious truth and nothing is ever taken at face value. We always look for alternative explanations and this is true in general areas of daily life, but is especially true in the religious or spiritual realm. There is nothing wrong with questioning and certainly the gospel of Jesus Christ will stand up to the most rigorous analysis and not be found wanting, because it is a faith that is founded on rock solid evidence and is built upon fact and truth.

Part of the truth problem for many people today is that they were told the stories of the Bible at school, in Sunday School, Kiddies' Club or Junior church and no progress has been made from that basic understanding of childhood. Stories such as "Jonah and the Whale", "Noah and the Flood" and "Daniel in the Lion's Den" were often told in dramatic form and captured our young imaginations. Yet there they have remained as simple stories lacking sophistication and viewed as hardly credible to adults in a scientific or thinking age. Therefore one is left with the feeling that such stories may be good for children to teach morality but are really little more than fairy tales, parables or myth. Indeed the term "flood myths" is often applied to any story found in any culture that mentions a flood in its primeval past. So the background to our reading on Noah, as found in Genesis 6-9 is reduced in the minds of many people to just another "flood myth". They assume that it must be an exaggerated account of a local flood that got bigger with the telling.

Yet there is no suggestion in the Bible that the account is other than sober history and there are very good reasons for accepting the account as it stands. We will look at three aspects of the story, the flood, the ark and the man: Noah.

THE FLOOD

One of the great books on the subject of "the flood" is entitled, *The Genesis Flood—the Biblical Record and its Scientific Implications* by Whitcomb and Morris. It is an impressive work and a formidably argued thesis and has done great service in demonstrating that the Genesis account of "the flood" has credibility and is not simply a work of imagination. Thus the Bible highlights many details about "the flood" though it is not an exhaustive account.

THE CAUSE OF THE FLOOD

The flood was caused by the Lord and was the direct result of the awful wickedness and evil that was being practiced by the people of that time. Firstly, the minds of the people were sinful for we read, *"…every imagination of the thoughts of his heart was only evil continually"* (Gen. 6:5). Secondly the actions of the people were sinful as we read, *"And God saw that the wickedness of man was great in the earth…"* (Gen. 6:5) and again, *"The earth also was corrupt before God, and the earth was filled with violence"* (Gen. 6:11). There is, of course, a great and very direct connection between thinking and doing. It is true that we 'sow a thought and reap an action'. Therefore we must guard our thoughts and be very careful what we allow our minds to dwell upon. Today the biggest battle is for control of minds and there are many means of stimulating evil, lustful and corrupt thoughts so that the thought processes of mankind today can become corrupted like those of mankind in Noah's day. Thus the flood was the result of sin and sin's awful and varied manifestations. God never has and never will take a light view of sin and therefore as Christians we must do our utmost to root it out and crush it from our lives. This is an on-going battle and is never easy.

THE EXTENT OF THE FLOOD

This factor focuses upon a debate as to whether the flood was universal across the globe or localized to a part of the Middle East. It would seem that the Bible gives us no room for alternatives but states that it was a universal flood. It says in Genesis 7:19, *"And the waters prevailed exceedingly upon the earth; and all the high hills, that were under the whole heaven, were covered."* Today we ask whether such words are credible and whether such an event could ever be possible. The modern mind is, to say the least of it, sceptical.

It is easy to be sceptical, especially when brought up with certain basic presuppositions in our thinking. If such assumptions are correct then clearly a universal flood could not have happened. Let me focus upon two such presuppositions.

Firstly, we are brought up with the principle of naturalism and this states that God is ruled out. This principle excludes God either as an entity at all and therefore he cannot influence life on earth and send an extended flood, or as an active entity on the globe. The latter sees Him at best as a disinterested on-looker. If there is no God then the flood could never have happened as recorded in Genesis. Naturalism as a prerequisite rules out God and insists that He must never enter the realm of science. Yet clearly if the God of the Bible is a true entity then the universal nature of the flood is no problem at all to such a great being. Indeed we cannot rule out the concept of God simply because naturalism tells us we must!

Secondly, we are brought up with the principle of uniformitarianism. This rules out the possibility of catastrophe because all the processes we see going on today have always gone on more or less at the same rate. Such processes are erosion, sedimentation and solidification. Therefore a giant flood must be ruled out. This principle has been modified, but essentially remains a cornerstone of evolutionary theory.

Yet there is evidence other than the Bible for a universal flood. This evidence includes the fact that accounts of a flood are found in all major cultures and anthropology has uncovered this fact time and again. Also the great sedimentary formations in various parts of the world were laid down by water in far greater quantities than anything we see today. There was a mechanism we call a catastrophe that laid down those great formations which are hundreds of feet thick and some have even contained a fossilized fully grown tree. If the sedimentation process had taken eons of years then the upper part of the tree would have long gone or been very greatly distorted, but the sedimentation must have happened very quickly as only a great flood could have achieved. There is also the theological aspect that says if mankind were universally evil, then the punishment through the deluge of flood water had also to be universal.

THE EFFECT OF THE FLOOD

The effect of the flood was both terrific and horrific as every man and beast were swept away to destruction. *"And all flesh died that moved upon the earth, both of fowl, and of cattle, and of beast, and of every creeping thing that creepeth upon the earth, and every man"* (Gen. 7:21). This was God's purging of the earth of all the wickedness and evil that had become so offensive to His holy and righteous character. God hates evil and sin and ultimately all such activity will be dealt with by His judgment. The flood stands as a reminder of God's universal judgment—God will punish sin. The God of history is the same God today and He will not tolerate sin and this account in Genesis is a warning for us today. All will stand before God's tribunal and give an account of their lives and will face the terrible consequences of their sinfulness unless they have found forgiveness through faith in Christ.

THE ARK

We read, *"By faith Noah, being warned of God of things not seen as yet, moved with fear, prepared an ark to the saving of his house"* (Heb. 11:7). Clearly Noah had never seen rain, never mind the huge flood that was to come upon the earth. Yet because of his deep reverence for God he built the ark and saved his family. The book "The Genesis Flood" goes into great detail about the ark. The word "ark" is probably taken from an ancient word that meant "chest" or "coffin" and that gives us a clue about its formation. The ark was a sort of floating box, which would have been highly suitable for extremely turbulent waters.

THE BUILDING OF THE ARK

God commanded Noah to build the ark and it took up to one hundred and twenty years to construct. It was built to clear and concise specifications. Firstly it had to be made of gopher wood and had to be 300 cubits (or 450 feet long). It was 50 cubits wide and thirty cubits high. It had to be sealed and made waterproof with bitumen and had three storeys with a long window just under the roof. It was a gigantic barge, big enough for the animals, for storage areas and for waste disposal areas. It was the biggest boat ever built until modern times. It was a huge undertaking for Noah and his family but they did it in simple obedience to the Lord's commandment. It took 120 years to build and was used for one year only.

THE PURPOSE OF THE ARK

The ark was God's means of safety and for the preserving both of human and animal life on planet earth. Only eight people were saved and that was Noah and his family. Just by way of interest the Chinese character for boat contains the number eight, which significantly reminds us of the eight people who were saved in Noah's ark. All around there was turmoil, trouble, destruction and death, while in the ark and in the ark alone was safety and security. The ark was God's chosen place of salvation.

THE APPLICATION OF THE ARK

The ark reminds us that there is a future judgment, not by water this time but by fire. There is only one place of safety in the face of that coming judgment and that is not the local church or some religious creed or ritual. The one place of security and salvation is the Lord Jesus Christ. He is the only one who is capable of protecting us from the judgment of God that is come upon mankind because of sin. He alone can take us safely to heaven and I do hope that we have found that safe haven of faith in Christ.

THE MAN—NOAH

The outstanding characteristic of Noah was his faith as we read, *"By faith, Noah...became heir of the righteousness which is by faith"* (11:7). His faith was seen in a number of ways.

1. **He believed the Word of God**: this was the foundation of his faith. When God spoke to him and warned him of coming judgment he believed the voice of God. When God spoke of a judgment, the like of which had never been seen on earth before, his faith never wavered. There had never been rain on the earth up to his time and even though it is very hard to imagine something one has never experienced he utterly believed God's words. When the storm came it was totally amazing and there has never been another storm like it. It rained continuously for forty days and forty nights with the most torrential downpour and it was accompanied by the most violent geological and seismic disturbances with water gushing from the ground. Yet Noah and his family were safe because he had believed the Word of God. Never forget that

you too can fully trust and rely upon the Word of God, the Holy Bible.

2. **He obeyed the Word of God**: faith is not just something held in the heart and the mind but finds expression in obedience. Noah expressed his faith by obeying God's commandment. God said, "Make an ark!" and so Noah did just that. I am sure that there were few people apart from his family that gave him any form of encouragement and no doubt he was mocked for his efforts, while others tried to hinder him. Some might even have thought that he was mentally unstable and unbalanced. To walk a path of obedience to God is not to walk a road to popularity and acceptance. Obedience means saying, "No" to the accepted wisdom of men and swimming against the tide of current opinion in society and even being considered a bit odd! Today it seems odd that a couple refrain from living together before marriage simply to obey God. It is strange that man restores what he once stole simply to obey God. It seems incredible that a man will not compromise his principles for honesty and integrity to further his career, simply because he wants to obey God. Noah knew this lesson centuries ago and as he was richly blessed by the Lord, so we can be as we also learn to obey our God each day.

3. **He preached the Word of God**: Noah's work went further than quiet belief and practical work. He was also a *"preacher of righteousness"* (2 Peter 2:5). Undoubtedly he warned the people about the coming judgment and urged them to repent and leave their sinfulness. It was hopeless work as he tried each day to curb the violence and corruption in society as no one listened to him or repented of their sin. At least his family respected him and followed his lead. There at least in his own home he carried credibility and it was there that they saw him as a righteous man who practiced what he preached.

Finally Jesus said, *"But as the days of Noe were, so shall also the coming of the Son of man be. For as in the days that were before the flood they were eating and drinking, marrying and giving in marriage, until the day that Noe entered into the ark"* (Matt. 24:37-38). Thus Jesus highlights three things. Firstly, *"eating"* and this is the lust for food and we certainly live at a time, at least in the Western world, where gluttony and over-eating are socially accepted sins. We have cheap food, junk food, fast food and eating out places all in abundance. Is it similar to the times of Noah? If it is then the time of Christ's return is very near. Secondly, He mentions *"drinking"* and this is the lust for alcohol. We live in times where alcoholic binging is epidemic and we live in a society with millions of alcoholics with many of them young people. Drink is freely available at all times of the day and night. Is it similar to the times of Noah? If it is then the time of Christ's return is very near. Thirdly there was *"marrying"* and this means wide scale sexual indulgence. This rings a bell with a modern society where corrupt, debased, pornographic activities are widespread and widely distributed and we have become a society that views the intimacy of relationships in a very shallow and short term way. Is it similar to the times of Noah? If it is then the time of Christ's return is very near.

We are warned to live in purity, to trust Christ through obedience and to be ready for His return in glory. In the meanwhile we should take every opportunity to convey the glad and glorious good news of the gospel to everyone we meet. May we be like Noah and live in faith and righteousness for the glory of our great God and Saviour Jesus Christ.

"In the midst of an age of moral darkness, Noah was perfect in his generation."

Herbert Lockyer

CHAPTER 6

THE FAITH OF ABRAHAM
PART 1

"When Abraham went out, he was not sure of his destiny, but he was sure of his company."

John Blanchard

By faith Abraham, when he was called to go out into a place which he should after receive for an inheritance, obeyed; and he went out, not knowing whither he went. By faith he sojourned in the land of promise, as in a strange country, dwelling in tabernacles with Isaac and Jacob, the heirs with him of the same promise: For he looked for a city which hath foundations, whose builder and maker is God. Through faith also Sara herself received strength to conceive seed, and was delivered of a child when she was past age, because she judged him faithful who had promised. Therefore sprang there even of one, and him as good as dead, so many as the stars of the sky in multitude, and as the sand which is by the sea shore innumerable. These all died in faith, not having received the promises, but having seen them afar off, and were persuaded of them, and embraced them, and confessed that they were strangers and pilgrims on the earth. For they that say such things declare plainly that they seek a country. And truly, if they had been mindful of that country from whence they came out, they might have had opportunity to have returned. But now they desire a better country, that is, an heavenly: wherefore God is not ashamed to be called their God: for he hath prepared

*for them a city. By faith Abraham, when he was
tried, offered up Isaac: and he that had received the
promises offered up his only begotten son, Of whom
it was said, That in Isaac shall thy seed be called:
Accounting that God was able to raise him up, even
from the dead; from whence also he received him in
a figure.* Hebrews 11:8-19

Though there are many fascinating and important characters to come in this great chapter of Hebrews 11 we have now
arrived at the one man who totally dominates this list of wonderful Old Testament saints. His name is Abraham and there
are more verses devoted to his exploits through faith than any
of the other Old Testament heroes mentioned in this passage. In
fact Abraham's life is one of the best documented in the whole
of Scripture. His name appears in twenty-seven books of the
Bible, though his life story is given to us in great detail only
in Genesis 11-25. However in the book of Galatians, especially
chapters three and four, Abraham is used as an illustration of
the Apostle Paul's argument that it is faith and faith alone in
Christ that is the basis of salvation and acceptance with God.

It is significant that Abraham should be so prominent in
the Galatian epistle, for that was Martin Luther's favourite
Bible book. He was the man who rediscovered for the church
from the Scriptures the truth of justification by faith and who
was used by God to usher in the Reformation in Europe, the
good of which we stand in today. That great reformer was
deeply influenced by the experience of Abraham who knew
that message of faith as long ago as 2,000 years before Christ
was born in Bethlehem. Abraham all those years ago was justified by faith. Abraham is also cited as an example in chapter
four of the Book of Romans to again highlight the truth of
justification by faith. We read the following words, *"For what
saith the scripture? Abraham believed God, and it was counted unto
him for righteousness"* (Rom. 4:3). This is the central message of
the Word of God and of the gospel of Jesus Christ that a man
is not justified by what he does but by faith in Jesus Christ.

So salvation is not personal achievement but a wonderful gift from God brought about by Christ's work on Calvary.

It has been rightly said of Abraham that, "He uttered no prophecy, wrote no book, sang no song, gave no laws. Yet in the long line of Bible saints he alone is spoken of as 'the father of the faithful' and as 'the friend of God'." It has also been said that, "Abraham is revered by more people than any other man except the Lord Jesus." Indeed that great exception our Saviour, the Lord Jesus quoted the example of Abraham to illustrate His teaching while here on earth. The Lord said, *"I say unto you, Before Abraham was, I am"* (John 8:58). Clearly the Lord Jesus was emphasizing to His listeners that He was truly deity, because though Abraham to Jewish eyes was deeply revered—here stood One in the person of Christ who was greater than their father Abraham.

ABRAHAM'S BACKGROUND

Abraham was born in Ur of the Chaldees which is located in today's modern Iraq, so he came from the Fertile Crescent, the area watered by the rivers Euphrates and Tigris. His early name was Abram which means "father of heights" and his father's name was Terah and he appears to have been born when Terah was 130 years old. We read the following words in Genesis, *"And Terah lived seventy years, and begat Abram, Nahor, and Haran"* (Gen. 11:26). It would seem that Terah had no children until he was seventy and then had three sons over a sixty year period culminating with Abram at the age of 130. This time span would help to explain why Haran, Abram's brother died in Ur, the land of his nativity (Gen. 11:28) and left a son named Lot who seems to have been comparable with Abram in wealth in later years and could well have been comparable in age as well. So Abram's name appearing first in the list of Terah's sons does not denote age but reflects importance.

Genesis 11:32 tells us that Terah died at the age of 205 and that Abram left Haran (to which he had travelled from Ur) only after his father had died. We are told this fact in Acts 7:4, *"came he out of the land of the Chaldaeans, and dwelt in Charran: and from thence, when his father was dead, he removed him into this land, wherein ye now dwell."* Abram was seventy-five years old when he left Haran (Gen. 12:4) and so must have been born when Terah was 130 years old.

A GREAT STEP OF FAITH

The first great act of faith by Abraham was to leave his home and go to an unknown destination, simply because God had called him to do so. We read, *"By faith Abraham, when he was called to go out into a place which he should after receive for an inheritance, obeyed; and he went out, not knowing whither he went"* (11:8). This act of faith meant that Abraham took God at His Word and fully trusted in the true and living God.

The city of Ur was a large and wealthy city but was also dominated at that time by heathen practices that included sin, idolatry and immoral activities. It was from this pagan environment that God chose Abram and called him to journey to the south west to the land of Palestine. God did not call Abram's father Terah, nor his brother Nahor or even his nephew Lot. It was a personal and distinct call to Abram and we are not absolutely sure why or how that call came to him. Certainly Abram must have had a deep appreciation of the true God despite living in such a pagan society. God must have recognized in the heart and life of Abram a genuine spiritual desire for holiness and integrity and so God called him out of the world of heathendom to a life of wandering in the Promised Land of Palestine.

Abram's response was immediate but it would seem not total and to begin with he simply went as far as Haran, which is a city to the west of Ur and is on the way to Palestine. Also Abram did not travel alone but was certainly accompanied by his father and his nephew Lot. Haran was still in Mesopotamian culture and it therefore took time for Abram to fully act upon God's call. Yet when his father died in Haran he moved on and left certainty for uncertainty. He left Mesopotamia with its sophisticated culture, its wealth and security. He left home, family and friends and embarked upon a trip which could prove dangerous and could put his whole family in jeopardy. He had to go and had no idea where the final destination would be and we can well imagine the wrench of departure. There may have been tears on the face, fears in the heart, heartache and all sorts of inner turmoil but he went with the certain knowledge that he would never return. He went because God had commanded him to go and he chose to obey God. He went because God had promised him blessings and Abram wanted to experience God's blessings.

What a man of faith he was and therefore no wonder he is called the father of the faithful. It was as if he said, "God, I trust you completely. Lord, I will follow you to the ends of the earth, if you want me to do that!"

GOD'S PROMISES TO ABRAHAM

"Now the LORD had said unto Abram, Get thee out of thy country, and from thy kindred, and from thy father's house, unto a land that I will shew thee" (Gen. 12:1). Then God gave to His servant Abram a threefold promise.

A LAND

This land would turn out to be the land of Canaan otherwise known as Palestine. It is a small country about the size of Wales and is squeezed between the Mediterranean Sea to the west and the River Jordan to the east. The northern boundary is the mountains of Lebanon and the southern boundary is the desert wastelands of Sinai. This was the first part of God's promise to Abram.

In that land Abram made his home and yet he owned none of that territory except a small burial plot near Hebron where he buried his wife Sarah. He bought that plot of land and it was the only part of the Promised Land that he could call his own. Yet we read, *"By faith he sojourned in the land of promise, as in a strange country, dwelling in tabernacles with Isaac and Jacob, the heirs with him of the same promise"* (Heb. 11:9). Thus it was very much a nomadic existence that Abraham experienced in the land of promise. He was constantly on the move living with his family, servants, flocks and herds and never living in a permanent dwelling but always in tents.

It would be hundreds of years before the promise would be fulfilled and the descendants of Abraham would possess the Promised Land. Ultimately they would invade the land under the leadership of Joshua and become the dominant force in the land of Canaan. Yet Abraham, together with his son Isaac and his grandson Jacob lived in the expectation of something greater, *"For he looked for a city which hath foundations, whose builder and maker is God"* (Heb. 11:10). Surely Ur was a city with a foundation but that was merely material and man made and eventually it crumbled and for many centuries was covered with accumulated dust and rubbish. Abraham clearly saw a spiritual city which he would inhabit for eternity and that would be the wonder of dwelling in the presence of God. So his view was lifted above the earthly to the heavenly and that was the final resting place of his faith. So each day, in the words of the hymn he pitched his tent, "a day's march nearer home"(*Forever With The Lord*, James Montgomery).

It is true that we as Christian people anticipate the wonder and glory of our heavenly home. That is our true home and not this passing, material existence we experience in the present time. My grandmother died at the age of eighty and her last words were, *"In my Father's house are many mansions: if it were not so, I would have told you. I go to prepare a place for you. And if I go and prepare a place for you, I will come again, and receive you unto myself; that where I am, there ye may be also"* (John 14:2-3). My grandmother also looked for that glorious, heavenly city and like Abraham before her dwells today in the presence of God.

So God's first promise to Abraham was that a land had been provided.

THE FAITH OF ABRAHAM: PART 1

A PEOPLE

The Lord promised Abraham, *"I will make of thee a great nation"* (Gen. 12:2) and this greatness was to be seen in two ways. Firstly, the greatness is seen in the large number of descendants described by the Lord as *"the stars of the heaven"* (Gen. 15:5) and as *"the dust of the earth"* (Gen. 13:16). The idea is that as it is impossible to add up all the stars in the heaven and all the grains of dust on the ground so Abraham's descendants would be too numerous to truly give an accurate count. This was a promise to Abram even though his wife Sarai was barren and it would seem as though they would be childless.

Abram's name was changed by God to Abraham (Gen. 17:5) and that means "father of a multitude". So God encapsulated the promise in the new name that He gave to His servant.

Secondly, the greatness would also be witnessed not simply in numbers but in influence. The nation that would be formed from the descendants of Abraham would be a powerful and influential people. Those who treated the nation well would be blessed and those who did not would be cursed (Gen. 12:3). Indeed in the Old Testament Abraham's descendants would be the premier people, namely the people of God. This proved to be the case and even today the Jewish nation are a very influential people.

A SPIRITUAL PROMISE

This is summarized as follows, *"and all peoples on earth will be blessed through you"* (Gen. 12:3, NIV). This focuses our attention upon one particular descendant of Abraham and that is our Lord and Saviour, Jesus Christ. It is because of the work of this greatest descendant that people out of every tribe, nation, tongue and people have been blessed with the richness of salvation and the joy of eternal life. Christ through His work on the cross and by His resurrection is enabled by God to bring the blessings of forgiveness to anyone who believes on Him. Maybe Abraham did not have the full details of this wonderful eternal promise but it is given to him in embryo form and today we are the recipients of its blessing.

So, on the basis of God's command and God's promises, Abraham set out on a journey into the great unknown. It was an adventure that must have caused him on many occasions to be afraid and wonder about the outcome but he trusted God and as such is highlighted as a great man of faith. It was faith that pleased God and that brought God's commendation to Abraham.

We are called to take God at His Word and to implicitly obey Him in all areas of our lives. We must never forget that God's command to us is to go and preach the gospel to those who need to hear that message. Will we obey in our workplace, in our home, in our neighbourhood and in our society? Certainly William Booth heard the call of God and obeyed in his time which was nineteenth century Britain. He saw the gin parlours, with small children climbing to the counter and buying their tots of liquor. He saw the squalor of prostitution, of criminality and the filthy, dirty living conditions of children and families in industrial London and other great cities of Britain. He assembled a salvation army of concerned Christians and they went out in faith and knelt in the centre of those industrial areas and claimed them for God. They took a courageous stand and were often the centre of jeering and violent crowds, who spat at them and threw rotten vegetables and dead animals at them. Yet they prayed, preached the Word of God and helped the poor. They had caught the same faith as Abraham and they too had set out on a journey and could not imagine the final destination of their travels. They did a tremendous amount to relieve the spiritual and physical suffering of many people at that time.

In the 1950s a young preacher from Pennsylvania was so moved by God as he saw the face of a young murderer in "Life" magazine, that he went out in faith to be God's witness to street gangs amongst the tenements of New York City and there to found "Teen Challenge". He set out on a journey and could only trust God as he had no experience of city life and its terrible subculture of drug addiction and violence.

"Abraham's place in the Bible's portrait gallery is altogether unique and unapproachable."
Herbert Lockyer

CHAPTER 7

THE FAITH OF ABRAHAM

PART 2

"Success is never final, failure is never fatal; it is the courage to continue that counts."

Winston Churchill

We have already noted that Abraham is the outstanding character in this list of great Old Testament people who achieved so much for God. Each one was an outstanding example of faith and is commended by God for their trust in Him. None of them was perfect as each sinned and failed God, sometimes in terrible ways but their faith caused them to rise above their failures and become utterly dependent upon the Lord. More verses in this chapter are devoted to Abraham and his exploits through faith than any of the other characters who are mentioned. He above all was the man of faith and no wonder he is called the "father of the faithful" and "the friend of God". He truly was a man of faith.

His first great act of faith was to leave his home and country and travel on a journey of which he did not know the destination. He went on that journey out of simple obedience to God and arrived at the Promised Land that his descendants would afterwards inherit. We now come to his second great act of faith. Our reading says, *"Through faith also Sara herself received strength to conceive seed, and was delivered of a child when she was past age, because she judged him faithful who had promised. Therefore sprang there even of one, and him as good as dead, so many as the stars of the sky in multitude, and as the sand which is by the sea shore innumerable"* (Heb. 11:11-12). God had promised him a son and Abraham was utterly convinced that God would give him a son, even though he was very old and his wife Sarah was well past child bearing age. He actually believed that God could perform a miracle in two people who as far as child bearing was concerned were actually dead. Humanly it all seemed so impossible.

Yet when we read the account of Abraham's life in the Old Testament we find that it took him time to arrive at the place of total faith and trust in God. Indeed in chapter 15 of Genesis Abraham seemed to be in despair and said to God, *"Lord God, what wilt thou give me, seeing I go childless, and the steward of my house is this Eliezer of Damascus?"* (Gen. 15:2). It would seem that at that stage Abraham had given up all hope of having a son to inherit his wealth and that it would all go to his servant, a faithful man called Eliezer. But God replied to Abraham in the following terms, *"This shall not be thine heir; but he that shall come forth out of thine own bowels shall be thine heir. And he brought him forth abroad, and said, Look now toward heaven, and tell the stars, if thou be able to number them: and he said unto him, So shall thy seed be. And he believed in the Lord; and he counted it to him for righteousness"* (Gen. 15:4b-6). So God had clearly stated that Abraham would be the physical and natural father of his heir and no adopted son from his household would come into the inheritance.

Yet it still took time for Abraham to appreciate the full extent of what God had said to him, for we read in Genesis 16 of Abraham's relationship with Sarah's servant girl Hagar.

ABRAHAM AND HAGAR

By the time we read of the events in Genesis 16 Abraham knew very clearly that he was to have a son, a natural son that would be heir to the wealth and covenant promises that Abraham had received from God. This knowledge makes the events of chapter sixteen all the more terrible and tragic and to some extent we still reap today the consequences of Abraham's failure.

Up to this time it would seem that Abraham had been faithful to one wife, namely Sarah. It would also seem to be right to assume that Abraham had been promised a son of his own but that there had been no direct word from the Lord that Sarah would be the mother but that was very much assumed. We can well imagine Abraham pondering upon the Lord's words and wondering how God could possibly fulfil His promises when Sarah was so old and barren. It all seemed an utter impossibility and so when Sarah mentioned a plan, her words must have seemed like the answer to his dilemma.

No doubt Abraham desperately wanted God's words to be fulfilled and he seized upon Sarah's plan with eagerness. Perhaps he thought that he could help make God's plans come true with human ingenuity and guile. We imagine that his motive was good but his actions amounted to failure and sinfulness. Yet Abraham hardly waited and failed to notice that essentially three things were wrong with the elaborate plan of Sarah.

ABRAHAM FAILED TO THINK

Abraham accepted the argument of his wife Sarah as valid because it seemed so credible. Her plan had a plausible sound to it, especially as it was couched in religious or spiritual terms. She said, *"the LORD hath restrained me from bearing: I pray thee, go in unto my maid; it may be that I may obtain children by her"* (Gen. 16:2). It was almost as if she were arguing that her plan was God's will and that the Lord had implanted these thoughts into her mind. Abraham listened to her words and then implemented her plan. No doubt he too felt that God's seal of approval was upon his actions because if the plan worked then the servant girl would give birth to a child who would be Abraham's own son and would therefore become heir to his estate.

Abraham at this stage in his pilgrimage failed to ask any questions and ignored the obvious factor that even if God had kept Sarah barren then He could just as easily reverse the process. Abraham moved ahead upon the basis of no reflection upon Sarah's words and upon the faulty spiritual logic with which the plan was framed.

We need to be very careful to think and to think in a biblical manner. It is too easy to be ensnared in false cults and to accept heretical teaching because they are put forward in spiritual language and often with kind words of comfort and love. We must learn not to be fooled and we can only gain an ability to see right from wrong by regularly reading and studying the Word of God with an open mind and an open heart. As we learn to understand what God states clearly in His Word then we will be better able to reflect upon what people say and what churches teach and be enabled with the Spirit's power to compare what is taught with what the Bible says. It is a pity that Abraham fell for the spiritual sounding argument of Sarah.

ABRAHAM FAILED TO BE DIFFERENT

In accepting the plan and putting it into operation Abraham was simply following and imitating the common practices found in the pagan societies of those days. In the heathen communities amongst whom Abraham dwelt it was usual for a servant girl to produce children and raise them up in the name of her barren mistress. It was a way of affirming the status of the chief lady of the family and also of perpetuating her offspring where she would be seen as the mother or matriarch of the household. So Abraham copied the heathen practices of his day and compromised his position of trusting in God and in his commitment to one woman, which is always God's way for marriage.

We must be so careful as Christians that we are distinct in our outlook, behaviour and attitudes. We must never simply imitate what is going on in the world and must be prepared to appear odd as we trust the Lord and obey Him in every part of our lives. In the area of making decisions we should for example be very different from how our society would expect us to make decisions. At the very least we would spend a great deal of time in honest prayer before God and seeking His will, wisdom and direction upon our major decision making processes. The end result is that we become certain that the person we marry, the church we attend, the place of work where we are employed, the course of study we pursue and the place where we live is as a result of following the direction of the Lord. Guidance is never easy but we must never simply rely upon accepted practices, upon personal logic or intelligent analysis of information. We need, as Christians, that extra dimension of knowing the leading and directing of the Spirit of God.

ABRAHAM FAILED TO PRAY

Abraham failed to consult God and there appears to have been no recourse to prayer. There was no seeking the mind of God and instead he rashly went ahead with a course of action for which God had given him no sanction. Unfortunately, many Christians today are in no position to criticize for is it not true that in many Christian activities there is far too much discussion, argument and consultation, and far too little prayer? We talk with many people about a whole host of matters instead of talking it over with our heavenly Father. Five minutes of genuine prayer is worth hours of discussion. Let us never be guilty of neglecting to spend quality time in prayer with God our Father.

The result of Abraham's failure was that Ishmael was born to Hager, the Egyptian bondservant. There were sad and continuing results because of Abraham's sinful and thoughtless actions and it is important that we remember that there are always consequences to any actions we take. Nothing is done in isolation and we must always try to think through the results of decisions we take and their effects upon other people. We will consider three consequences of Abraham's failure.

IT PRODUCED PRIDE

The servant girl Hagar became a proud person and developed an arrogant attitude especially towards her mistress Sarah and this is made clear as we read the words, "... *her mistress was despised in her eyes*" (Gen. 16:4). So obviously a deep tension entered into their relationship and Sarah became the object of scorn in the eyes of her servant. The wise writer of the book of Proverbs knew about such tension when he wrote, *"For three things the earth is perturbed, Yes, for four it cannot bear up: For a servant when he reigns, A fool when he is filled with food, A hateful woman when she is married, And a maid-servant who succeeds her mistress"* (Prov. 30:21-23, NKJV). The outworking of that statement and its truthfulness are very evidently seen in the reaction of Hagar to Sarah.

IT PRODUCED BITTERNESS

Sarah's reaction was severe and she complained to Abraham and blamed him for the consequences of his actions. She obviously conveniently forgot that she had pushed him into the relationship with Hagar and now she says, *"My wrong be upon thee: I have given my maid into thy bosom; and when she saw that she had conceived, I was despised in her eyes: the LORD judge between me and thee"* (Gen. 16:5). It all seems a bit unfair to blame Abraham but Sarah's words reflect the bitterness and resentment she felt towards Hagar and the unborn child she was bearing.

Abraham's reaction was simply to say that she was Sarah's servant and she had full control over her servants. Sarah began to ill-treat Hagar in such a way that it all became too much for the servant who decided to run away. It was a desperate action by a desperate woman but the Lord sent her back to Abraham's household with the promise that she would have a son and from him a great and powerful nation would be created.

The net result of Abraham's foolish action was a household riddled with tension, division and antagonism. It was all due to his moral compromise and his failure to consult God in prayer.

IT PRODUCED CONTINUING DIVISION

The results of Abraham's actions produced consequences that have lasted for thousands of years and we still live with those consequences today. The descendants of Hagar's son Ishmael are the Arab nations. The descendants of Sarah's son Isaac are the Jewish nation. Through the centuries and even into our own day we have seen the antagonism between these two great people nations and the fearful tensions and violence that have been witnessed in the Middle East as a consequence of that antagonism. We live in a tense and divided world caused in part by the actions of this one man Abraham who lived all those years ago.

It is true, as Abraham found out, that we cannot sin with impunity. Compromise in spiritual things never succeeds. We must never as Christians take matters into our own hands, without consulting God and His Word with open hearts and minds. We must be wary of making quick, snap decisions and also take care that those who are close to us do not lead us astray, even unwittingly. We must work out the principles for Christian behaviour from the Scriptures through regularly reading and studying the Bible.

Yet we can take encouragement that in spite of Abraham's failure he is held up as a model of faith. Thus when we fail the Lord, and we do all too often, we need to remind ourselves not to remain failed. God has called us to triumph and victory in spiritual things. Each believer has a real part to play in the overall great victory of God. We thus must be like Abraham and not remain guilt-ridden, defeated, mediocre and failed but we must rise up in confession of sin, repentance and faith. Only then will we like Abraham know God's power and victory in our lives. Eventually Abraham learned to trust God for that great son of promise, who was his own natural son and who was also the natural son of his wife Sarah. What a day of rejoicing for Abraham and Sarah when that son, Isaac was born! God's promise was fulfilled, Abraham's joy was complete and this was the line of succession through which came our Saviour the Lord Jesus Christ.

"It is better to fail in a cause that will ultimately succeed, than to succeed in a cause that will ultimately fail."

Peter Marshall

CHAPTER 8

THE FAITH OF ABRAHAM
PART 3

"A religion which costs nothing is worth nothing."
J. C. Ryle

As we read through this great chapter of Hebrews 11 we are struck by the fact that Abraham dominates these verses. More is said about him and his faith than about any of the other great Old Testament saints. His first great act of faith was to set out on a long journey and leave the safety and comfort of his homeland and his extended family. It was made worse by the fact that he did not know where he was going and the final destination of his travels was unknown to him. He went simply because God had commanded him to go and in faith he obeyed the requirements of God. His second great act of faith was to trust God for a son, even though he and his wife Sarah were very old and his wife had never conceived. She had been barren, having never given birth to any children. Yet despite their age and medical history Abraham believed that God would give them a son. It was the son of promise and his name was Isaac.

Abraham had to wait patiently for the fulfilment of God's personal promise to him and it must have seemed like a long time in coming. It seems that the greater the faith, the greater the trials but eventually there was joy in his heart, in the heart of Sarah and in their extended household as the waiting was at last over and Sarah conceived. We read, *"For Sarah conceived, and bare Abraham a son in his old age, at the set time of which God had spoken to him"* (Gen. 21:2). That longed-for son was given the name of Isaac and was the cause of much rejoicing and celebration. He was the son that would inherit his father's wealth, influence and also the wonderful covenant promises that God had made with Abraham. Yet with that son came another test of faith for Abraham. This was the famous incident as recorded in Genesis 22 of God calling Abraham to offer up his son Isaac as a sacrifice upon an altar.

I can hardly imagine Abraham's thoughts and feelings as God said to him, *"Take now thy son, thine only son Isaac, whom thou lovest, and get thee into the land of Moriah; and offer him there for a burnt offering upon one of the mountains which I will tell thee of"* (Gen. 22:2). Possibly his thoughts were confused and his feelings anguished but there is nothing of that reflected in chapter 22 of Genesis. There simply seems to have been instant obedience and total faith and confidence in the provision of God.

THE REASON

The reason for this act of sacrifice is found in verse one and we read, *"after these things...God tested Abraham"* (Gen. 22:1, NKJV). This was a test for Abraham to demonstrate his loyalty and trust in God. God knew the heart of his servant and knew the devotion and commitment he had to serving God. The test was to demonstrate that the priority of Abraham's heart was the Lord God Almighty. The first call upon Abraham would always be God and that would take precedence over family, friends, neighbours and colleagues and even his own precious son of promise. The test demonstrated that there was no idol in Abraham's life. There was nothing that could break his communion with God and this was to be openly demonstrated on Mount Moriah where he would be willing to sacrifice his son. Abraham through all his travels and through the ups and downs of his spiritual pilgrimage had finally come to total faith and commitment to God and this fact was demonstrated by his willingness to obey God without question and without dragging his feet. The very next day after the call of God to sacrifice his son he got up early in the morning to do as God had commanded him. Such instant obedience is remarkable and reveals how deeply and totally Abraham had come to trust in God.

THE PURPOSE

We notice that Abraham travelled with his son and two servants. They carried the wood, the fire and a knife and went to the place that God had directed Abraham to go. Eventually, Abraham left the servants and travelled on with Isaac with the words, " *I and the lad will go yonder and worship, and come again to you*" (Gen. 22:5). These are remarkable words because Abraham knew that he was going to sacrifice his son on the altar he would build on Mount Moriah and yet he fully expected to return with his son Isaac. This seems almost contradictory and at the very least paradoxical. If his son died on the altar then there was no way they could both return and it would not be the two of them returning but Abraham alone.

However, his words express his sincere and deep rooted faith and confidence in the Lord God Almighty. He now knew God and had for a long time had wonderful dealings with the true and living God and so we read that Abraham, *"Accounting that God was able to raise him* [Issac] *up, even from the dead; from whence also he received him in a figure"* (Heb. 11:19). So Abraham actually believed that God was so great that he could raise his son to life again, even if he were offered as a sacrifice upon the altar at Mount Moriah. This again reflects the wonderful faith of Abraham; it was an unquestioning assurance that God would keep His promises and would supply descendants and produce a great nation through the son of promise, namely Isaac.

Yet the purpose of going to Mount Moriah was to worship God. The people of God are expected to worship the Lord and this was Abraham in worship to Jehovah. Worship is a demonstration of deep love for God because of His "worthship", namely that He is worthy to receive praise, adoration, love, thanksgiving and devotion. To truly worship the Lord involves sacrifice and in Abraham's case it would have been an enormous sacrifice of the most precious part of his life. Nothing was more precious to Abraham than his son and he was willing to sacrifice him to the Lord.

We notice that true worship flows from a number of factors.

1. **Communion:** Abraham was in deep and constant communion with the Lord and his act of worship flowed from those times he spent in prayer with God. We cannot automatically turn on worship, like a tap, just when we enter a church building. It is not simply a matter of place because we will never truly worship the Lord as a company of Christians if as individuals we are not in constant communion with the Lord. By communion we are not talking about "holy communion" or the "breaking of bread" service, but the reality of fellowship with God. We are talking about being in touch with God and enjoying the presence of God as a daily constant reality. This is found through the daily quiet time of reading God's Word to hear His voice and spending time in prayer. Throughout the day we should lift up our hearts in prayer and praise to our Saviour and so maintain the presence of God in our lives and enjoy companionship with the Lord. It is really impossible to worship if we are out of communion with God. Certainly Abraham was in such deep communion with God that it enabled him to know the will of God for worship on Mount Moriah. He knew the heartbeat of God and was in close companionship with the Almighty. True worship flows from communion with God.

2. **Communication:** this is closely linked with communion and involves speaking and listening. Certainly God listens to the prayers of His people, when they come from a holy and righteous heart and have a deep desire for His glory. So motive in prayer is important if God is going to listen and answer our requests to Him. Also we need to read God's Word in such a way that we hear Him speaking to us. The reading of the Bible should be an everyday activity for the true Christian. It must be read slowly, prayerfully and perhaps a few times so that God can speak to us out of

the passage before us. Certainly Abraham was in deep communication with God and clearly heard His directive to go and offer Isaac on the altar at Mount Moriah. True worship flows from communication with God.

3. **Obedience:** certainly Abraham had come to the place of total and unquestioning obedience to God's will. That is why he is known as *"the Friend of God"* (Jas. 2:23). The Lord Jesus told His disciples, *"Ye are my friends, if ye do whatsoever I command you"* (John 15:14), and again He said, *"If ye love me, keep my commandments"* (John 14:15). So obedience to God flows from love for God and as Christians we obey the Lord because we love Him and want to please Him because He has saved us from sin and its consequences. Abraham through his many experiences of God had learned to obey the Lord and obey Him implicitly. Certainly Abraham was obedient to God and that enabled him to worship on Mount Moriah. True worship is always tainted and weakened by sin and disobedience.

4. **Faith:** this was the outstanding quality of Abraham's spiritual response to the Lord. Firstly, when Isaac his son asked the question, *"Behold the fire and the wood: but where is the lamb for a burnt offering?"* (Gen. 22:7), Abraham answered with complete confidence, namely the confidence of faith in God. He said, *"God himself will provide the lamb for the burnt offering, my son"* (Gen. 22:8, NIV). It is impossible to truly worship the Lord without having total confidence in the provision of the Lord for salvation. Secondly, Abraham had faith that God would restore Isaac to him, even if he were offered as a sacrifice. Certainly Abraham had deep faith in God that enabled him to worship God on Mount Moriah.

5. **Sacrifice:** Abraham was willing to make sacrifices in order to worship God. His first sacrifice was to get up early and travel three days by donkey to go to the

right place in order to worship God. No cost was too great for Abraham in order that he might offer acceptable worship to God. His second great sacrifice was much more costly and that was his willingness to offer up Isaac upon the altar. Ultimately there was nothing that Abraham would withhold if God demanded it by way of sacrifice. If he was willing to give his son, then he was willing to give everything he possessed. It was as if he viewed everything as unimportant before his relationship with God. We remember in the New Testament in John 12, the lady who poured expensive perfume upon the feet of Jesus. The cost was nearly a year's wages and she offered it in worship to her Saviour. Certainly worship is nothing if it costs us nothing. What sacrifice do we make in order to worship the Lord? Do we give up time, expend energy, exercise discipline and go without sleep and food so that we might truly worship the Lord? Abraham was willing to pay any price in order to worship God and that enabled him to worship on Mount Moriah.

So Abraham worshipped God as one who had learned the blessing of communion with the Lord as well as communication. He had also become committed to the Lord in obedience and faith and was willing to sacrifice everything, even what was precious so that God would be truly worshipped.

THE RESULTS

A number of positive and wonderful results came from Abraham's act of devotion to God. Firstly, his confidence in the Lord was seen to be well founded and he did return to the servants and subsequently to his household with his son Isaac. God had not let him down. Secondly, it demonstrated what a true servant Abraham was to his God. There was nothing he would withhold from the Lord and the test that the Lord had given him was passed with flying colours. Of course it was not Isaac's life which God desired, it was Abraham's heart. Abraham did not fail, for he was willing to give to God his precious son. In effect he was saying, "Lord, take everything". In Abraham's life there was no idol, nothing to break communion with God and this was so openly demonstrated on Mount Moriah. This then, was Abraham's faith – total commitment of all he had to the Lord. So he becomes a great example to the people of God of all generations of what it means to live by faith.

"Faith is not blind unbelief. Faith is not superstition. Faith works by reason. It does the thing that seems contrary to expectation, but it does it, reckoning on God by faith, being sure of God; being sure that after Abraham had done his utmost, and his son was blotted out of his heaven, God was able to raise Isaac up. By faith Abraham offered up his son. That was the supreme activity" (G. Campbell Morgan). So in the offering up of his son we are seeing Abraham as supremely trusting in God. Would we be willing to give up in order to obey God? Would we ever give up something precious in order to live as God wants us to live?

I have read of parents who have watched their son or daughter go to the mission field and face the debilitating conditions of living in impoverished countries. It is not easy for parents to let their children go and trust God for their welfare. Some parents have refused to give their blessing and have remained bitter towards both God and their children. Others have given their blessing hardly understanding what their child might be doing but knowing that they are moving outside the security and material standards of Western society. They like Abraham have learned to trust God and were willing to let go and rejoice in the calling the Lord has made upon their son or daughter.

The great missionary and former cricketer C. T. Studd gave up wealth to go to China and preach the gospel. Later he went to India and then for the last fourteen years of his life went to Central Africa and during that time only saw his wife for two weeks. It was an incredible sacrifice for them both as he served on the mission field and she served in the home office of the mission. Yet it was all given to God without rancour or a bitter spirit. They walked in the footsteps of Abraham all those years ago.

God provided a ram as a sacrifice and this pointed to the Lord Jesus who was our substitutionary sacrifice on Calvary's cross. As the ram died instead of Isaac, so Christ died instead of us. He took our place because we deserved to be punished for our sins but Christ died for us. How we thank God for the wonderful love that caused Jesus to bleed and die for our sins.

Finally, in this whole incident we see an allegory of something greater. In Isaac we see a son willing to die because his father said so and that reminds us that Christ in obedience to His Father willingly died on the cross for our sins. No wonder in some churches Genesis 22 is frequently read at the communion service. It provides a vivid picture, a prophecy in historical narrative of the greater work that would be achieved by Christ, who died for our sins on the cross. We rejoice today in the finished work of Christ.

So Abraham was a mighty man of faith. May we too learn to live by faith and trust God in every situation and serve Him with true faithfulness and utter devotion.

> *"He is no fool who gives what he cannot keep to gain what he cannot lose."*
> *Jim Elliot*

CHAPTER 9

THE FAITH OF SARAH

"The woman who became the mother of nations."

Herbert Lockyer

Through faith also Sara herself received strength to conceive seed, and was delivered of a child when she was past age, because she judged him faithful who had promised. Therefore sprang there even of one, and him as good as dead, so many as the stars of the sky in multitude, and as the sand which is by the sea shore innumerable. Hebrews 11:11-12

Sarah is the first lady to be mentioned in the list of Old Testament saints in Hebrews 11. She was an outstanding woman of God, though throughout her life she was very much overshadowed by her famous husband Abraham. She is described by Herbert Lockyer as, "The woman who became the mother of nations." That description alone is remarkable because for most of her life she was infertile and unable to produce children, but in old age and by a miracle of God she was given the privilege of motherhood when Isaac was born. That son was the result of God's promise and he became the second patriarch or founding father of Israel after Abraham.

HER BACKGROUND

Sarah came from Ur of the Chaldees and was the daughter of Terah, who was also the father of Abraham. So when Sarah married Abraham, who was ten years older, she was marrying her half-brother, because they had a common father, but different mothers (Gen. 20:12). Such marriages between close relatives were eventually outlawed amongst the people of Israel but in Sarah's days they were much more common. "Marriages between near relatives were countenanced in those days and were sometimes common for religious reasons, but not marriages between those actually by the same mother" (Lockyer).

Her name was originally Sarai, which means "princely" or "a princess" and identifies her as coming from an honoured and well connected family. Her name was later changed by God to Sarah and that signified that the Lord had blessed her and that she would have a son and become the mother of nations. Indeed God said, *"As for Sarai thy wife, thou shalt not call her name Sarai, but Sarah shall her name be. And I will bless her, and give thee a son also of her: yea, I will bless her, and she shall be a mother of nations; kings of people shall be of her"* (Gen. 17:15-16). She thus became the honoured matriarch or founding mother of Israel and is held up as an outstanding example of faith in Hebrews 11. Thus eventually in fulfilment of God's promise the years of frustrated barrenness gave way to the joy and delight of motherhood. So we read, *"By faith Sarah herself also received strength to conceive seed, and she bore a child[a] when she was past the age, because she judged Him faithful who had promised"* (Heb. 11:11, NKJV).

Her devotion and obedience to Abraham her husband was total and unquestioning. She journeyed with him from Ur to Haran and then from Haran to the Promised Land of Canaan. She ran his household, exercised hospitality to his guests and entered into the same wonderful faith in God that he enjoyed. The Apostle Peter holds her up as an example of a model wife when he writes, *"For after this manner in the old time the holy women also, who trusted in God, adorned themselves, being in subjection unto their own husbands: Even as Sara obeyed Abraham, calling him lord: whose daughters ye are, as long as ye do well, and are not afraid with any amazement"* (1 Pet. 3:5-6). So Sarah is held up in the New Testament as an example of an outstanding wife who supports and respects her husband and contributes positively to the working of their marriage relationship.

HER BEAUTY

Sarah was blessed with outstanding natural beauty and indeed this is the testimony of the Bible. We read, *"I know that thou art a fair woman to look upon"* (Gen. 12:11), and *"when Abram was come into Egypt, the Egyptians beheld the woman that she was very fair"* (Gen. 12:14). Her physical attractiveness made Abraham nervous and even frightened on a number of occasions. The first was when he travelled to Egypt to escape a famine in Canaan. In Egypt he feared that he would be killed so that his wife could be taken into the royal harem. So he and Sarah devised a plan in which they would claim to be siblings and not a married couple. In a way their words were true because they were half brother and sister, but the idea was to deceive the Egyptians and at that point in their lives they had lost their trust in the Lord. Sarah was taken into the royal harem but God preserved her from violation and she was returned to Abraham and the couple were loaded down with wealth but ordered to leave the country.

Sarah's beauty must have been remarkable for it lasted well into old age and she was even deeply attractive at the age of ninety. This is evident because the experience of Egypt was repeated when Abraham moved into southern Canaan and the King of Gerar took Sarah into his harem on the understanding that she was Abraham's sister and not his wife. Again God preserved Sarah from violation and again Abraham was protected from violence and given great wealth by the king of Gerar (Gen. 20). It was another sad example of Abraham failing to act in faith.

Hebrew folklore "has kept alive stories of her remarkable beauty and ranks her next to the most perfect woman the world has known, Eve" (Lockyer). Her beauty was all the more remarkable because she had endured the strains and stresses of travel through terrible heat and dusty deserts. Indeed Orientals have always considered travel as the most unfavourable factor for continuing beauty and even consider travel as fatal to it. That explains why Abraham sounds so surprised and utters the words, *"I know that you are a woman of beautiful countenance"* (Gen. 12:11, NKJV).

Yet beauty is much more than the surface and is not just skin deep. It is the enduring qualities that truly make a person beautiful and these were also evident in Sarah. She had certainly inner strength and resolve. She had respect and devotion to her husband. She came to a total commitment of faith in the Lord. These are wonderful qualities that also make her character beautiful that goes very much with the physical beauty with which she was endowed.

As Christians we are to focus much more upon development of character and the inner part of our lives than ever we should upon the outward aspects of physical beauty. This does not mean that we should go around looking scruffy or unkempt. We should have our hair done, keep clean and do our best to look attractive. However, this must not be the driving force of our lives and we should make much more effort to develop the beauty of character which is the fruit of the Spirit in our lives. This requires a determination to spend time each day with God in prayer and to listen to His voice through regular reading of His Holy Word. We should obey without question the commandments of the Lord and trust Him in any and every situation. We need to also look for the fullness of the Holy Spirit in our lives and let the Spirit direct, guide and lead us and this should certainly be true of every major decision we ever make. We should know the Spirit's leading about marriage, work, church and where we live. Our prayer should constantly be:

> "Let the beauty of Jesus be seen in me.
> All His wondrous compassion and purity.
> Oh thou Spirit Divine all my nature refine.
> Till the beauty of Jesus be seen in me."
> —*Let the Beauty of Jesus*, Albert Osborn

HER JOY

Sarah shared with her husband one abiding sadness and that was that she was childless. Their long life together as husband and wife had produced no offspring and this was a great grief to them both. Yet it is often much harder for a wife to be barren than for a husband and that was especially true in those days. "To a Hebrew woman, barrenness was looked upon as a gnawing grief, and sometimes regarded as a sign of divine disfavour" (Lockyer). This embarrassment to her pride and standing forced her to make an arrangement that did not have divine approval. She offered her servant girl Hagar to Abraham as a concubine and hoped that she would produce a child who could be raised up in her name. This was a common practice in those days where a servant would raise up a child in the name of her barren mistress.

Sarah knew the promise of God and yet she still pushed forward her plan and encouraged Abraham to follow heathen practices rather than to trust God for an heir. The result was that Ishmael was born to Hagar and there was terrible tension between Hagar and Sarah. Hagar became arrogant and despised her mistress and eventually she and her son were driven out of Abraham's camp but were eventually cared for by that patriarch. We must remember that there are always serious and often prolonged negative consequences when we disobey God or when we try to do things without His specific direction or approval. It is so important that before we make any major decision we seek the Lord's clear direction.

God renewed His promise that a son would be born to Abraham and Sarah and both of them reacted with laughter. However, Abraham's laughter was that of faith for we read, *"Then Abraham fell upon his face, and laughed, and said in his heart, Shall a child be born unto him that is an hundred years old? and shall Sarah, that is ninety years old, bear?"* (Gen. 17:17), though even in his case he seemed unable to truly believe that such a thing were possible. Sarah overheard this promise of a son being reaffirmed to Abraham and *"Sarah laughed within herself…"* (Gen. 18:12). Her laughter was the laughter of doubt and disbelief and when confronted by the messengers of God she instantly sobered up and out of fear denied that she had laughed. No doubt from that point onward she took the promise of God very seriously indeed.

When God fulfilled His promise and Sarah bore a son she was overcome with delight and so was Abraham. They called that son of promise by the name of Isaac, a name that means 'laughter'. Truly Sarah's laughter had become one of deep joy and satisfaction in what God had done in enabling her to hold in her arms her own child. We read, *"And Sarah said, God hath made me to laugh, so that all that hear will laugh with me. And she said, Who would have said unto Abraham, that Sarah should have given children suck? for I have born him a son in his old age"* (Gen. 21:6-7). This miracle that was wrought by faith was an anticipation of a far greater miracle that would take place hundreds of years into the future, namely the miracle of the incarnation. It would take place in Palestine when God the Son would be born of Mary in Bethlehem and grow up to die on a cross in order to be the Saviour of the world. Certainly at His birth there was great joy as the shepherds in the fields heard the announcement of the news by the angels of God.

HER DEATH

Sarah is the only woman in Scripture whose specific age is stated. She died at the age of one hundred and twenty-seven (Gen. 23:1). This means that she died thirty-eight years before her husband but her life had found a fulfilled satisfaction in the birth and development of her son Isaac. She was buried in a tomb and her grave is the very first to be mentioned in the Bible.

When it came to burying his wife Abraham decided to do away with the nomadic customs of desert people. They buried their loved ones in graves out in the desert where there were shifting sands and that meant that vultures and beasts of prey could dig up those bodies and eat the dead. Abraham wanted a more permanent burying place for Sarah and so he bought a piece of ground in Canaan and in the cave of Machpelah he entombed his dear wife. Later when he died his sons buried him with Sarah and "thus, in death, symbolically, they were unseparated as they had been through their long and eventful life together" (Lockyer).

THE FAITH OF SARAH

Lockyer further writes, "There is a legend that Sarah died of a broken heart as she learned of God's command to Abraham to offer their son Isaac as a sacrifice on Mount Moriah. The sword pierced her heart, as it did Mary's when she witnessed the slaying of her illustrious Son at Calvary. When Sarah saw her husband and son leaving the tent, taking with them wood and a large knife she became terrified with shock and died. When Abraham and Isaac returned— Isaac brought back from the dead as it were—it was only to mourn and weep for Sarah. Had she lived she might have received her dead son back from the hands of God, and heard from her husband how his hand had been restrained by the angel...But in the legend it goes on to tell us, eye and ear of the devoted wife and mother were closed to earthly things, and her heart stilled forever beyond the reach of the terrors, to which human flesh, and especially mothers' hearts, are heirs." Such a legend may be true but it is not found in the Bible but certainly Sarah died and was buried in a tomb in the land of Canaan. Her tomb was the first piece of land ever to be owned in Canaan by the nation of Israel.

HER EXAMPLE

In the book of Galatians the apostle Paul describes Sarah as the freewoman and Hagar as the bondwoman, though he only mentions Hagar by name. He indicates that the gospel which speaks of faith and promise is descended from the freewoman, while the Law which speaks of works and bondage derives from the bondwoman. He urges the Galatians to delight in their freedom in Christ and to never again come under the bondage of sterile religious activity (Gal. 4:19-31).

The Apostle Peter uses Sarah as the example of an outstanding wife in his first epistle. Sarah was strong willed, determined and clearly very strong in her character and was even known to lose her temper but she never disobeyed her husband and always showed him the greatest respect and reverence. The reformer Martin Luther, who was happily married, once said that if he wanted an obedient wife he would have to carve her out of marble. However Peter points to Sarah as the great example of an obedient wife who has her husband's best interests at heart. All Christian wives says Peter can learn from the example of Sarah.

She suffered a great deal but lived in close harmony with her husband. She went through terrible sorrows but eventually experienced the grace of God that enabled her to say "Your will be done". She had learned to trust God and to rely upon His promises and she became the mother of Israel and the mother of all who have entered into the family of faith. She is the mother of the faithful and an abiding example of consecration to the Lord. She was an outstanding servant of God.

"Nothing is so infectious as example."
Charles Kingsley

CHAPTER 10

THE FAITH OF ISAAC

"Isaac was a man of submission and meditation."

Anonymous

By faith Isaac blessed Jacob and Esau concerning things to come.　　　　　Hebrews 11:20

Having devoted twelve verses to a review of Abraham's faith the writer of Hebrews 11 seems to almost dismiss the next three patriarchs as of no consequence. Isaac, Jacob and Joseph are given one verse each and we almost get the impression that they are brushed aside as the writer rushes on to consider the next great servant of God, Moses.

Yet the truth is that the Spirit of God does not dismiss them. They are named in this great list and their faith is highlighted as spiritual mountain top experiences in the history of Israel. The faith of each one, Isaac, Jacob and Joseph, is old age or death-bed faith. It is faith that has endured and reached its pinnacle at life's end. They had overcome sins, doubts, difficulties, failures and troubles to be at the point of absolute trust in God. As their life journey on earth was nearing the end so they had become utterly committed to the Lord. This is a challenge to us as our faith needs to grow constantly and we need to be committed to being steadfast to the Lord right to the end of our life on earth.

Isaac was second in the line of the three founding fathers of Israel. He succeeded Abraham his father to the covenant promises and he preceded his son Jacob. His name appears in twenty-one books in the Bible, but usually in a list with the other two patriarchs. He lived to be 180 years old and was married to Rebekah. His life story is told in the book of Genesis 21-35, but chapter 26 is the only chapter that is solely devoted to him.

Isaac's life was very much a passive life. It was undistinguished and almost colourless. It lacked the great energy and initiative which so clearly characterized Abraham and Jacob. His life was so lacking in vitality that he has been described as "the ordinary son of a great father and the ordinary father of a great son". So squeezed between the greatness of Abraham and Jacob is the ordinariness of Isaac. If you are ordinary then this message is for you, if you are great and above the ordinary then I doubt that this message is for you.

Isaac was a faithful husband but a weak father. He seemed to be so lacking in any aspect of greatness but the tremendous fact is that God blessed him. God in His grace and mercy accepts all kinds of people, the ordinary as well as the extraordinary, the passive as well as the active, the weak as well as the strong. This must be a very great blessing and encouragement to us and we need to constantly remember that in Christ we are accepted by God and we can be used and blessed for His glory. In the nineteenth century a man by the name of John Henry L. Ewen travelled to Argentina and founded churches as a result of preaching the gospel. He was described as "not one of exceptional ability or attractive presence, but one who believed God and trusted implicitly in Him." Today there are more than one thousand churches in the movement he initiated in Argentina.

ISAAC WAS PASSIVE

Isaac's life reveals a temperament that was passive and not active. We see this in three examples.

1. **The experience on Mount Moriah:** Abraham had been instructed by God to make an altar and offer up his son Isaac as the sacrifice on that altar (Gen. 22). At that time Abraham was very old and Isaac was a young man and it would seem that he could have easily resisted his father's actions, but he did not. Some commentators have suggested that Isaac was at least in his late teens, while others have put him older in his twenties or even in his thirties. So he could have refused to be bound and killed on the

altar but he passively accepted what his father was doing, so that Abraham could reveal his obedience to God. Many others with different characters might have resisted or at least have very closely questioned their father's actions but not Isaac. The result is that he becomes a terrific picture of the Lord Jesus who was willing to die on Calvary's cross for our sins in obedience to the will of His Father.

2. **The experience of Marriage**: in Genesis 24 we read of Abraham's plan to find a wife for Isaac. He did not want Isaac to marry a woman from the pagan people amongst whom they lived in Canaan and so he despatched his faithful servant to Haran in order to find a wife for Isaac from his distant relatives of that area. Isaac did not question his father and simply accepted the plan and married Rebekah who was brought back from Haran by Abraham's servant. In the end it is a beautiful story of love and faithfulness but essentially reveals Isaac as accepting the choice of others. His was faith but not adventurous faith. His was not initiative and action but passive acceptance. He had a contentment in the Lord's choice and such contentment is a wonderful blessing for each Christian, as the New Testament tells us that *"godliness with contentment is great gain"* (1 Tim. 6:6).

3. **The experience of Digging Wells**: in Genesis 26 we read of Isaac's servants digging wells of water and Isaac is remembered for such wells. Actually he redug the wells which Abraham had dug before him and on two occasions Isaac dug wells only for the Philistines to demand them. His approach was to give them up and move on and when the third well was dug he was left in peace. Isaac's approach was a refusal to argue or contend with the Philistines; even though he had dug the wells. He simply gave them up and moved on. It is very hard to imagine either Abraham or Jacob being

so accommodating but Isaac just quietly moved on and continued digging for water. At the third attempt he was left in peace to water his flocks and herds.

We notice that he redug wells and that was because the original wells had been filled with rubble and debris. In our own lives it is possible that we have allowed sin and selfishness to stop the flow of life-refreshing water to reach out to others. We may need to once again experience the true blessing of the living water of God in our lives. We notice too that Abraham's experience was not enough for Isaac. He had to redig the wells himself and it simply reminds us that we cannot live from another's spiritual experience even if that person is a close relative such as a father or brother. I well remember a young man who had professed faith in Christ over a number of years who constantly talked about his father's spiritual life and he never mentioned anything of his own. It was as if he tried to live his Christian life through his father. It is imperative that we constantly have a fresh personal experience of the Lord in our own lives.

There are times when we should be like Isaac and display passivity, as there are times to be passive and times to be active. We remember that the Lord Jesus just before He launched out on His public ministry was found in prayer (Luke 3:21). He was prayerful or passive before He went out to actively preach and conduct his public ministry. The apostle Paul was found in prayer before he started to preach the gospel in the city of Damascus. Also the early church was in prayer for a prolonged period of time before they launched into gospel preaching in the city of Jerusalem (Acts 2). We need to remember that it is important to be passive before being active in the service of Christ, to be prayerful before preaching the gospel. Thus there are times to wait before we go out and witness to people. Thus there is much to be learned from the passive life of Isaac.

ISAAC BELIEVED GOD

Our particular verse that focuses upon Isaac, Hebrews 11:20, mentions a strange incident to be marked out as faith in the life of Isaac. It is strange because when we read about that incident in Genesis 27 it is very clearly failure and not faith. It was all about the time when the patriarchal blessing was to be bestowed. Isaac wanted to bestow this blessing upon his oldest son, Esau and not upon his youngest son, Jacob. Isaac had now taken to his bed and his passivity had become total and he loved his eldest son. The one reason for this love was the savoury stew that Esau made for his father.

Isaac planned to bestow the blessing upon Esau and so instructed his son to go and get some venison and make the stew. Esau was then to bring the stew to his father and would receive the blessing after his father had eaten. However Rebekah made a plan and put Esau's clothes on Jacob, put skins on his neck and hands because Esau was hairy but Jacob was smooth skinned. She made savoury stew and Jacob took it into Isaac who because he was blind was unable to recognize his son. The stew tasted like Esau's, the clothes smelled like Esau's because he lived in the open air and the skin felt hairy like Esau's. So three senses told Isaac that this was Esau. The result was that Jacob received the patriarchal blessing from his father Isaac. It is this incident that is highlighted as faith in Isaac.

Sadly Isaac's passive nature had become totally self-indulgent and this led to two tragic consequences.

1. **He had a divided home**: he and Rebekah did not see eye to eye and his favourite son was Esau, while his wife's was Jacob. This led to tension and the necessity of Rebekah and Jacob resorting to intrigue and trickery to deceive Isaac into bestowing the blessing on Jacob. There is something deeply tragic about a divided and tense home and selfishness will always be at the heart of such tension. The wonder of Christ is that He has healed many a divided home as people have welcomed Him into their hearts as Saviour.

2. **He had blurred spiritual perceptions**: Isaac knew right from the birth of the twin boys and even before

their birth that *"the elder shall serve the younger"* (Gen. 25:23). Yet here he wanted to bestow the blessing upon the older son Esau at the expense of the younger son Jacob. It was a vain and futile attempt to thwart the purposes of God. God's purposes were vested in Jacob as he would continue the promised line to see God's promises fulfilled. Yet Isaac was tricked into giving the blessing to Jacob and not Esau. This incident incredibly is held up as an example of wonderful faith. How can this be?

We can say two things to underline the genuine faith of Isaac. Firstly, the words of the blessing reflect his absolute and total confidence in God. They are words of total trust for his offspring in God's great and glorious provisions. He may have believed that he was giving the blessing to Esau but the very words he used showed that he truly trusted God. Indeed it could be said that he was not trying to alter the purposes of God, just the method by which they would come about. He wanted the promise to flow through Esau and not Jacob. So the words of the blessing are a true indication of his faith.

Secondly we can say that Isaac's faith truly shines when he understood the trick that Rebekah and Jacob had played. This was when he realized that he had blessed the "wrong" son. He instantly recognized that the deceitfulness of his family had worked in the interests and purposes of God. He accepted their deceit as God's interference and he laid aside his foolish plans and refused, utterly refused to remove the blessing from Jacob. In fact he underlined the blessing to Jacob by saying, *"yea, and he shall be blessed"* (Gen. 27:33).

Esau's reaction was upset and fury and he did his utmost to make his father change his mind. We read in Hebrews 12:16-17, *"Esau...was rejected: for he found no place of repentance, though he sought it carefully with tears."* Thus Esau wept before Isaac his father and tried to get him to change his mind and remove the blessing from Jacob and transfer it to himself. Yet this could not be done because Isaac would not change his mind. No doubt Isaac was sorry and even ashamed when he realized that God had outwitted him. He saw God's hand in what had taken place and he refused to remove the blessing. A lesser blessing was bestowed upon Esau.

So often it is true that genuine faith, deepest faith is revealed when a person faces up to failure. Isaac seems to have acknowledged his wrong-doing, his false motives and sin and as he faced up to them his true faith was revealed. This was true of king David when after the terrible sin with Bathsheba he cast himself upon God for mercy and acknowledged his sin in the outpouring of Psalm 51.

So we see that out of absolute failure, resulting from the failure of faith, at last true faith burned brightly and triumphed in the heart of Isaac. Isaac, self indulgent and spiritually weak is not excluded, neglected or forgotten by the Spirit of God in Hebrews 11. His deeply embedded faith eventually triumphed over personal weakness and God chooses to highlight his faith. The failure is forgotten and Isaac is given a place with the great people of God.

So we read, *"...the God of Abraham, of Isaac, and of Jacob"* (Ex. 3:16). We would expect Him to be the God of Abraham who was clearly a man of vision, energy and faith. We would expect Him to be the God of Jacob who was a trickster made good, who had great energy and ingenuity. However He is also the God of Isaac, yes weak, faltering, failing, ordinary Isaac. Surely that is a very great encouragement to us today who so often may falter in our walk with the Lord. How many times has our faith failed and we have been weak in the face of temptation? Yet the same God who was Isaac's God will be our God and will strengthen us and bring us to ultimate victory.

In this chapter we are reading about the great people of God. Yet they all had their sins and weaknesses and the essential point is that God made them great.

William Carey was an ordinary shoemaker in Northampton in the eighteenth century and also pastor of a small Baptist Chapel. He heard a call from God to go to

India and out of that inconsequential background he moved forward in response to God's will. It was not easy as the British Government was against him and he had formidable obstacles to overcome. Yet he said, "Attempt great things for God and expect great things from God." That man set out on an impossible task and became perhaps the greatest linguistic missionary ever known. He, with his colleagues, established churches, translated the Bible into Indian languages, wrote grammars in those languages, established schools for boys and girls, helped stop immoral and violent practices and had a great influence for positive good upon the sub-continent.

Carey's faith was a total commitment to God and to His Word and he gave himself sacrificially for India. Today he is hailed as a great man and a great man of faith, yet he knew his low times when his wife was mentally ill and when fire destroyed vital manuscripts and printing equipment. Yet for him faith triumphed and today as we serve the same great and wonderful God may we too know the triumph of faith and may we learn total devotion to Jesus Christ. All this would be for the glory of God.

"In the gospels, Jesus often rebukes weak faith, but never rejects it."

John Berridge

CHAPTER 11

THE FAITH OF JACOB

*"Jacob's blessing—a hope that can
never be disappointed."*

Anonymous

> *By faith Jacob, when he was a dying, blessed both
> the sons of Joseph; and worshipped, leaning upon
> the top of his staff.* Hebrews 11:21

In our study of Hebrews 11 we have now come to the next great Old Testament hero and his name is Jacob. He was the third patriarch or founding father of the nation of Israel. He was the son of Isaac and grandson of Abraham. As with Isaac before and Joseph afterwards the faith that is highlighted in Jacob is end of life or deathbed faith. He had come through many traumas, difficulties, sins and deceptions to a point where he could show the reality of his faith by blessing his sons and worshipping God. It is wonderful when faith has grown and reaches the pinnacle at life's end. However, towards the end of his life when Jacob stood before Pharaoh the king of Egypt he described his years in terms of being *"few and evil"* (Gen. 47:9).

Certainly his life was shorter than the other two patriarchs. Abraham lived to be 175 years old, while Isaac lived to be 180. Jacob lived to the comparatively short age of 130. Also his life was filled with difficulties, some of them were of his own making and at times he found life grim and he had to work extremely hard before he became the great and wealthy man of later years. Yet in the end his faith triumphed over all his struggles, difficulties, suffering, disappointments, sins, failures and deceptions.

Jacob was the second son of Isaac and Rebekah and was the result of the prayers of his father Isaac. We read, *"Isaac intreated the LORD for his wife, because she was barren: and the LORD was intreated of him, and Rebekah his wife conceived"* (Gen. 25:21).

Jacob was the younger son of twins and his older brother was named Esau. Thus both sons were the direct result of the prayers uttered by Isaac on behalf of his wife.

It was this relationship with Esau, which at times was filled with bitter rivalry that was at the heart of Jacob's life. The struggle even started before the boys were born because they jostled each other in the womb of Rebekah as we read, *"The babies jostled each other within her..."* (Gen. 25:22, NIV). As they grew up the boys competed for parental approval and favour and even after their deaths the rivalry continued. It has been maintained to this very day. The descendants of Jacob are the Jews, while the descendants of Esau was the nation of Edom, which in many respects can be equated to the Arab nations of today. The bitter struggle between Israel and Edom historically has been maintained into modern times as the Arab – Israeli dispute. So today we feel the effects of that former sibling rivalry on an international scale.

JACOB AT HOME

For many years Jacob lived at home with his parents Isaac and Rebekah. His brother Esau also lived in the same tented encampment. Yet there were significant pressures in their family and the home was sadly divided. Esau was an outdoor man, a tough, rough fellow who enjoyed hunting and with the catch made savoury stew which delighted his father's heart. So Esau was Isaac's favourite son, one of the reasons being he enjoyed his son's good food. Jacob seems to have been more homely and stayed around the family settlement. He was Rebekah's favourite son. It has been said that "men are what their mother's make them" and certainly Jacob grew up to reflect the ability of his mother's family to deceive, scheme and gain the best for themselves. He was in many ways a product of his mother's personality and learned how to gain advantage through being a good "in fighter". Certainly in his earlier life he was a true deceiver or as Luis Palau calls him, "The Schemer".

The sons knew that there were two gifts to be granted to them by their father and the one to receive those gifts would be the most important and his descendants would hold the covenant promises that had first been given to Abraham. The two gifts were as follows.

1. **The Birthright**: this gift carried the spiritual or priestly responsibility for the family. Here was the task of acting as a go-between or mediator between God and the family. The responsibility involved the work of offering sacrifices, building altars and leading the family members in worship to God. The one who received the birthright was in line to receive the renewal of the covenant that God had given to Abraham. In those days it was usual to invest such a gift in the oldest son.

    Jacob seized the birthright in a bargain he made with his brother Esau. His brother returned home from hunting and felt fatigued and hungry and he begged Jacob for some food. Jacob only fed him on the basis that the birthright would be his and so Esau traded his birthright for a "mess of pottage" or put more simply a "bowl of stew". Essentially Esau despised the birthright and considered it of little importance as he was a man of action and not one of spiritual contemplation. He was more materially inclined than spiritually inclined and no doubt would have fitted in well with the materialism of the twenty-first century.

2. **The Blessing**: this was the father's special blessing that was bestowed upon the favoured son. It meant that the one who received the blessing entered into the full enjoyment of both family headship and family wealth.

    Jacob seized the blessing by deceitful means that was planned by his mother. The time had come for Isaac to bestow the blessing and he wanted to bestow it upon Esau his oldest. His main reason seems to have been that Esau made savoury stew that Isaac thoroughly enjoyed. So Esau went hunting for the venison to make the stew and in the meanwhile Jacob dressed in Esau's clothing, with skins on his arms and neck because he was smooth skinned while Esau was hairy and with his mother's lovely savoury stew went in to see his father. Isaac who was bed ridden and blind heard Jacob enter and was deceived by the smell of Esau's clothes, the touch of goat's skins that gave a hairy feel and the taste of good stew. Thus he bestowed the blessing upon Jacob and clearly this was the ultimate desire of God. Esau was furious and threatened death to Jacob but was prudent enough to wait for Isaac's death before carrying out retribution. This enabled Jacob to escape. We read, "...*Esau, who for one morsel of meat sold his birthright. For ye know how that afterward, when he would have inherited the blessing, he was rejected: for he found no place of repentance, though he sought it carefully with tears*" (Heb. 12:16-17).

So by deceit and lying Jacob obtained both the birth-right and blessing, yet he paid a high price for such guile. He had to leave home to avoid his brother's anger and go to his uncle Laban's home in Haran. The deceiver would himself be deceived by his uncle Laban; his wife Rachel and by his sons. It is absolutely true that, "*whatsoever a man soweth, that shall he also reap*" (Gal. 6:7). Jacob had many lessons to learn and some of them very painful before he entered into the fullness of faith. It would seem that Jacob had no experience of God while he lived at home. There is no record of him praying to the Lord or of God visiting him while he resided in his father's home. He had to leave home before he came into personal contact with God.

JACOB AWAY FROM HOME

So with both Isaac and Rebekah's blessing Jacob left home and set out on the long journey to Haran in Mesopotamia. On the way he slept on the open ground with a rock for his pillow and during the night he had his first visitation from God in a dream. In that dream God renewed the covenant with him. The covenant that had been invested in Abraham and Isaac was now affirmed in Jacob. Also God gave him the promise of total protection and this promise must have been a wonderful blessing to Jacob in the years of danger and trouble that lay ahead for him.

The place where Jacob had chosen to rest was known as Luz but Jacob changed its name to Bethel which means the "house of God". It was not a building but it was the place where Jacob met with God. The important thing for us is not primarily that we have attended a service in a church building but that we have personally experienced God through Jesus Christ His Son. So Jacob experienced the presence of God and was given a promise that God's presence and protection would continue with him.

In Haran Jacob had "bitter–sweet" experiences as firstly he was received warmly as Rebekah's son and then gradually he was deceived and eventually driven out. He cared for the flocks of his uncle and endured the intense heat of daytime and the severe cold of night as he looked after those sheep.

Jacob fell in love with Laban's youngest daughter whose name was Rachel and the deal was struck that Jacob would work for seven years and then receive Rachel's hand in marriage. Yet after seven years Jacob was deceived and found himself married to the older daughter Leah and he had to work a further seven years to be joined in matrimony with Rachel. Thus Jacob had two wives and two concubines who were the maidservants of the two wives. His family grew and grew. Leah had six sons and one daughter, Zilpah (Leah's maid) bore him two sons, Bilhah (Rachel's maid) bore two more sons and eventually Rachel gave Jacob two sons, Joseph and Benjamin. She died in childbirth when they had returned many years later to Canaan.

Eventually Jacob worked a further six years for his uncle Laban and this was for proper wages. Yet despite the fact that those wages were frequently changed eventually Jacob became a very wealthy man with flocks, herds and servants. God richly blessed him and then the pressure built up. Laban and his sons became deeply angry towards Jacob and so he decided to run away with his wealth and family. The plan worked well but Rachel deceived everyone by stealing her father's household gods and this caused Laban to pursue Jacob with the intention of destroying him, but God intervened and in a dream instructed him to do Jacob no harm.

So Jacob was free from entanglement with Laban but it was really a case of out of the frying pan and into the fire. He now had to face his brother Esau, whose seething anger might be far worse after twenty years of separation. His fears must have increased when he heard the news that Esau was coming to meet him at the head of a group of four hundred men. Esau was now a powerful leader and Jacob had to face him and no doubt he was traumatized at the thought of it.

However again God intervened and at a place that was eventually named Peniel Jacob wrestled all night with God. There he had two experiences. The first was that his name was changed from Jacob which means "the supplanter" to Israel which means "a prince with God". He had prevailed with God and his new name became the name for the nation that would ultimately develop from his children.

Secondly, God touched his thigh muscle and caused him to walk with a limp. From now on there would be no more running away. God had touched him at his point of strength and had weakened him physically but spiritually he was now powerful.

At Peniel Jacob prevailed with God. Has there ever been a Peniel experience in our lives? Have we wrestled in prayer with God until we knew with a deep certainty that God had answered our prayers? Have we ever known the removal from our lives of something dear to us? Always remember that God removes to replace it with something more precious and something of more eternal worth. God's strength is made perfect in weakness. Jacob went on to face Esau and bowed in humility before him seven times. Yet Esau welcomed him with affection and love, the anger had evaporated. Their estrangement was healed and Jacob was able to move on to Bethel where he buried the idols Rachel had stolen and built an altar to worship God where the covenant promises were renewed to him. It is a reminder that idol worship and worship of the true God cannot coexist. We must destroy the idols in our own lives whether these are the idols of metal or the mental idols we build in our minds.

JACOB AND HIS FAMILY

There can be no doubt that Jacob must have often seen himself mirrored in the actions of his sons. His second and third sons, Simeon and Levi massacred the inhabitants of Shechem in revenge for violating their sister. They used deceit and cunning (Gen. 34). Reuben his eldest son committed adultery with Bilhah, his father's concubine (Gen. 35). Judah the fourth son had twins borne by his widowed daughter in law, Tamar (Gen. 38). The ten oldest sons all conspired to sell their brother Joseph into Egyptian slavery and deceived their father by claiming that a wild beast had devoured him (Gen. 37).

The loss of Joseph was a deep and abiding grief to Jacob and nothing could relieve him of the deep gloom he felt in his soul. Yet eventually the gloom was penetrated by light and the grief was lifted as he was reunited with Joseph who had become the most important official in the land of Egypt. Joseph's provision of food stocks enabled his family to move to Egypt and be preserved from the famine that had overtaken Canaan.

Eventually in Egypt Jacob's faith rises to the pinnacle. As he was dying he pronounced a blessing upon the two sons of Joseph. He had already pronounced a blessing upon his own sons. Finally while leaning upon his staff he worshipped God. He had recognized that through all the trouble, grief and sorrow God's hand had always been upon him and he had been chosen by God to continue the promised line of covenant succession. Jacob may have at times strayed from the pathway of God's will but in the mercy of God he had always come back to it. Ultimately he had come to appreciate God in three ways.

Firstly, he knew God, not as a vague generality but personally in his life and that had started at Bethel. He had to leave home in order to gain an awareness of God and His greatness. There may be too many who have never really got away from the long shadow of spirituality which their parents had and have never truly come to know God for themselves. This is a particular problem for those brought up in Christian homes, where they know how to speak and behave in a Christian manner but might never have come to know God personally in their lives through faith in Christ.

Secondly, he had seen God at work in his life through the provision of wives, children, wealth, material goods and the renewal of the covenant promise in him. He had seen God preserve his life in miraculous ways and also he had experienced six visitations directly from the Lord. This was much more than his father Isaac, though not as many as his grandfather Abraham. So he saw God at work and experienced the presence of God with him.

Thirdly, he had come to trust God totally. He had become utterly dependent upon the Lord especially since Peniel when he could never run away again. So in old age he could only lean upon his staff and trust God for the preservation and blessing of his children and grandchildren. Also he could worship the Lord with genuine praise, humility and a sense of God's abiding blessing upon him. Jacob's days on earth may have been "few and troublesome" but his days in heaven are "long and glorious". I hope we have all come to the place where we know God, see God and trust God. Like Jacob we too can have a great spiritual impact upon people and situations and know the blessing of being a "prince with God". Let us learn to trust Him with our lives and to live each day for His glory.

"Jacob's blessing—a salvation that can never be cancelled."

Anonymous

CHAPTER 12

THE FAITH OF JOSEPH

"A man whose dreams came true."

Herbert Lockyer

> By faith Joseph, when he died, made mention of the departing of the children of Israel; and gave commandment concerning his bones. Hebrews 11:22

The delightful life story of Joseph is found in Genesis 37-50 and he was the concluding patriarch or founding father of Israel. He followed in the footsteps of his father Jacob, his grandfather Isaac and his great grandfather Abraham. He was the eleventh son of Jacob and was the first son of Jacob's favourite wife Rachel. He was his father's favoured son and he is remembered to this day as the one son singled out by Jacob, with the favoured status being recognized by a gift of a *"coat of many colours"* (Gen. 37:3). This action announced to the other brothers that Joseph was special in the eyes of their father and their jealousy of him spilled over into an intense hatred, which could have easily led to them killing him. Instead they put him in a pit, a sort of dried out well and then sold him as a slave into Egypt. Yet Joseph is an outstanding example of devotion to God and of a man with a powerful intellectual capacity and clear sighted spirituality. He had a forgiving heart and a caring ministry that not only saved the nation of Egypt from starvation but also his own family. He was certainly an outstanding Old Testament servant of God.

His life can be summarized as follows, "boy sold into Egyptian slavery by jealous brothers, who makes good in adversity and from an unjust imprisonment rises to the highest offices of state. By wise planning he averts the scourge of famine, thereby saving Egypt, Canaan and his family from starvation. Reconciliation with his brothers follows and the family settles in the pastures of Goshen in the North East Nile Delta area."

THE FAVOURITE

Joseph was his father's favourite son and that was undoubtedly to begin with due to the fact that he was the first son of Jacob's favourite wife Rachel. It had seemed as though Rachel would never bear a child but by a miracle of God and in answer to prayer she conceived and gave birth to Joseph. The child grew to be a sensitive and caring boy who was grieved by the sins of his brothers and he reported their activities to his father. He also had an awareness of God through dreams that focused upon himself as one day being so great that his family would bow down before him. Therefore he knew from an early age that God had destined him for great things. Yet he was hated by his jealous brothers, both for the coat and the dreams, who when they were away from home grabbed him, tore off the coat of many colours and sold him to slave traders who were on their way to Egypt. They sold him despite his tearful pleadings with them. So he was ripped away from his father, family and familiar surroundings and entered the service as a slave in the house of Potipher a royal commander in Egypt. Joseph must have been distraught at that particular time, but even there his faith shines through.

THE SLAVE

There was no indolence in Joseph and he worked hard as a slave and it was soon realized that he was completely trustworthy and everything that he did prospered. God was with him and he learned to trust God in the loneliness of a foreign country, where he found himself no longer being free but being in slavery. Potipher soon gave Joseph full authority for the running of his household and everything was going well until the master's wife wanted to conduct an affair with Joseph, the good looking head slave. This was Joseph's greatest test and he knew that he must not yield, because it would violate his master's trust and would also be an iniquity against God. Joseph knew the sacredness of intimate sexual relationships and also the terrible sin that adultery is in the sight of God. So he reasoned with the woman, ignored her entreaties and eventually ran away from her grasp, only to be falsely accused. His master in anger had him flung into prison. It was another dark day in his life and he must have wondered whether things could get any worse?

THE PRISONER

In prison Joseph's integrity shone through and all matters relating to prison life were entrusted to him by the head jailer. In the course of his duties he served two notable prisoners who had held high office in the court of the king. They were the king's cupbearer and baker. One day they were troubled by dreams they had experienced the night before and Joseph with insight given him by God was able to interpret those dreams. The dreams revealed that the baker would be executed and the cupbearer restored to his former position. The interpretations turned out to be true and Joseph urged the cupbearer to make a plea to the king for his release, but on gaining freedom the cupbearer forgot all about Joseph. Did Joseph wonder at this point whether it was all worth it? He had lived his life with integrity and now he was worse off than a slave, namely a prisoner languishing in an Egyptian prison.

Do we sometimes wonder whether living the Christian life with integrity and godliness is really worthwhile? It may seem to be an easy option to give up and simply indulge in lust and selfishness and join those who do not know Christ as Saviour. Yet we must keep going no matter how hard it might seem, for ultimately there is fulfilment and eternal life only in the Lord Jesus. Someone sent me a little framed poem at one time when they sensed that I was feeling down and was finding my ministry difficult and discouraging. I have cherished that poem and have kept it on my desk ever since. It says,

When things go wrong as they sometimes will.
When the road you're trudging seems all uphill.
When the funds are low and the debts are high,
And you want to smile, but you have to sigh.
You never can tell how close you are,
It may be near though it seems so far:
So stick to the fight when you're hardest hit—
It's when things seem worst that you must not quit.
—Edgar A. Guest

I thank God for that poem and it seems as though it could have been written for Joseph. Even when things seemed at their darkest he did not quit and eventually the break came and he took on his life's responsibility for which God had been preparing him. The king of Egypt had two dreams one night and in the morning they deeply disturbed him and no wise man or magician in Egypt was able to interpret those dreams for the king. It was then that the cupbearer remembered Joseph and that led to the most rapid rise from rags to riches ever experienced in history.

THE CHIEF OFFICIAL

Joseph was hurriedly washed, shaved and given decent clothes to wear before being ushered into the awesome presence of the king of Egypt. There he was confronted with the dreams and with God's help, which he freely acknowledged, he gave interpretation which was that there would be seven years of abundant harvest for Egypt and then seven years of severe famine would follow. He then dispensed sound advice that surplus should be collected in the years of plenty to sustain the people through the years of famine. The king was so impressed that he made Joseph the chief man in Egypt and gave him full authority to run the country and make provision for the years of famine. So Joseph became the most powerful official in the land of Egypt. His prison days were over; as were his days of slavery and with the King's full authority he set about his task with his usual diligence and hard work. He constantly lived his life in the light of God's presence and so everything he did he did well, working to the best of his ability. He set up store houses where grain could be collected and from which the corn could be distributed in the time of famine. It turned out to be a magnificent system and it worked brilliantly.

So the people of Egypt had plenty of food when the surrounding nations were starving and those hungry people came to Egypt to buy food. They included Joseph's own family who were facing starvation in the land of Canaan. They came and unbeknown to them they were fed by Joseph and cared for by the supreme official in Egypt. The one over whom they had once exercised power now had the power of life and death over them. It was the most remarkable change of fortunes but God had clearly revealed this to Joseph in the dreams he had experienced while still living with his father and family.

THE RECONCILER

The brothers were horrified when they found out the identity of the chief official of Egypt, before whom they had so humbly bowed. However, they must have been even more astonished when Joseph freely forgave them and held no bitterness or resentment over their former treatment of him. He cared for them, showed them kind generosity and fulfilled what the apostle Paul would later write, *"be ye kind one to another, tenderhearted, forgiving one another…"* (Eph. 4:32). Joseph fully and totally forgave his brothers and held no grudge against them and there was no sense of him ever trying to get even with them or of extracting revenge for their past deeds and terrible actions.

The Christian faith is essentially about forgiveness. It is God forgiving us in Christ and us forgiving others because God has forgiven us. Indeed the atheist Bertrand Russell recognised this truth. He wrote, "Forgiveness is not a specifically Christian virtue, but I am not aware of any other sect, except Christian, which is committed by its very terms of reference to cultivate a forgiving spirit as a central and constructive force of both individual and social life." He is absolutely right and this was wonderfully exemplified in the life of Joseph. I hope it is seen in all our lives as Christian people.

The Apostle Peter once asked the Lord the following question. *"Lord, how many times shall I forgive my brother or sister who sins against me? Up to seven times?"* (Matt. 18:21, NIV). Peter no doubt felt very superior because he was willing to forgive someone seven times and perhaps he thought that he would be congratulated by the Saviour and be affirmed as the forgiving type. However, the Lord said, *"not seven times, but seventy-seven times"* (Matt. 18:22, NIV). That must have been a great shock to Peter. Seventy times seven is four hundred and ninety times. Jesus was not saying keep a strict count and then when you have passed four hundred and ninety times you need never forgive again. He was in effect saying you should always forgive and there is never a time when you should not forgive. It would be impossible to commune with the God of forgiveness if we were unwilling to forgive others. So we must always be ready to forgive and never let past events interfere with present relationships.

The brothers of Joseph had the terrible thought that when their father Jacob died then Joseph would exact revenge. They thought that Joseph was only showing them kindness to keep their father happy but of course nothing could have been further from his mind and he reassured them. Indeed he said, *"Fear not: for am I in the place of God? But as for you, ye thought evil against me; but God meant it unto good, to bring to pass, as it is this day, to save much people alive"* (Gen. 50:19-20). He reassured them and spoke kindly to them, even pointing out that their evil intentions had been turned by God into very great good. Clearly Joseph saw the big picture and had learned to trust God in absolute totality.

THE PROPHET

When Joseph knew that his time on earth was drawing to a close he gave instructions to his family. He indicated that the land promised to Abraham, which was reaffirmed to both Isaac and Jacob would indeed become the home for the descendants of Israel. Joseph who died at the age of one hundred and ten insisted that his bones be preserved for the future journey to the Promised Land. So he was not to be buried in Egypt his adopted home but in the land of Canaan that had been promised to the people of Israel. His faith stretched forward into the future when Israel would no longer be dependant upon the food of Egypt and the protection of an Egyptian king. They would eventually leave that land and travel to the Promised Land and live in the land that God would give to them.

At the time of his death it would have seemed very unlikely that they would ever get to Canaan. Certainly they were as a people simply a small wandering family of animal keepers, who barely numbered a hundred. They had never really had a settled existence and there certainly were not enough of them to inhabit a country the size of Canaan. The only part of the Promised Land they possessed was the cave of Machpelah which had been purchased by Abraham as a burial place. This was the burying place for Abraham and Sarah, Isaac and Rebekah and Jacob and Leah. Yet as Joseph viewed the future he knew that God would fulfil His promises and he wanted to be part of that great movement from Egypt to the Promised Land. So his body was embalmed and held in waiting until the time came to move to the Promised Land. This happened four hundred years later when the Israelites were a numerous people and they left Egypt under the leadership of Moses carrying the remains of Joseph in a coffin.

Joseph was truly a great man of God. His faith shines out throughout his life and even in the darkest times of being sold, of being made a slave or of being a prisoner there seems to be just a deepening of his reliance upon God and his relationship with the Lord simply grew stronger. He had absolute assurance that the Lord's hand was very much upon him. There is very little of negative comment made about Joseph in the Bible. He was an outstanding servant of God and that is why his name appears in this glorious chapter of Hebrews 11.

Let me finish by quoting R.W. Moss, "A very high place must be given Joseph among the early founders of his race. In strength of right purpose he was second to none, whilst in graces of reverence and kindness, of insight and assurance, he became the type of a faith that is at once personal and national, and allows neither misery nor a career of triumph to eclipse the sense of Divine destiny." In a similar way may nothing ever divert us from doing good, fulfilling the will of God and bringing glory to our Saviour's name.

"Faith in God will always be crowned.""

William S. Plumer

CHAPTER 13
THE FAITH OF AMRAM & JOCHEBED

"Give me a generation of Christian mothers, and I will undertake to change the whole face of society in twelve months."
Lord Shaftesbury

> By faith Moses, when he was born, was hid three months of his parents, because they saw he was a proper child; and they were not afraid of the king's commandment. Hebrews 11:23

In Hebrews 11:23 we come for the first time in this chapter to the name of the great Lawgiver of Israel. His name is Moses and he was a mighty man of faith, yet in this verse it is not his faith that is highlighted but that of his parents. Indeed if they had not exercised the faith they did, then there might have been no Moses. His great contribution to the history of Israel and the inspired literature of Holy Scripture would have been lost and we would have been infinitely the poorer spiritually. So we thank God for this faithful couple whose youngest son grew up to be the great leader of Israel. The names of the parents of Moses are not well known today and indeed Campbell Morgan has written, "I do not believe one out of a hundred could tell me the names of his parents" and further describes them in these terms, "two unknown, hidden people, two of the slave crowd!" Their names were Amram and Jochebed, they sound strange names to us today but they were spiritually great people of God.

Their names are not mentioned in Hebrews 11 but they stand out as the only married couple to be mentioned who seem to have shared equally in their faith. Sarah has been mentioned as the wife of Abraham but was very much in a secondary role as far as faith is concerned, as her husband was primarily the man of faith. Thus though Jochebed is not mentioned by name she becomes the second Old Testament lady whose faith is highlighted in this glorious chapter.

BACKGROUND

Amram and his wife Jochebed were descendants of Jacob's son Levi. They were a married couple living in Egypt together with the other members of the Israelite nation who had now grown into a great and substantial people. They now lived under an Egyptian king who could not remember the blessings that their ancestor Joseph had brought to the land and this new king forced the Israelites to become the slaves of Egypt. Taskmasters were set over the slaves and they worked on major building projects for the Egyptians. It would seem that the Israelites built walls, towers and even the great pyramids that became one of the wonders of the ancient world.

The end result was that God blessed Israel with a high birth rate and their numbers seemed to grow very quickly. This alarmed the Egyptians who feared that if enemies attacked their land the slaves would join the invading armies, become victorious and the roles would be reversed with the Egyptians being the slaves and the Israelites the masters. To avert such a happening the King of Egypt wanted to weaken their birth rate and so instructed the midwives of the Israelites to kill any baby boys that were born but to keep the girls alive. However the midwives feared God and were unprepared to do such terrible things and steadfastly refused to carry out infanticide. Finally Pharaoh instructed that every baby boy born to the Israelites should be thrown into the River Nile (Ex. 1:15-22). We can only imagine the horrified reaction to such a decree. The river would be death for baby boys and families would be struck with deep sorrow as their babies drowned or were eaten by crocodiles that infested the river.

This was the regime under which Amram and Jochebed lived. They were slaves in Egypt and knew the king's dreadful and terrifying commandment. They already had two children, a daughter named Miriam and a son named Aaron. Those children did not experience the death sentence because they were above the age for execution and in Miriam's case she was a girl and the decree only applied to male children. However, we can imagine the horror of the parents when they realized that Jochebed was pregnant with their third child. Throughout her pregnancy she must have wondered, "would it be a boy or a girl?" If a girl then all would be well, but if a boy then he would have to be thrown to his death in the river Nile, what a terribly horrendous thought. So in the midst of maternal joy there was an awful grief, even terror because of the king's command. We can well imagine some of the thoughts that went through Jochebed's mind when the midwife said, "A boy". Those same thoughts would also have afflicted Amram. They would have been thoughts of horror, dread and fear.

The king's decrees were terribly cruel and caused dreadful sorrow to the lives of many Israelite families. We wonder whether parents and especially mothers ever recover from the loss of their children, as it is such an awful experience. Despots in ancient times and even to the present time have often proved to be cruel dictators and we remember that at the birth of Jesus King Herod killed all the baby boys of two and under who lived in Bethlehem and the surrounding countryside. We thank God that Jesus escaped that infanticide by being taken to Egypt. Yet even today there is wide scale "murder of the innocents" as we see high abortion rates with some statistics saying that only 13 in 100,000 are for health reasons.

THE PARENTS

Amram and Jochebed were closely related even before they were married. They were both born into the same Israelite tribe having descended from Levi, who was the third son of Jacob. Also Jochebed was Amram's father's sister and therefore that makes her his aunt. So a nephew married his auntie and she became his wife. We note in passing that such marriages between close family members became unlawful for members of the nation of Israel when God gave the laws that governed His people to their son Moses many years later. However at the time of their marriage it was common practice and this was true for the various people groups throughout the whole of the Middle East. Today we know very well why God made such practices unlawful because the problem of inbreeding can produce all sorts of disabilities and needs to be avoided at all costs.

Clearly Hebrews 11:23 (NIV) indicates that both parents exercised faith in the preservation of their son Moses because we read, *"By faith Moses' parents..."*. They both demonstrated and exercised true faith and shared together in the work of preserving their younger son from the dreadful fate which awaited him if the king's decree was carried out. Yet when we read the account of this incident in the book of Exodus it seems as though everything was done by Jochebed and there is little mention of Amram being involved in the process. It was Jochebed who did the hiding and the planning for the preservation of their baby son. The lack of Amram's name may be simply a reflection of the fact that he was called upon by the Egyptian taskmasters to work all day as an able bodied Israelite. It is even possible that he worked away from home for long periods of time and if these two scenarios are true then it would fall to Jochebed to put together the practical details for their son's preservation and well being. Yet it would seem that they both agreed and both worked for the one aim of maintaining Moses alive.

The meaning of the name "Amram" is unclear as it might mean "inexperience" or "exalted people". However it is interesting to note that Jochebed's name means "glory of God" or "God is her glory" and it is a very unusual and special name. It is the first name in Holy Scripture that is compounded with the name of God. It is such a striking name that some believe that this was a special title that Moses bestowed upon his mother as he thought back and remembered what she had done for him. However, this can only be speculation but certainly God was her glory and this was wonderfully revealed in her children. Miriam was a gifted poetess and musician, who became a leading lady in Israel during the wilderness wandering. Aaron became the first High Priest of Israel and it was his direct descendants alone who could fulfil that sacred position and thus enter the "Holy of Holies". Yet the glory was most clearly and most powerfully witnessed in Moses who was the most famous of her children. He became the great leader of Israel and is universally recognised as an outstanding national leader and legislator. He also wrote the first five books of the Bible and throughout Scripture is given a prominent place. Indeed in Hebrews 11 more verses are devoted to Moses than anyone else except Abraham. So Moses too was very much a man of faith, as well as a man of action.

THE SON

Every proud parent considers their child to be the most beautiful and the most wonderful baby that was ever born. Parents take pride in their newborn child and they have pleasure in showing him to others. They rejoice and rightly rejoice in the birth of their children and this was certainly true of Amram and Jochebed. Yet they saw in Moses something very special. There was some sort of quality, an extra dimension that they had not seen in either Miriam or Aaron. Our reading says, *"because they saw he was a proper child"* (Heb. 11:23). It would seem that even as a baby they recognised something of greatness about their youngest child.

The point is also emphasized in Acts 7:20 where we read, *"In which time Moses was born, and was exceeding fair"*. The footnote says, "was fair in the sight of God", while the Authorized Version translates it "exceeding fair" and indicates that those words mean "fair to God". There stood out in baby Moses a quality of heavenliness and a special awareness was given in the hearts of Amram and Jochebed that this child was like no other and was truly destined for greatness. The point is made in Exodus 2:2, *"...And the woman conceived, and bare a son: and when she saw him that he was a goodly child..."*. So right from birth God's touch seems to have been upon Moses and to begin with only his parents saw that mark of true greatness. However, eventually the whole nation of Israel would recognize the greatness of God's chosen leader, as would the king and the people of Egypt who would even learn to fear him. Finally all the people of God have come to acknowledge the greatness of God in Moses and all civilisations and civil law have been based upon the laws he formulated for Israel under the hand of God.

THE ACTION

There are times when it is right to break the laws of the land but such times are very few and far between. Essentially Christians are called upon to be model citizens who indulge in no criminal activity, pay their taxes on time, obey the laws of the land, give respect to those in authority and never engage in shady or doubtful practices. Yet there are a few times when God's people broke the laws of their country to obey the higher laws of God.

We remember that Daniel refused to obey the king's decree and continued instead to openly pray to the true and living God. God honoured his faith and devotion and spared him from being consumed by the lions when he was thrown into their den. In the New Testament the early apostles were instructed, even ordered not to preach in the name of Jesus. Their response was that they should obey God rather than men and so they continued to proclaim the gospel of Jesus Christ and the impact on the world of the first century was enormous. It brought about a spiritual and social revolution as God honoured their faith. No law should ever stand in the way of us being able to talk to God in prayer and of us being able to talk to people about the Lord and His saving mercy.

In Amram and Jochebed's case they disobeyed the king's command in order to save life. They did not react with fear at the king's edict but simply chose to listen to the voice of God and to trust in their Lord. Their great act of faith is very simply and briefly put in Hebrews 11 but it was an enormous step of courage, love and ultimately cooperation with the purposes of God. We read, *"By faith Moses, when he was born, was hid three months of his parents"* (Heb. 11:23) and their actions changed the course of history. It was a very great act and it required tremendous courage.

In this action we realize the deep love those two people had in their lives. They deeply loved their baby son and at all costs they wanted to keep him alive. No doubt too this reflected their love for God from whom they knew that they had received their son. Secondly, their action revealed their genuine and very real courage. It is no small matter to defy the decree of a cruel despot such as Pharaoh, king of Egypt. He was a king who ruled with absolute power and there were no democratic checks and balances to counteract his despotic rule. He held the power of life and death over his subjects and especially over the Israelite slaves. Such courageous action meant that these parents risked their lives to keep their son alive. Yet it was all a reflection of their faith in God. They trusted God throughout those months when they hid their baby from prying eyes. Faith at the risk of one's own life is genuine faith and so no wonder they are held up as mighty examples of faith. Do we possess in any measure similar love, courage or faith as was seen in Amram and Jochebed.

THE OUTCOME

For three months Moses was hidden and that must have been no mean feat. A baby boy from birth to three months old was hidden from prying eyes and the many spies who would have reported the news to the authorities. How the parents did it we do not know but with wisdom given them by God and protection granted by the Lord they were able to do it. However, as we can well imagine the baby would have cried at inconvenient times and it must have got harder and harder to keep him quiet, so a plan was devised. We can imagine the little basket of reeds being made and the waterproofing taking place. We can see with our mind's eye the parents placing their infant son into that ark of reeds, no doubt with sincere and heartfelt prayers that God would protect that child. Jochebed then placed the baby in the place decreed by the king, namely the place of death, the river Nile. Miriam stood a little way off and watched what would happen.

Pharaoh's daughter came to the river to wash and bathe and spotted the basket. She sent a slave girl to collect the basket and when it was opened the princess saw the baby crying and her heart went out to the child. She clearly claimed the child as her own and through Miriam's intervention Jochebed was called and acted as wet nurse for the baby and eventually Moses was introduced to the Princess' household and was adopted as her son. This would undoubtedly mean that Moses may have been in line to the throne of Egypt or at least he carried some very great influence in court circles as he grew up. He received the education that was usual for royals in those days and through his writings that high quality education shines through.

Moses left Egypt at the age of forty and it was really an escape as he had killed an Egyptian taskmaster. We don't know how long Amram and Jochebed lived after the birth of their son and it seems likely that by the time he left Egypt they had already died. He lived in the Midianite desert for forty years before returning to Egypt and leading the Israelites out of Egyptian slavery and into the freedom that would eventually enable them to inherit the Promised Land. He forged them into a nation and laid down the laws for humane, hygienic and moral behaviour that would bene-fit the nation into the indefinite future. He was a man who lived close to God and knew the heart beat of the Almighty. His greatness was due in no small measure to the faith of his parents. May we be faithful in all we do and walk in the footsteps of this humble couple whose son became so great.

"All that I am or hope to be I owe to my angel mother."
Abraham Lincoln

CHAPTER 14

THE FAITH OF MOSES
PART 1

*"Faith makes things possible—
it does not make them easy."*

Anonymous

> *By faith Moses, when he was come to years, refused to be called the son of Pharaoh's daughter; Choosing rather to suffer affliction with the people of God, than to enjoy the pleasures of sin for a season; Esteeming the reproach of Christ greater riches than the treasures in Egypt: for he had respect unto the recompence of the reward. By faith he forsook Egypt, not fearing the wrath of the king: for he endured, as seeing him who is invisible. Through faith he kept the passover, and the sprinkling of blood, lest he that destroyed the firstborn should touch them.*   Hebrews 11:24-28

In Moses we have one of the greatest leaders who have ever lived in history. His story is a remarkable tale and reveals time and again that he was a specially chosen person to accomplish wonderful and great things for God. His name is deeply revered and yet he experienced times of failure, weakness and disappointment. However his deeply established faith enabled him to triumph over every adversity and be counted as a true hero of faith. Moses has been described as "historian, orator, leader, statesman, legislator and patriot." His exploits are legendary and he was the favourite Bible hero of the great Scottish explorer and missionary in Africa, the famous Dr. David Livingstone. He has been described as "the greatest man among mere men in the whole history of the world."

There were all sorts of strange twists and turns in the life of Moses. He was born into the Hebrew nation of Israel when they were experiencing the terrible oppression of slavery. The king's decree ordered that all new born baby boys of Israel be thrown into the River Nile, but the parents of Moses refused to commit murder and protected their baby son. Eventually they put him into a basket of reeds and placed him in the river, where the Princess of Egypt, the king's daughter found him and adopted him as her own son. That in itself is a fascinating story of God's protection and care over the infant Moses.

So Moses grew up in the opulence of the Egyptian court but he always knew that he rightly belonged to the slave people who inhabited the area of Goshen. This knowledge may have been instilled into him by his real mother who was employed as his wet nurse in his early years. Thus for his first forty years Moses enjoyed the comforts of court life. He became accustomed to the ways and manners of the Egyptians and was clearly well educated in both reading and writing. This would later manifest itself when he had the privilege and responsibility of writing the first part of what became known as the Old Testament. The first five books are referred to as the "books of Moses". They include the early history of the world, of the nation of Israel and reveal all the laws that God gave to His people to enable them to live happy and contented lives in all areas of life as individuals, as families and as a nation. That section of the Bible has come to be known as "The Law".

The life of Moses is divided up into three very clear sections. The first forty years he spent as a prince in the court of Pharaoh, king of Egypt. The second forty years were spent in the desert as a shepherd caring for the flocks of his father in law. The final forty years were spent leading the nation of Israel through the Sinai Desert towards the Promised Land. Moses died upon Mount Nebo where he was able to view but not enter the Land of Promise and he is the only man to have had "God as his undertaker" (Deut. 34:6), as God buried him in an unknown place. His name is extensively mentioned throughout Scripture and is found in over thirty books of the Bible. We also remember that when Jesus and three of His disciples went up a mountain, which today we call "The Mount of Transfiguration", they were joined by two Old Testament saints, namely Elijah and Moses. The former represented the prophets, while the latter represented the Law. They spoke of the exodus of Jesus, namely His death on a cross. Also after His resurrection Jesus was walking along a road to the village of Emmaus and talked with two disciples. He used the writings of Moses and of the prophets to clearly teach that they had written of Him. Moses long ago had written about the Lord Jesus, who was the Messiah, the Saviour of the world.

The name Moses means "drawn forth" or "taken out of the water" and it was given to him by the Princess of Egypt because she had literally drawn him out of the water of the River Nile. Moses had an older brother Aaron and an older sister Miriam and they all became great leaders in the nation of Israel but by far the most important was God's servant Moses.

HIS FAITH LED TO RENUNCIATION

In our verses we see three things concerning Moses. Firstly, he refused, secondly, he chose and thirdly he regarded.

HE REFUSED

This is remarkable and would have seemed totally incredible to the people of his time. We read that his faith led him to renounce his privileged position and this is what our verses say, *"By faith Moses, when he was come to years, refused to be called the son of Pharaoh's daughter"* (Heb. 11:24). We must remember that Moses must have had every privilege that was available in Egypt. He would have lived in luxury in the king's palace and would have enjoyed the glory of being the son of Pharaoh's daughter. Thus the king of Egypt was effectively his grandfather and this would have made him a powerful man. He may even have had some claim to the throne and so possibly one day could have been king.

His life could hardly have been of greater contrast with the conditions in which his real family and their people lived. They were humble slaves, who were cruelly treated by their

Egyptian overlords. They had no national self determination and served their masters under total duress. Yet his was a life with everything that was best in terms of clothes, food, education, standing and privilege, servants and officials and everything that earthly beings could want in material terms. Yet the day came when he was grown up and no longer a youth that he refused these things and turned his back upon them.

He refused to be known as the son of Pharaoh's daughter. He relinquished the privileges of royalty and gave up any right or claim he might have had to the throne. He saw through the shallowness and superficiality of everything that Egypt had to offer him. He gave up materialism for something much more worthwhile. Today we live in a similarly privileged nation where there is every kind of consumer good available and more disposable income available to people in the West than ever before in history. We are a materially oriented society that focuses upon "things" and the goods that money can buy. We are taken up with the latest technology in phones, computers, TVs and entertainment. We are taken up with constant house improvements whether we need them or not. We are a totally self consumed society with everything centred upon personal gratification.

That gratification is always an instant gratification and with every kind of financial credit available then just about anything is within our grasp for the immediate meeting of our desires. In the headlong race to get on and to get we forget to consider with any serious intent the future. We fail to think about the long term consequences of our actions and attitudes and we fail to ask the question, what does God think? It would seem that Moses came to the point where he saw the worthlessness of it all and realized that material things do not satisfy the deepest spiritual needs of the human soul and so he renounced that lifestyle in order to take on something totally different. He turned his back upon the court of Egypt and simply refused to be part of the Royal household. He gave up the pampered luxury of life in the palace. It was faith that led him to do this and we realize that at some stage he must have come face to face with the reality of God and the ultimate truth that we are all accountable one day before that God.

HE CHOSE

He chose to leave the place of opulent splendour and identify with the Israelite slaves. This was an amazing change and we might not understand his motives but we are given the reason for it. He did not want to simply *"enjoy the pleasures of sin for a season"* (Heb. 11:25). Clearly there were many pleasures in the court of Pharaoh but unfortunately many of them were sinful. Yet we are clearly told here that there is pleasure in sinning and no one could possibly deny such a statement. Everyone who indulges in sin does so for the pleasure they derive from it. Unfortunately the pleasures of sin do not last but are only for a short while. At best they are temporal and earth bound, they give enjoyment only at an earthly level.

How often must this be realized by so many people and yet they do nothing about it? There are short term gains in committing sin but long term pains. For example the pleasure of consuming alcohol in large quantities is negated by the hangover, financial loss and maybe the loss of dignity when drunk. Also the need to maintain the same level of pleasure requires consumption of ever increasing quantities of alcohol and so the danger emerges of alcoholism and total dependence upon drink. This is true of every sinful indulgence and yet so many people seem to be blinded to the danger. Sin is breaking the laws of God and in the short term there is pleasure but in the long term there are serious dangers both in this life and in the world to come. So we are well warned.

Moses made a clear decision and humbled himself to leave the palace and be identified with the slave people of God. Yet the start he made in trying to identify with the Israelites was anything but impressive as we read the account in Exodus 2:11-15. He went out to see the Israelites working hard under the watchful eyes of taskmasters. He saw one of the Egyptians cruelly beating an Israelite and so he killed that Egyptian and buried him in the sand. The next day he saw two Hebrews in conflict and asked the one in the wrong, "Why are you hitting your fellow Hebrew?" This produced an antagonistic answer from the Hebrew who made it clear that Moses had no jurisdiction over him and asked rather insolently whether he intended to kill him as he had killed the Egyptian the day before.

The result was that Moses had to leave Egypt because the king of Egypt wanted him executed for murder. So we see that early in life Moses tried to intervene on behalf of the people of Israel which ended in failure. At this point in his life he was trying to do things in his own strength rather than by faith. At this stage he had not yet learned to trust God completely.

Yet he had made a most momentous decision to leave the great palace of Pharaoh and identify with the slaves of Israel. This was a huge act of humbleness. It is said that when Richard Daley was mayor in Chicago that one day he left the mayor's mansion and spent a day with the winos, drug addicts and homeless who lived on the streets and survived as best they could on very little. The next day the local newspaper carried a banner headline that read, "The World's Greatest Stoop". The writer presumably could think of nothing greater than a stoop from the mayor's mansion to skid row. However Moses made the stoop from the palace of a king to being part of a group of slaves. He turned his back on sinful pleasures knowing that they could only give short term benefits at best. Thus through faith he made a choice and it was a life changing decision that affected not just his own life but that of a nation and in many ways that of the world and future generations. We all owe an enormous debt to Moses.

However his great stoop is as nothing compared with that of our Lord and Saviour. Jesus left the highest pinnacle of heaven for a drafty stable at Bethlehem and ultimately the dark and painful death of crucifixion. He came to die the death we deserved and then rose to life in order that we might experience the life that we never deserved to enjoy. In Christ we can know forgiveness and salvation and rejoice in the wonder of what was truly the greatest stoop this world has ever seen.

HE REGARDED

We read these words, *"He regarded disgrace for the sake of Christ as of greater value than the treasures of Egypt, because he was looking ahead to his reward"* (Heb. 11:26, NIV). The word *"regarded"* has been translated as "accounting" and "the word merely means balancing things in order to come to a decision of some sort, putting this by the side of that, and weighing the evidence on both sides..." (G. Campbell Morgan). So he preferred the disgrace of associating with Christ and found it to be of greater value than all the treasures he could enjoy in Egypt. Many people have given up this world's riches to be identified in service for Christ. Some have given up fortunes, others have given up their freedom, some have given up their home and country and others have even given up their lives.

Such sacrifices can amaze us and we may wonder why Moses made the decision he did and the answer is that *"he had respect unto the recompence of the reward"* (Heb. 11:26). He realized, as every true Christian has come to realize that this world is only fleeting and our real destiny lies with Christ. It is not true to say that we have only one life and it ends with death. The Bible says that *"it is appointed unto men once to die, but after this the judgment"* (Heb. 9:27). Clearly there is more to life than death. Yet so many refuse to acknowledge their own mortality and fail to give serious consideration to that moment when they will have to face God as their Judge. Jesus came to earth to enable us to be prepared for that momentous occasion and all those who truly know Christ as their Saviour and are prepared to serve Him as their Lord are looking forward to the day of reward or as we read in Hebrews 11:6, *"he is a rewarder of them that diligently seek him."* Like Abraham before him the focus of Moses was ultimately upon eternity and the reality of a future kingdom and city that would be realized in heaven.

In the New Testament we read that we should set our affections on things above and not on things of the earth. We must constantly remember that this world is transient and that there is a richer and much more glorious place called heaven. The riches of earth are subject to decay, robbery and corruption and we can never take such wealth with us. Yet the riches of heaven are indestructible and utterly safe and secure. They are of eternal value and enjoyment and we should do our utmost to secure such wonders even if that means giving up the pleasures of sin and the treasures of Egypt here on earth. Like Moses we must set our eyes upon the future, the glorious future where as Christians we will reign with Christ in heaven.

So by faith Moses weighed matters up between this life and the next, between the glory of Egypt and the glory of heaven. On the basis of his considerations he made a choice and decided to identify with the slaves, the downtrodden people of God. He humbled himself and chose to be part of Israel. This was his choice but in some ways he already belonged to them by birth but through adoption he could have distanced himself from them and lived a different life. There have been people who have claimed that they are Christians but do not want to be part of the local church.

It might be that they are ashamed to be part of the visible kingdom of God on earth and their pride keeps them away. It may be that they do not want the responsibility that membership of a local church entails. It may be that they are deliberately disobedient to God's commands. Christianity is a shared and corporate activity, where together we worship and serve God under the guidance and direction of spiritual leaders. God has called His people not to live in isolation as Christians and certainly not to live in a materialistic manner, but to give up on riches here on earth and be part of the local body of Christian people and to gain a great reward in heaven in a coming day.

I hope you are fully involved with your local church and take your responsibilities very seriously. In a coming day you will have to give an account.

"No local church is perfect—but there is no way in which it can be improved by the absence of spiritually-minded Christians."

John Blanchard

CHAPTER 15

THE FAITH OF MOSES
PART 2

"For Thee all the pleasures of sin I resign."

Dr. Gordon

It is incredible to think that one of the men most revered in Hebrews 11 as a man of faith was in fact a murderer. This was Moses who in his early days had killed an Egyptian taskmaster who was being cruel to an Israelite slave. Later in life Moses was given the Ten Commandments one of which said, *"Thou shall not kill"* (Ex. 20:13) and the word *"kill"* in that context means "murder". It is a commandment that is delivered with no qualifications and simply states that life is sacred and there are no circumstances where it is ever right to commit murder. I wonder how Moses felt when God gave him this commandment. It is also of interest to note that the Bible does not gloss over the sins of God's people and their fallibility is not only noted but so often highlighted. They are revealed as warnings to us that we must avoid similar pitfalls in our own lives. So Moses the one time murderer became the great leader of Israel and is held up as one of the greatest saints in the Old Testament.

His first great act of faith was to turn his back upon the privileges of being the son of Pharaoh's daughter and become identified with the slave people of God, the Israelites (Heb. 11:24-26). Two further things are revealed to us as actions of faith by Moses. The first is the decision to leave Egypt and the second is to keep the Passover.

LEAVING EGYPT

We read these words, *"By faith he forsook Egypt, not fearing the wrath of the king: for he endured, as seeing him who is invisible"* (Heb. 11:27). This verse has caused some dispute and division amongst Bible scholars and the question has to be asked as to which incident does this refer. It may be argued that this verse refers to the time when Moses killed the Egyptian task-master and departed from Egypt to be a fugitive and eventually a shepherd in Midian. Yet quite clearly at that time he did fear the king of Egypt's anger. He knew the king wanted to bring charges against him and indeed to kill him (Ex. 2:15). So this verse cannot possibly refer to that first departure from Egypt when he and he alone of the Israelite nation left the land of Egypt.

It must refer to what happened forty years later in what today we term the "Exodus". That was the time when Moses under the hand of God led the people of Israel out of Egyptian bondage and into freedom. It had certainly been an act of faith to return to Egypt and confront the king with a message from God to let the Israelites go free. Moses was by then a man of very great spiritual stature and power. He had no fear of the king's anger at such an audacious suggestion and the result was that Egypt experienced ten dreadful plagues. These all happened as a result of the king's refusal to obey God's message through Moses. Time and again the king said "No" and he would not let the Israelites go free. Indeed he even increased their workload and multiplied their burdens. This produced grumbling complaints from the Israelites towards Moses and some of them wished that he had never come back to deliver them.

However, Moses did not give up but persevered. His faith made him keep going in his dealings with the king as he was utterly assured that God was with him and would ultimately bring about a successful conclusion. This was due to the fact that Moses had come into direct contact with the living and true God. It had been a miraculous encounter when in the desert he had turned aside to see a remarkable sight. It was one of the bushes of the desert burning, with flames leaping out of it and yet the bush was not consumed. The flames were real but the bush was totally unaffected and did not blacken or turn to ash. In those flames was the presence of God and Moses had to realize that he was approaching holy ground and so he had to remove his shoes.

At the place of holiness he was commanded by God to go back to Egypt and instruct King Pharaoh to let God's people go free. The king was to release them from their slavery and bondage and let them leave Egypt in peace. Moses was a reluctant servant of God and found it difficult to accept and obey God's command to him. He made all sorts of excuses such as an inability to speak properly and so God said that Aaron his brother could speak on behalf of Moses. In the end there seems to have been nothing wrong with Moses' aptitude for addressing the royal personage of Egypt.

Moses foresaw a further reason that might make such a journey futile and maybe he remembered the reaction of the Israelite who was ill-treating another Hebrew that had led to his first departure from Egypt. The Israelite had essentially said that Moses commanded no authority over the nation of Israel and so had no right to question him. Thus Moses said to God at the burning bush about the Israelites, *"But, behold, they will not believe me, nor hearken unto my voice: for they will say, The LORD hath not appeared unto thee"* (Ex. 4:1). He felt that he might not be accepted as the God-ordained leader and deliverer of the nation. God assured him with two signs. The first was that when he threw down his staff it became a snake on the ground and when he picked the snake up it became a staff again. Secondly when he placed his hand inside his cloak it came out leprous and diseased but when he put it back and pulled it out a second time it was healed. These would be signs that God had truly sent Moses to be the deliverer of Israel. Finally if the Israelites still did not believe then Moses was to take some water from the River Nile and pour it onto the ground where it would instantly turn to blood (Ex. 4:9).

So Moses returned to Egypt and with unusual boldness spoke to the king of Egypt and demonstrated supernatural power in his presence. Yet the king refused to let the people go and so started the terrible plagues that were to afflict the Egyptians. Throughout it all Moses was not diverted from his task and refused to give up but persevered *"because he saw him who is invisible"* (Heb. 11:27, NIV). He was deeply aware of God and knew God personally and had a deep and close relationship with the Almighty. It has been said, "His greatest honour, however, was the privilege of being known as 'the friend of God.' What holy intimacy existed between God and this prophet so supernaturally guided and aided in his life and labours" (Herbert Lockyer).

Moses knew God and it caused him to persevere in the work God had given him to do. This work not only involved facing Pharaoh and delivering the people from bondage but of guiding and leading them through the desert for forty years. It was a thankless task and at times deeply disheartening. He had to face sinful behaviour amongst the people, wars, rebellion, grumbling, complaining and unbelief. However he stuck to his task steadfastly because he saw what was invisible. He experienced the presence of God and appreciated the power of God in his life and ministry. I trust that we will know that quality of perseverance in the work that God has given us to do. It requires personal discipline and determination but in the end these can very easily become depleted. We need to know the reality of the call of God upon our lives and to daily know the true joy of God's presence through genuine prayer and the reading of His precious Word. Only God can truly sustain us in what is often a difficult and fraught time in Christian ministry these days. May we know God's sustaining grace and appropriate it by faith in the same way that Moses did all those years ago.

KEEPING THE PASSOVER

This is the final act of faith that was attributed directly to Moses in Hebrews 11 and we read, *"Through faith he kept the passover, and the sprinkling of blood, lest he that destroyed the first-born should touch them"* (Heb. 11:28). The word *"kept"* has been translated as "instituted" and that was exactly what Moses and the people of Israel did in the land of Egypt. This turned out to be the tenth and final plague that God would bring upon the Egyptians and it would be the means of Israel being released from slavery and bondage and being given their free-dom to leave Egypt and make their way to the Promised Land of Canaan in fulfilment of the covenant promise that God had made to their forefathers, Abraham, Isaac, Jacob and Joseph. We read of this very first Passover which was instituted by God through Moses in Exodus 12:1-30.

THE PROCEDURE

Moses was given elaborate plans for celebrating the Passover. These plans were passed on to the people of Israel and were essentially given for their own protection. The whole community of the Israelites were instructed that each family was to take a year-old male lamb and it was to be a perfect lamb, totally without defect. It was to be selected on the tenth day of the first month of the year. Small households who could not afford a whole lamb were to share the lamb of others but every family were to have access to a lamb. After the careful selection the lamb was to be properly looked after during the following four days and then at twilight the lamb was to be killed.

The blood of the lamb was then to be collected and some of that blood was to be smeared on the doorposts and lintel of the home where the lamb was to be eaten. So the putting of blood on the doorframes was applied to every household of the Israelites. Then in the same night the lamb was to be roasted, eaten with bitter herbs and taken with unleavened bread. The meat was not to be eaten raw and was not to be boiled or cooked in water. It had to be roasted and totally consumed that night, if any was left then it had to be destroyed with fire.

They also had to dress correctly as they ate the food. The commandment was to Israel, *"And thus shall ye eat it; with your loins girded, your shoes on your feet, and your staff in your hand; and ye shall eat it in haste: it is the LORD's passover"* (Ex. 12:11). Clearly they were to eat the Passover as if they were ready for travelling and on the point of going on a long journey and that was precisely what they were going to do. This was the last action before what would become the acclaimed exodus of Israel from the land of Egypt. This would be their dash for freedom but it would be done with the full permission of the Egyptian authorities and with the desperate desire of the Egyptians to see the back of their slaves. The plagues instituted at the hand of Moses had given the Egyptians very real fear at his God-given power and authority.

Certainly in faith Moses instituted the Passover as the prelude to departure and Israel obeyed the words of Moses and indicated their faith in the Lord.

THE PURPOSE

To do all that God had commanded was a great act of faith and yet it was to be done for a purpose. The reason had been given to the people through Moses. That very night the tenth and final plague would come upon Egypt and would even affect Israel if they were not protected by the blood of the Lamb. God would pass through the land of Egypt that night and would come as a destroying angel. Every firstborn of men and animals would be slain. The gods of Egypt would be seen for what they really were, namely useless, worthless and impotent creations of men. The idols may have been elaborately and skilfully made and were worshipped with deep reverence and sincere devotion, yet they could not protect the Egyptians. God's power was awesome and beyond compare and would be demonstrated in the most awful judgment upon the Egyptians.

Essentially God was announcing *"I am the LORD"* (Ex. 12:12). He is the one and only true God and there is no one else. All other gods are false and fail to protect their followers from judgment. God was emphasizing the supremacy of who He was and the reality of His power. The Egyptians would experience that power through destruction that would bring terrible pain and sorrow. The Israelites would experience that power through protection and safety. Thus God said, *"when I see the blood, I will pass over you, and the plague shall not be upon you to destroy you, when I smite the land of Egypt"* (Ex. 12:13). Thus the hardness and sinfulness of the king of Egypt and his people were to be punished with one final plague. However the faithfulness and obedience of the Israelites were to be rewarded with no deaths and very quick release from bondage. They had trusted the word of God through Moses and had acted in obedience to the commandments of the Lord and so they were safe from the terrible destruction that was to come.

Today we do not need to put blood around our doors. We have a lamb who has died for us. He is the Lord Jesus, the perfect Lamb, described as *"a lamb without blemish and without spot"* (1 Pet. 1:19). He died as a sacrifice for our sins on the cross at Calvary and through faith in Him we can avoid the terrible consequences of our sin. We can find forgiveness and cleansing in the shed blood of Christ and when we are sheltered in Him it is as if the Lord says *"when I see the blood, I will pass over you"* (Ex. 12:13). We are secure from the moment we trusted Christ as our Saviour and received Him into our lives by faith. We thank God for the blessings that derived to Israel because they trusted the Lord but we are even more thankful for the wonderful, eternal blessings that we receive when we trust in Christ and receive His glorious salvation.

So Israel obeyed God and made the elaborate preparations for the Passover because they were promised deliverance from the awful plague that was to descend on Egypt that very night.

THE PERPETUATION

The assurance that Israel would be saved from destruction and perpetual bondage as slaves in Egypt is given in Exodus 12:14-28. Every year the people of Israel were instructed to perform this ritual and they were to do it as families followed by the Feast of Unleavened Bread. For one whole week every year they were to only eat bread that was made without yeast. Every time their children would ask the inevitable question "Why?" the answer was to be that the Lord had spared them as a people when destruction came upon Egypt. They were to constantly remember the day of their deliverance. This was an instruction to be obeyed *"for an ordinance to thee and to thy sons for ever. And it shall come to pass, when ye be come to the land which the LORD will give you, according as he hath promised, that ye shall keep this service"* (Ex. 12:24-25).

So the Passover Feast was instituted as a means of protection. It was God who gave them the means of protection and the people simply obeyed God. They took God at His word and *"did as the LORD had commanded Moses and Aaron"* (Ex. 12:28). The Israelites trusted God and obeyed His word and the result was that they were safe and their families were secure. They also set up the means for commemorating the event for future generations and this in itself was an act of faith in the promises of God.

Today we simply trust Christ and accept Him into our lives as Saviour as we realize that He died for our sins on the cross. We remember His work not as a Passover but through our Breaking of Bread Service or Communion Service. There we realize that "richer blood has flowed from nobler veins, to purge the soul from guilt, and cleanse the reddest stains" (*No Blood, No Altar Now*, Horatius Bonar). The blood of Jesus Christ God's Son cleanses us from all sin. We thank God for that wonderful victory and the assurance of salvation and eternal life which only Christ can give.

"Every doctrine that is not embedded in the cross of Jesus will lead astray."

Oswald Chambers

CHAPTER 16

THE FAITH OF ISRAEL
PART 1

"God had commanded, and, however tremblingly they marched..."

G. Campbell Morgan

By faith they passed through the Red sea as by dry land: which the Egyptians assaying to do were drowned. Hebrews 11:29

So far in this glorious chapter of Hebrews 11, that gives us a list of Old Testament saints who achieved great things for God through faith, we have encountered particular individuals and married couples. Now for the first time we have come to a collective group of people. This group is much larger than a family or a clan and it is actually the whole nation of Israel. Their faith is highlighted as a mountaintop experience in the history of God's dealings with His people. The incident where faith is highlighted is one of the greatest miracles in the whole of human history and is certainly one of the miraculous glories of the Old Testament. It is of course the crossing of the Red Sea.

Israel as a nation was moving out of Egyptian bondage and was experiencing national freedom for the first time in a very long time. Their numbers may have been in the region of one or two million and they were not simply a small clan of a few hundred. We can work out roughly how many people belonged to Israel at that time when we read the lists of numbers of the fighting men in the nation and they only represented men between the ages of thirty and fifty. They were a mighty nation. God had brought them out of Egypt under the leadership of Moses and it must have been a great relief and a deep joy for the people to no longer be slaves for the

Egyptians. Yet after three days into their journey they had come into a sort of cul-de-sac. They were face to face with the Red Sea and with desert and mountains all around they were hemmed in and then to make matters worse the Egyptians had changed their minds, their armies were mustered and they pursued the Israelites with the intention of recapturing them. So in front of them was the sea, behind them was the aggressive Egyptian army and on either side were the impenetrable desert and mountain regions of Sinai. It must have been bewildering for the people of Israel.

However we must remember:

GOD IS NOT TAKEN BY SURPRISE

The Egyptians were led to believe that *"They* [the Israelites] *are entangled in the land, the wilderness hath shut them in"* (Ex. 14:3). It seemed as though the newly freed slaves were in the most dangerous situation but we must remember that God had led them to that position. In the daytime God led them in a pillar of cloud, while at night time He appeared as a pillar of fire. The whole situation looked dangerous from a human perspective but God was not taken by surprise. Israel had yet to learn that they could depend upon the Lord but at this stage when they saw their dangerous situation their reaction was one of fear.

FEAR IS REAL

Fear is often based upon the unknown and Israel at that moment in time only knew a small part of the picture. They saw their progress blocked by the sea and a hostile army approaching and it looked like the end of their new found freedom. Their initial reaction was essentially due to their fearful hearts.

1. **Their focus of attention was wrong**: they looked at the Egyptian army instead of focusing upon the Lord and His greatness. Is that not so often true for us? When things go wrong we focus upon the problems

and are very slow to seek the Lord's help. Yet we must remember that the Lord knows everything and is greater than all our concerns. He is utterly dependable and has promised to meet all our needs and carry our burdens.

2. **They Attacked Moses**: their fear turned to anger and they vented their frustrated anger upon God's chosen leader. They expected to die by the Red Sea and claimed that they would have preferred slavery in Egypt to death in the desert. How often do we do the same? When we make mistakes and things go wrong we look for someone to blame. We are quick to blame others when things go awry but slow to praise when things go well.

3. **They Cried to the Lord**: unfortunately this was not the cry of faith or prayer but of anger, frustration and asking the question "why?" So often we too can be in the same situation and we turn our anger upon the Lord.

The people of Israel failed to realize the true greatness of God and that He was in control of all things. They failed to remember His miracles in Egypt and that nothing is impossible for Him. They failed to realize that nothing ever takes God by surprise. Fear had engulfed them but there is an antidote to fear and that is faith.

FAITH WAS NEEDED

The antidote, the answer to fear is faith. The leader of Israel, who was Moses possessed such faith in abundance. He urged the people to "trust the Lord" and to not be afraid. His words to them were to "stand still" or "stand firm" and the idea is that of clinging. It is like a limpet that clings to a rock by the beach and it is so hard to pry it off the solid surface. In a similar way God's people should cling to Him in every circumstance of life and never let go of their faith in Him. Instead of noise, anger and frustrated shouting there is need to look to the Lord and seek for His deliverance and

Moses was reminding the people that God is never taken by surprise and indeed He had actually drawn them into their present situation. To them it looked like a predicament but to the Lord it was a wonderful opportunity to demonstrate His power and exercise His authority.

So Moses calmed the people and called them to be at peace and to watch for what God would do. He stated very clearly that God would fight for them and bring them through their present situation victoriously. So the first great truth is that God is not taken by surprise.

GOD IS ALWAYS IN CONTROL

In hindsight now through reading the Word of God we can see that God always knew what He was going to do. He knew the actions He would perform to save His people from death in the desert. The situation was not beyond the Lord and we must remember that no situation is ever beyond the Lord's ability to control and bring blessing. When we are at the extreme of circumstances we must never forget that our heavenly Father is still in control and He ultimately sets the limits for man's behaviour. This should encourage us as we see the spiritual and moral condition of the world today and of our nation. It should give us encouragement as we see the weak state of so many churches in our land today. The truth is that God can do something at any moment and change the situation in ways beyond our wildest imaginings. This is what He did for Israel at the Red Sea.

1. **He Commanded Moses**: through Moses the people of Israel were commanded to "Go forward". It was no longer the command to "stand still" but to make an advance and move on. There was need for them to make progress but there was a terrible barrier in front of them and their circumstances were extremely dangerous but still God said, "Go forward".

It is always true for the people of God that we must go forward and that applies to us as individual Christians. We must make progress in our prayer life, in our understanding of Scripture, in our evangelizing and sharing of our faith with others, in our attendance and involvement at church and generally in our spiritual lives. However there are so often barriers that seem to hold us up, such as getting a good education, our family responsibilities, watching television, going out, our sports, our hobbies and we have every excuse to avoid making progress. Indeed to make progress in our Christian lives requires commitment, determination and obedience.

It is also true that as corporate bodies of Christians, namely the local church we need to make progress. We must maintain and develop our evangelistic thrust, our care for the needy and develop new areas of bringing the gospel and the love of Christ to more people. However, we may find that our workers are declining, our money is not enough, our time seems limited and our collective vision, devotion and commitment has become weak and we are going backwards instead of obeying the injunction to go forward. Now is the time to alter and start to make progress.

Let us heed the command and no matter what the obstacles may be we will go forward and gain new ground in our Christian lives before God both individually and collectively.

2. **He Divided the Sea**: so in response to God's command Moses raised his staff by stretching out his arm over the sea and God caused an east wind to blow and the waters of the sea were divided. There was a wall of water on one side and a wall of water on the other side and in between there was a pathway. It was a spectacular work and the Israelites moved forward to take advantage of that path. They did not slosh through mud and silt but walked on dry ground. This was a wonderful path through the sea that eventually led them to safety. Today we have a wonderful path and His name is Jesus. He said, *"I am the way…no one comes to the Father except through me"* (John 14:6, NIV). He created a way for us to go to heaven that penetrates the barrier of sin that excluded us from the Father's

presence and so through Him a way was made for us to reach the place of safety.

So *"By faith they passed through the Red sea as by dry land"* (Heb. 11:29). They had learned to trust God and took the means He had created for them to escape from the danger they faced.

3. **He Destroyed the Egyptians**: firstly throughout the night the pillar of cloud moved behind the Israelites and came between them and the Egyptian army. It acted as darkness for the Egyptians and as light for the Israelites. So it delayed the Egyptians with the chariots and horses and as a result the people of God had time to cross the Red Sea. When eventually the Egyptians arrived at the Red Sea they must have been deeply surprised to see the pathway, but they decided to follow and pursue the Israelites. This was their undoing. The Lord caused confusion to come over the Egyptians and wheels came off their chariots and so they had difficulty driving them. The Egyptians began to fear the Lord and were deciding to retreat away from the Israelites when God caused Moses to lift up his arm with the staff in his hand and the waters flowed back and destroyed the Egyptians including chariots and horsemen and at long last Israel was free from their evil and cruel taskmasters. So we read, *"which the Egyptians assaying to do were drowned"* (Heb. 11:29).

This was a glorious miracle and reminds us of the awesome power of God. If God is God then we have no difficulty in believing that He could form a path through a sea. He doesn't do this every day of the week but at significant moments in history. He may use natural means and in this case it was caused by a strong east wind but the timing is absolutely remarkable, indeed it is miraculously remarkable. The miracle has been confirmed by underwater archaeology that has discovered parts of chariots and their wheels on the floor of the Red Sea. We rejoice in God's greatness and that was exactly what Israel did when they realized the extent of God's glorious work. At that point they must have wondered why they had ever doubted or been fearful when they were following such a great and Almighty God. They had come to realize that God is never taken by surprise and that He is always in control. The result was that Israel was blessed and God was honoured.

GOD WAS HONOURED

In Exodus 15 we read that Israel realized that God was the source of their deliverance and that the great miracle meant that they were free people. Their response was to praise God and they were led in thanksgiving and praise by Moses and Miriam. Let us never forget to praise and give God thanks for His many mercies and blessings to us. In their praise we find the following features.

1. **God is Unique**: there is only one God and He is holy, great and good. He is the God we will one day face as our judge. The idols of this world are pathetic and impotent before the greatness of the one true and living God. Let us never allow a place in our lives for an idol because that place should only be occupied by God. This is because God created us and because He loves us deeply and eternally.

2. **God is Worshipped**: the idea of worship is to recognize the glory of God and to offer Him the love of our hearts. It is much more than a church service and is the daily commitment of our lives to Him in service. It is enthroning Christ as Lord of our lives so that nothing else matters except His will for us. It is not good enough to say the Lord is present in my life or indeed that He is prominent in my life. He must have the pre-eminence in our lives. He must be the number one and everything else must be secondary to the primacy of the Lord.

3. **God is Feared**: the heathen nations heard what God had done for Israel and they started to fear the Lord. When the spies went into Jericho, they talked with

Rahab and she mentioned how God had led Israel miraculously through the Red Sea. That had been forty years before and it was very unlikely that Rahab was even alive when the event took place. However it carried such significance that it was still talked about in heathen circles decades after it happened and it caused those idol worshipping peoples to fear.

Fear is not always a bad thing and if it causes us to recognize danger and look for an escape from that danger then it is a good thing. Indeed it is a God-given mechanism within each individual that enables people to have an awareness of danger. The danger for us as Christians is that we can become cold in our hearts towards the Lord and we can become complacent and shallow in our devotion to Christ. When our lives become like that then God is not honoured and we do not focus upon Him as the unique One, the One who should be worshipped and the One who should be feared. Let us daily renew our commitment to the authority of God in our lives and serve Him with the totality of our being for His glory.

"To know the will of God is the greatest knowledge. To do the will of God is the greatest achievement."

George Truett

CHAPTER 17

THE FAITH OF ISRAEL
PART 2

Never doubt in the darkness what
God has shown you in the light.

Robert J. Morgan

By faith the walls of Jericho fell down, after they
were compassed about seven days. Hebrews 11:30

This is the second time in two verses that the Spirit of God draws our attention to the faith of a collective group of people, namely the nation of Israel. They had acted in faith, which was revealed in obedience and blessing as they crossed through the Red Sea on a pathway that God had miraculously made for them. It was a wonderful time of deliverance for the nation and it sealed their freedom from Egyptian bondage and the slavery which they had endured for many long years. They could have sung the words, "Jehovah hath conquered, His people are free." They rejoiced in God and sang His praise as they considered the glory and wonder of their deliverance. That was their first act of faith and is recorded in Hebrews 11:29.

We now come to the second act of faith and this took place forty years after the Red Sea crossing. It had taken such a long time because their faith had in fact failed and they had wandered about the desert while an unbelieving and disobedient generation died in the wilderness. The reason was that at times their trust in the Lord had given way to fear. This was especially seen when the spies, twelve in all, one from each tribe of Israel had come back from the Promised Land with their report. Ten spies talked of the impossibility of invading the land because of the well defended cities and the giants that seemed to live in the land. Two spies Caleb and Joshua urged immediate attack and emphasized that the Lord would help them conquer the land. The people chose the report of the ten and were consigned as a consequence to stay in the desert for a much longer period of time. They also as a nation had a tendency to complain, moan, rebel and disobey the laws of God. At times Moses their leader found them a very difficult and problematic people to control and lead. However eventually the wilderness wandering came to an end and Israel arrived on the East Bank of the River Jordan.

By that time Moses had died and a new leader had been appointed by God and accepted by the people. His name was Joshua and he had been one of the faithful spies. His faith in the Lord never seemed to falter and even when the nation had turned their back upon God in the desert he never forsook his trust in the Lord. He stands out as a faithful and consistent man who became an inspirational leader of his people. His leadership had led Israel to become a formidable fighting force. They had defeated the armies of the Amorites on the eastern side of Jordan and this had demonstrated the power of God to help them in their time of need. They were now poised on the East Bank ready to cross the River Jordan and attack the citadel of Jericho.

JERICHO

The city of Jericho traces its history to the very earliest of times and is believed to be one of the first cities known to human history. It is situated in the Jordan Valley and that means that it is below sea level. It is known as the "city of palms" which emphasizes its warm climate and it is just to the north of the Dead Sea and on the western bank of the River. It was an important city as it guarded the lower Jordan Valley and guarded the passes and routes into the western foothills that lead to what became known as the Judean hills. It was very strongly fortified and would have seemed to be an impregnable fortress, but it was the main city blocking the Israelite advance into the Promised Land of Canaan. The rest of Canaan would look on and see if Jericho would fall and if it did then fear would spread throughout the country. The city had to be taken if Israel were ever to advance into and gain control of the Promised Land. Up to this time the nation of Israel had never engaged in any kind of siege warfare and was utterly unused to this form of battle. Yet it was not going to be their experience or human ingenuity that would gain them victory but trust in the living God.

There can be in our lives as Christians new forms of work that God may want us to do. We may feel that we have no experience and even no aptitude but if God has called us then we will find that He will abundantly equip us for the tasks. David Wilkerson was called by God to go into the rough areas of New York and minister to violent youth gangs and drug users. This was a work he had never undertaken before but he obeyed the call of God and was wonderfully used by God. Certainly he made mistakes, but he learned on the job and eventually his work became a widespread ministry with branches in many countries of the world.

William Carey said, "Attempt great things for God, expect great things from God." He acted upon his own words and became the father of modern missions. He, against fierce religious and political opposition, went at the end of the eighteenth century as a missionary to India and his work was phenomenally blessed by God. In the first nineteen years of the work he and his colleagues baptized 600 people and they were very careful to make sure that each one was genuine in their faith. In thirty-one years they published 212,000 items (Bibles, New Testaments, Gospels, books and tracts) and printed in forty languages. These were mainly Indian languages but also included non-Indian languages such as Chinese. Carey and his companions set a very high standard for missionary work both with disciplined effort and deep integrity. They blazed a trail that no one had trodden for nearly 1800 years. It was truly a new work and led to great things.

Have we been called to do a work for God? If we have then the only response is obedience. We must as the hymn writer says, "trust and obey, for there's no other way to be happy in Jesus but to trust and obey" (*Trust and Obey*, John Henry Sammis).

So Jericho was a great fortress city and needed to be taken by Israel if they were to gain a foothold in the Promised Land.

JOSHUA

This man who took over the leadership of Israel at the end of the desert journey and succeeded Moses was a great military man. He has been described, "as the first soldier consecrated by sacred history". His name means "Jehovah is salvation" and he certainly proved that in his lifetime. He had been born as part of the slave nation in Egypt and had survived the forty years of wandering in the desert. He was a man who proved to be loyal both to Moses and to God and was totally obedient to the Lord. When the nation of Israel reacted with unbelief he did not, but steadfastly trusted the Lord. When the nation of Israel reacted with sin and disobedience he did not, but always did the will of God. Time and again he showed his determination to live for God and do the will of the Lord.

He was pre-eminently a military general who knew how to plan military campaigns, discipline his armed forces, use spies to gain valuable information but above all he prayed and trusted God. Ultimately his victories and conquests were the result of his faith in God. It has been said, that "many a general has closely studied Joshua's conquest of Canaan and followed his strategy". So Joshua was first and foremost "a good soldier of the Lord whom he encountered and obeyed as Captain of the Lord's host (Josh. 5:13-15)" (Lockyer).

There had been a great relationship between Moses and Joshua. Moses had acted as a mentor to Joshua and Joshua had learned the art of leadership from Moses. The teaching had been of two sorts, firstly what Moses said by way of instruction and secondly by the example of his actions and his life. So Joshua had been taught by the words that flowed from the lips of Moses and by the example that flowed from the life of Moses. The words were supported by actions. Certainly we teach and instruct others by what we say and how we live and we might have learned far more from non-verbal communications than we did from verbal teaching. How we need to be constantly aware of the need for consistency between what we say and what we do, between what we profess to believe and how we live our lives.

Joshua succeeded Moses not because he was related as a son but because he was marked out by unusual spirituality and devotion to the Lord. Joshua was filled with the Spirit of God (Deut. 34:9), enjoyed the presence of God (Josh. 1:5; 6:27), was indwelt by the Word of God (Josh. 1:8) and was always obedient to the will of God (Num. 32:12; Josh. 5:14). It is therefore of little surprise to learn that he was a great and successful leader. Lockyer writes, "No wonder his death at 110 years was deeply mourned and his eminent service universally acknowledged! The brief but noble epitaph of the historian is eloquent with meaning, 'before Joshua, the servant of the Lord'. Dead, he could yet speak, for the nation continued to serve the Lord all the days of the elders that outlived Joshua (Josh. 24:3)."

It was this man who sent two spies across Jordan to find out vital information about the defences and armed forces of Jericho. It was this man who led the Israelites across the River Jordan in a sort of re-enactment of the Red Sea crossing for the people crossed upon dry land as the river's flow was stopped long enough by a miracle of God for the people to cross safely. It was this man who led the attack on Jericho, an attack that was strangely muted but highly successful and entry was gained into the Promised Land of Canaan.

THE STORMING OF JERICHO

Blocking Israel's advance was the fortified city of Jericho. It was a city whose walls and gates could well withstand a long and drawn out siege. It was defended by an army which was no doubt well equipped with the usual weapons of the day. As the Israelites faced this great citadel many must have wondered how they would storm the walls and we can imagine some thinking of scaling ladders, battering rams and other weapons of siege warfare. However God gave the instructions and the people simply obeyed them and a mighty miracle took place.

The people obeyed God by simply marching. They fired no arrows, threw no spears and made no attempt to scale the walls or batter down the gates. They were told to take the Ark of the Covenant and the fighting men were to march around the city with the priests blowing on the trumpets. It seems such an absurd thing to do and could have no human connection with attacking the city, but Israel obeyed and that is the essence of faith. It was not their faith that eventually brought the walls of Jericho down but the power of Almighty God but "it is faith that makes possible the activity of God" (G. Campbell Morgan).

On day one the divine order was followed and the men marched around the city walls. The order apparently had no connection whatever with taking the city or with the falling of its walls. It really must have made no sense either to the Israelites or to the defenders on the city walls. Day two followed a similar pattern and the Israelites marched around once again and they did this for the next four days. So for six consecutive days they had marched around the city and then they went out again on the seventh day and this time they did not march around once but altogether seven times. It must have been a mammoth march and would have seemed utterly absurd. There they were marching around the wall of a city, blowing horns and carrying a box which they called an Ark. Such activity could never bring down a great wall and never take a city, except that in this instant God was working with them. At the end of the seventh circuit the silence of the Israelites was broken by a great and powerful shout and the walls of the city fell. We read these words, "...*the people shouted with a great shout, that the wall fell down flat, so that the people went up into the city, every man straight before him, and they took the city*" (Josh. 6:20).

This was a phenomenal miracle and has been ascribed by many to the work of an earthquake. Yet really there is no reasonable explanation and even if God used the natural world of earthquakes it happened at the exact moment when God ordained it. The breach in the defences of Canaan was complete and now the rest of the nations and the people of the other fortified settlements would look with awe and fear at the nation of Israel and the greatness of their God. So we see that *"By faith the walls of Jericho fell down, after they were compassed about seven days"* (Heb. 11:30)

God's command had seemed to be beyond reason but it was intended to remind the people of Israel that any victories they achieved were actually due to His greatness and not their military prowess. There can be times when we are called by God to do unreasonable things, activities that are out of the ordinary and seem ridiculous and it is only after we have obeyed that we have seen the richness of His blessing upon our lives. I remember a lady telling me that one New Year's Day she felt the Lord call her to go next door and wish the neighbours a happy new year. She had been reading her Bible and praying and she sensed this was a directive from the Lord. So she said to her husband that she was going next door to wish the neighbours a Happy New Year. He was surprised and said, "You've never done this before!" The neighbours had been living there for six years and this was the first time she had done anything like this and she felt somewhat foolish. However in obedience to the Lord she exercised faith and went next door. When the man opened the door she wished him and his wife a Happy New Year and promised to pray for them.

The man in astonishment opened the door wide and invited her into the house. There she found the man's wife deeply upset and they explained that she faced a serious operation in the next few weeks and they were asking themselves the question, "Who can we turn to?" and then this Christian lady had come promising to pray for them. She had the opportunity to bring something of the blessing of the Saviour to those people and to share the gospel message with them. It was a tremendous time simply because she had acted in faith.

The people of Israel were victorious because they had acted in faith. The city walls were destroyed and the city conquered. The people of the city were destroyed except for faithful Rahab and her family. The silver and gold as well as other valuables were put into the treasury of the House of the Lord. The city was then put under a ban and the warning was given by Joshua that if anyone rebuilt the city then they would lose their eldest son when the foundations were laid and their youngest son when the gates of the city were put in place. This actually occurred much later during the reign of Ahab when Heil the Bethelite fortified the city but in the process lost his two sons.

So Israel had entered the Promised Land as a victorious campaigning army and eventually the whole land would fall to them and they would inhabit the land that had been promised to their forefathers Abraham, Isaac, Jacob and Joseph. As we act in faith we will receive our blessed reward in the "land that is fairer than day" (*In the Sweet By and By*, Sanford F. Bennett) namely the glory of our inheritance in heaven. What a glorious prospect that is for every true servant of God.

"I am weak, but Thou art mighty."
William Williams

CHAPTER 18

THE FAITH OF RAHAB

"When we are tempted to look with contempt upon any human being for any reason whatsoever, let us remember Rahab."

G. Campbell Morgan

> *By faith the harlot Rahab perished not with them that believed not, when she had received the spies with peace.* Hebrews 11:31

Rahab is one of only three women that are singled out for mention in this wonderful chapter which lists Old Testament saints who achieved great things for God. One of the other two ladies was Sarah who is the only other one mentioned by name and she was the great matriarch of Israel. The other woman highlighted is mentioned by implication as a parent of Moses and she was Jochebed who saved her infant son from destruction. Rahab is the third member of this illustrious group and yet she was not born into the nation of Israel and was not originally a member of God's covenant people. She was a woman of Jericho which was a pagan city and yet God gives her an honoured place amongst the spiritually great. She is given an important place in Holy Scripture.

She illustrates the words of the apostle Peter after he had seen the vision, *"I perceive that God is no respecter of persons: But in every nation he that feareth him, and worketh righteousness, is accepted with him"* (Acts 10:34-35). Thus God accepts everyone and anyone who comes to Him in faith. It has to be true faith, a faith which is seen, a faith which is practical and a faith that works. Indeed James in his epistle later in the New Testament uses Rahab as an example of someone whose faith was seen in works and who was therefore justified by works. We can see Rahab's faith in four ways.

THE REQUIREMENT OF FAITH

Rahab certainly needed to believe. She was a Gentile and had none of the blessings of being born into God's people, the nation of Israel. Her people had no law such as that which had been given by God to Israel through His servant Moses. Thus Israel had a guiding moral code but the people of Jericho did not possess that vital standard for ethical behaviour and right attitudes. Her people had never seen anything like the Tabernacle, the place where Israel worshipped God and which emphasized the holy nature of God. There had been no patriarchs in her ancestry such as the outstanding godly men of Abraham, Isaac, Jacob and Joseph the great patriarchs of Israel. Her people had no history of miraculous deliverance and blessing such as had been experienced by Israel. So Rahab needed to come into the reality of faith because of her nationality.

It is incredible to think that this woman of faith is nearly always described in Holy Scripture as a prostitute. We cannot get away from the fact that God blessed, saved and commended the faith of a prostitute. Some people have tried to argue that she was simply an inn-keeper which is a similar word to that for a harlot. Some say that if she was a prostitute then that fact negates the story totally. Yet we must not condemn her on the basis of the moral light we have today but see her lifestyle and her response to God in the light of her own situation. In a pagan society evil and sexual practices were normal. She may not have been aware of any sin and was certainly not criticized by the people of Jericho. What she did was normal by the standards of that society. Today in the light of the Lord's teaching, in the light of the New Testament and in the light of the tradition of the church and Western Society generally we know that prostitution is wrong and utterly reprehensible to God. However in Rahab's day in Jericho it was part of every day life, an ingrained heathen and idol worshipping practice. This makes the faith and the work of God in her mind and heart all the more remarkable. She somehow had her spiritual horizon lifted to see the Holy

THE FAITH OF RAHAB

God of creation and submitted to Him and His laws in total surrender. It is a remarkable step of faith. She needed to come to the reality of faith not only because of her nationality but also because of her lifestyle.

Rahab was also a liar and we read of her lies in Joshua 2:4-5 where with the best of motives she spoke untruths. Her motive was to protect the spies that had been sent from Israel to spy out the city of Jericho. She deceived the Jericho secret police and sent them on a wild goose chase, which gave the spies time to escape. Rahab seems to have no compunction about lying and no doubt lying and deceit was an ingrained part of her character. Yet God puts her faith amongst those of the greatest believers. Praise God that He is no respecter of persons. If God could see faith shining in Rahab can He see it in us?

So she needed to come to the reality of faith because of her nationality, she was a Gentile; because of her lifestyle, she was a prostitute and because of her character, she was a liar. We praise God that she came into the reality of faith and her nationality, lifestyle and character were all dramatically changed. So we see the requirement for faith.

THE REALITY OF FAITH

The Israelites were now poised to enter the Promised Land of Canaan. The forty years of wilderness wandering were over and they were now camped across the Jordan directly opposite the city of Jericho. We can hardly visualize the enormity of that camp with well over a million people. It must have been a vast and impressive sight and would have filled the hearts of the people of Canaan with horror and dread.

Joshua had replaced Moses as leader of Israel and he was to become one of the greatest military commanders who ever lived. Like all good military leaders he wanted to know about the enemy. He needed intelligence about the city of Jericho. So he despatched two men of Israel to cross the River Jordan and slip into the city of Jericho on a spying mission. Unfortunately their presence was detected in the city and the security forces of Jericho arrived at Rahab's house with the words, *"Bring forth the men that are come to thee, which are entered into thine house: for they be come to search out all the country"* (Josh. 2:3). We then see two actions by Rahab that reveal the depth of her faith in the Lord.

Firstly, she hid the spies and misdirected the security forces of Jericho. We must always remember that she did this at the risk of her own life. Had she been found out then she could well have been executed as traitor and died for treason against the king. To harbour enemies of the state was a very dangerous undertaking. Faith at the risk of one's own life is real faith. No wonder God highlights her faith in Hebrews 11. So her first great act of faith was to hide the spies.

Secondly, she believed the words of the spies and hung out the scarlet thread from her window. They had said that if she put the scarlet thread in her window then she would be safe and so would everyone who was with her in the house. However if she did not put the thread in the window then she would perish as everyone else would in the city. It may have seemed an absurd thing to do but Rahab accepted the words of the spies as the message from God and she obeyed by putting that scarlet thread into her window.

Do we in any way exercise similar faith? Have we ever taken a step or a stand for God and moved out in faith? I remember a young teacher in a fairly rough comprehensive school taking courage in both hands and approaching the head teacher for permission to start a Christian Union in the school. She was given permission and swimming against the tide of prevailing thought in that school she started her work and the junior Christian Union grew to more than a hundred and eventually a senior group was also started and it might have been the only time those young people were ever exposed to the gospel of Jesus Christ. When you know the sense of God's calling into your heart move forward in faith and take courage in both hands to obey Him.

THE REASONS FOR FAITH

Why did Rahab believe? Why at the risk of her own life did she do a work of faith? There are essentially two reasons.

SHE HAD HEARD ABOUT ISRAEL'S GOD

Firstly she recalled how God had opened up the way through the Red Sea. That had been a great and mighty miracle which even the heathens still talked about. The Red Sea crossing had been forty years before and it is very unlikely that Rahab was even born at that time and so her mother or others must have related it to her and she grew up with a very deep knowledge about the greatness of the God of Israel. She knew that God did miracles in a way that the gods of Jericho had never done and never could do and in awed tones she said, *"we have heard how the LORD dried up the water of the Red sea for you, when ye came out of Egypt..."* (Josh. 2:10).

Secondly, she had heard of Israel's victories over the two kings of the Amorites, Sihon and Og. Those victories had happened very recently on the eastern side of the Jordan. So God's power was not just a historical event but was also a very recent phenomenon. In our own testimonies I hope we don't just dwell upon what God did for us twenty years ago but can also relate the reality of God's actions in our lives today. It is so important that our testimony can be updated and is not just moulded in history.

Thirdly, she recognised that everyone in Jericho was living in fear from the king to the least inhabitant of the city. She used words like, *"terror"; "faint"; "hearts did melt"* and *"neither did there remain any more courage"* (Josh. 2:9-11). She realized that the greatness and victories of Israel were due to the greatness and victory of God. Israel lived in victory because God is victorious. As a result Rahab had learned to respect and reverence the unseen God of Israel. That is the reason why she cared for the spies and protected them and she could say, *"...for the LORD your God, he is God in heaven above, and in earth beneath"* (Josh. 2:11).

So her first reason for faith was that she had come to understand the greatness of God.

SHE LOVED HER FAMILY

She not only risked her life for herself but also for her family and loved ones. She wanted them to be saved from the coming destruction and so she said, "...*that ye will save alive my father, and my mother, and my brethren, and my sisters, and all that they have, and deliver our lives from death*" (Josh. 2:13). She appealed for mercy and salvation not only for herself but also for her family and God honoured her faith. We should similarly love our families very deeply and remember them in prayer every day and seek to lead them to the Lord Jesus Christ who can save and bless them with eternal life and forgiveness.

So her second reason for faith was that she loved her family very deeply.

THE RESULTS OF FAITH

Rahab had trusted God with her life by hiding the spies. Then she had trusted the Word of God through the spies by hanging out the scarlet thread and now she had learned to trust God forever.

Initially her faith resulted in the spies escaping Jericho and returning safely to their camp on the eastern side of the Jordan River. Later when Israel marched around the city and the walls fell down Rahab and her family were delivered from the carnage and death in Jericho. Her house on the wall remained standing. She and her family were then allowed to dwell outside the camp of Israel for a time and then were invited to live amongst the Israelites. The stay outside was undoubtedly to instruct them in the ways of the people of God. It also meant that they were impressed with the privilege and responsibility of joining and becoming part of the household of Israel. No doubt too they were instructed in the laws and holiness of God and about true worship to Him.

THE FAITH OF RAHAB

So Rahab joined the nation of Israel and her nationality was transformed. She was now no longer a Gentile but a daughter of Israel. Also her lifestyle was changed and she no longer lived as a prostitute but became married to Salmon and therefore lived in commitment to one man. Some have considered that Salmon was one of the spies which is a very nice thought but that can only be conjecture.

Later she had the glorious privilege of being a direct ancestor of King David and in Matthew chapter one she is mentioned along with two other Gentile women, Tamar and Ruth in the genealogical line that led to Christ. It pleased God to use her to bring about the line of descent that brought His Son, the Lord Jesus into the world. God richly and abundantly blessed her faith.

Do we walk in the faith of Rahab? Is there truly in us a deep awe and reverence for the greatness and glory of God? Do we fully realize the awful terror of His judgment and seek through evangelism to save people from the consequences of their sins? Do we genuinely love the lost as Rahab did and do our utmost to win them for the Lord so that they can escape the awful destruction which is to come?

Let us remember that God honours faith. He blesses faith. We need to be men and women who will trust Him implicitly by obeying Him without question and regardless of the consequences we might fear. It is important that we do and say what is right and never just what is expedient. Let us look forward to the day when we will join Rahab in heaven and get to know more deeply this great heroine of faith.

As with Rahab God does not hold our sinful and failed past against us if we are true Christians. He says that in Christ there is now no condemnation. He says that our sins and iniquities He will remember no more and that *"as far as the east is from the west, so far hath he removed our transgressions from us"* (Ps. 103:12). We have a God who truly forgives the repentant heart and looks for us to act in faith and serve Him with total devotion and genuine commitment. We need to view our fellow believers in the same light as God sees them. They too are forgiven and their sins are not held against them and so we should be very ready to forgive one another and live in deep love and fellowship with each other. Together we can serve the Lord and the glory of Christ will be revealed, people will be saved and Christ's name will be glorified. May we "escape the curse of a useless life". Let us serve God by faith and live for His glory.

Rahab and her family were saved…

"under the protection of the scarlet line."

Herbert Lockyer

CHAPTER 19

THE FAITH OF GIDEON

PART 1

"Until a man is nothing God can make nothing of him."
Martin Luther

And what shall I more say? for the time would fail me to tell of Gedeon, and of Barak, and of Samson, and of Jephthae; of David also, and Samuel, and of the prophets. **Hebrews 11:32**

And the children of Israel did evil in the sight of the LORD: and the LORD delivered them into the hand of Midian seven years. And the hand of Midian prevailed against Israel: and because of the Midianites the children of Israel made them the dens which are in the mountains, and caves, and strong holds. And so it was, when Israel had sown, that the Midianites came up, and the Amalekites, and the children of the east, even they came up against them; And they encamped against them, and destroyed the increase of the earth, till thou come unto Gaza, and left no sustenance for Israel, neither sheep, nor ox, nor ass. For they came up with their cattle and their tents, and they came as grasshoppers for multitude; for both they and their camels were without number: and they entered into the land to destroy it. And Israel was greatly impoverished because of the Midianites; and the children of Israel cried unto the LORD. And it came to pass, when the children of Israel cried unto the LORD because of the Midianites, That the LORD sent a prophet unto the children of Israel, which said unto them, Thus saith the LORD God of Israel, I brought you up from Egypt, and brought you forth out of the house of bondage; And I delivered you out of the hand of the Egyptians, and out of the hand of all that oppressed you, and drave them out from before you, and gave you their land; And I said unto you, I am the LORD your God; fear not the gods of the Amorites, in whose land ye dwell: but ye have not obeyed my voice. And there came an angel of the LORD, and sat under an oak which was in Ophrah, that pertained unto Joash the Abiezrite: and his son Gideon threshed wheat by the winepress, to hide it from the Midianites. And the angel of the LORD appeared unto him, and said unto him, The LORD is with thee, thou mighty man of valour. And Gideon said unto him, Oh my Lord, if the LORD be with us, why then is all this befallen us? and where be all his miracles which our fathers told us of, saying, Did not the LORD bring us up from Egypt? but now the LORD hath forsaken us, and delivered us into the hands of the Midianites. And the LORD looked upon him, and said, Go in this thy might, and thou shalt save Israel from the hand of the Midianites: have not I sent thee? And he said unto him, Oh my Lord, wherewith shall I save Israel? behold, my family is poor in Manasseh, and I am the least in my father's house. And the LORD said unto him, Surely I will be with thee, and thou shalt smite the Midianites as one man.

Judges 6:1-16

The next character in this list of great Old Testament saints mentioned in Hebrews 11 is Gideon. His life story is found in the book of Judges and that book covers approximately four hundred years in the history of Israel. It was that period of time between entering the Promised Land as conquerors and the eventual rise of the monarchy. It was a saga of constant defeats, invasions by foreign powers and subservience to those invading armies. The reason behind each invasion was simply the hand of God. It was His judgment upon the nation of Israel because of their wicked and evil ways. Time and again they deserted the Lord and bowed down in worship to heathen idols. Those idols were dumb and quite incapable of hearing any prayers or incantations. They were simply the creations of man and no doubt were in some cases beautiful works of art, but it was a beauty that did not honour God. Also it led to the debasement of the people of Israel, because so often there were promiscuous and immoral practices associated with those pagan, idol-worshipping activities.

The result of such evil within the nation of Israel was that God sent invading armies as His means of discipline. Israel came under the iron hand of foreign powers and when matters reached extreme proportions they repented of their sins and cried out to God for deliverance. The Lord heard their prayers and sent deliverance to them in the form of a warrior-judge who led the nation to victory and established true worship to God as the central activity in Israel.

The first major judge was Othniel and he defeated the forces of Aram from Mesopotamia. The second was Ehud who defeated a confederation of Semitic people under the leadership of the country of Moab. There is a brief mention of a minor judge named Shamgar who defeated an army of Philistines (6:31), then there was the combination of the prophetess Deborah and the leader Barak. They defeated a northern invasion that had lasted twenty years made up of Canaanites. Gideon was the fourth major judge. His name is famous because the world-wide organization that distributes Bibles to hotels, schools, prisons, hospitals and other places as well as to key individuals takes its name from this man. The organization is known as "The Gideons International" and has branches in many countries of the world and does a wonderful work in distributing the Word of God.

THE INVASION OF ISRAEL

The invading army in the time of Gideon was headed by the nation of Midian. They moved in from the east and were confederated with the Amalekites and other peoples of the east. So this was a federation of various nomadic peoples who invaded from the desert regions of Arabia. They obviously arrived on camels and these may have been used in warfare to form a mounted army and would have given the invaders clear advantages when battles were conducted in the open countryside.

This invading force is described as being *"without number"* (Judg. 6:5). They are further described as being like *"grass-hoppers for multitude"* (Judg. 6:5). There are clearly two senses in which the invading army could be considered similar to a plague of locusts.

Firstly, the sheer number of them: A plague of locust contains millions of insects and is very hard to number accurately. In a similar way the number of soldiers in this army was almost too many to count. Certainly 120,000 were killed in the battle that eventually came (Judg. 8:10) and even that huge number does not exhaust the extent of this confederacy because we read that Gideon went on to pursue, defeat and capture many more. It was like a plague of locusts in the great number of people that invaded Israel.

Secondly, their destructive quality: A plague of locust can strip a countryside bare of anything and everything that grows. The following is a description of such a plague, "In their march they devour every green thing and with wonderful expedition. A large vineyard and garden…was green as a meadow in the morning, but long before night it was naked and bare as a newly ploughed field or dusty road…I saw with my own eyes not only a large vineyard loaded with young grapes, but whole fields of corn disappear as if by magic…". Locusts strip the countryside bare and leave everything as a waste and barren desert. This was essentially what the Midianite forces did to Israel.

That huge army camped on the lands of Israel and destroyed the crops upon which the nation depended. This happened every time Israel planted their crops. So as the nation was very much an agricultural community, to lose its crops would have meant long term disaster because it would have deprived them of a staple food for the rest of the year and also of seed to plant for the following year. The invading hordes trampled the crops and presumably took what was left for their own needs. In addition they *"left no sustenance for Israel, neither sheep, nor ox, nor ass"* (Judg. 6:4). It was a brutal and savage regime that took everything and anything they could and the nation of Israel was effectively deprived of its means of survival and prosperity. The purpose of the invasion is thus clearly demonstrated and was to strip Israel of its wealth and is described in these words, *"they entered into the land to destroy it"* (Judg. 6:5). So the simile of locusts was very apt because it suggests both destructiveness as well as multitude.

So the result was that Israel was utterly impoverished and was reduced to servitude and its people were forced to try to eke out an existence to simply survive. This may not have applied to the whole of the nation because we read of the Midianites *"destroyed the increase of the earth, till thou come unto Gaza"* (Judg. 6:4). It may simply be that the main agricultural and central areas of the land were particularly affected and that there was less direct control by the invading force in other areas of Israel. However the Israelites were seriously dislocated and many had to leave their homes and *"made them the dens which are in the mountains, and caves, and strong holds"* (Judg. 6:2). So the Israelites had to leave the towns and villages and move into the hills and mountains. They had to leave the lowlands and move into the highlands for protection and safety. This might not have been for all the year round but only when the Midianites were rampaging over the countryside.

It was a terrifying and desperate time for the people of God and that oppression lasted for seven years. The whole outlook seemed to be utterly hopeless and their only recourse could be to seek the help of the Lord.

THE CRY OF ISRAEL TO GOD

In their desperate and impoverished condition Israel engaged in the only sensible course left to them, *"the children of Israel cried unto the Lord"* (Judg. 6:6). When we are in the most extreme situations it is so often that at that stage we think of the Lord. It is so easy to forget the Lord when all is going well. As Christians we must learn to maintain our contact and fellowship with the Lord and not to just seek Him at our more difficult or dangerous moments.

So Israel cried to God and the people must have been well aware of how the Lord had miraculously intervened in their nation's history in the past. Yet this time there was a prophetic message from the Lord. God sent them a prophet. He is an unnamed and therefore unknown prophet but he came to Israel with a message from their God. It was a short message and was really a rebuke to the nation.

The prophet said, *"Thus saith the Lord God of Israel, I brought you up from Egypt, and brought you forth out of the house of bondage; And I delivered you out of the hand of the Egyptians, and out of the hand of all that oppressed you, and drave them out from before you, and gave you their land; And I said unto you, I am the Lord your God; fear not the gods of the Amorites, in whose land ye dwell: but ye have not obeyed my voice"* (Judg. 6:8-10). This was a terrible indictment upon Israel and was clearly the reason for their present troubles. Can we imagine the awfulness of ignoring the voice of God? Can we imagine how God's heart was broken when the people He loved and whom He had blessed would not listen to Him? Yet we cannot stand in judgment upon ancient Israel because it could be true that we too go about our daily lives and fail to acknowledge the Lord or allow Him to lead, guide and direct us. It may be possible that we as Christians can be guilty of not listening to the Lord. This will certainly be so if we live such busy lives that we fail to find time for prayer or for reading and studying the Bible. These are the means of making contact with our Lord and Saviour and to neglect them will mean that we lose that sense of the voice of God into our hearts and lives.

However, God had a deliverer ready for Israel and that man was Gideon and he becomes one of the greatest leaders in the history of the nation.

THE CALL OF GIDEON

Clearly Gideon was a discouraged and disheartened man. He belonged to the Israelite tribe of Manasseh (Judg. 6:15) and his father's name was Joash. Joash is described as *"the Abiezrite"* (Judg. 6:11), which means that he belonged to the Abiezer clan or sub tribe of Manasseh. This part of Manasseh was found on the western side of the River Jordan and not on the eastern side. Manasseh was the only tribe that had tribal areas on both sides of the River Jordan.

Gideon was involved in clandestine activities so that the Midianites would not see what he was doing. It was secret work, but exhausting at the same time. He was simply threshing wheat. Such an activity was usually done in places where there was a breeze and that helped to make the job more pleasant but more importantly it helped to separate the wheat from the chaff. Gideon was doing this work in a winepress where there was certainly no breeze and was probably working on very small quantities of wheat. In the oppressive heat of that activity the Lord appeared to him.

This seems to have been a theophany or Christophany, being one of those occasions when the Lord appeared on earth before His birth at Bethlehem. The person who appears beside Gideon is described in two ways. Firstly an, *"angel of the Lord"* (Judg. 6:11, 12, 21) and then as *"the Lord"* (Judg. 6:14, 16, 18). It could be that in speaking to the Lord's representative, namely an angel it was as if Gideon was speaking to the Lord Himself or more likely it was the Lord appearing to him as an angel.

So the Lord came in the form of a person and directly called Gideon to his life's work. The Lord *"sat under an oak which was in Ophrah"* (Judg. 6:11), the location of which is not really known anymore and spoke to Gideon. The words used were startling words, *"The L*ORD *is with thee, thou mighty man of valour"* (Judg. 6:12). This certainly seemed an absurdity to Gideon's mind because how could he be a mighty warrior when here he was threshing wheat secretly because he was afraid of the Midianites.

Gideon's reaction was one of utter disbelief. Indeed he felt that the Lord had abandoned them. He knew of the great wonders the Lord had done for Israel as a nation in the past yet that was history, and he says, *"but now the L*ORD *hath forsaken us, and delivered us into the hands of the Midianites"* (Judg. 6:13). Clearly Gideon had been instructed in the history of his people but now it seemed as though God was far away. Certainly if he had heard the message from the unknown prophet then that would have added to his discomfort and sense of utter dejection as he looked upon the present circumstances of Israel. However the call to Gideon to lead his people against the Midianites was clear and unmistakable. *"And the L*ORD *looked upon him, and said, Go in this thy might, and thou shalt save Israel from the hand of the Midianites: have not I sent thee?"* (Judg. 6:14).

In words reminiscent of Moses when God called him to his most important task Gideon replied in a personally disparaging way. He thought it utterly inconceivable that he could undertake such a great task, and so he answered the Lord by saying, *"Oh my L*ORD*, wherewith shall I save Israel? behold, my family is poor in Manasseh, and I am the least in my father's house"* (Judg. 6:15). Here was a man whom God could use because he was humble. There was no sense of inflated self-importance, no arrogance and no pride. He had been reduced to the lowest point and could not imagine any life apart from one of subservience to the Midianite hordes.

It is often amazing whom the Lord chooses to serve Him. In His sovereign will He chooses some very unlikely candidates to be heroes of faith. Here was one of the most insignificant men in Israel and yet he is singled out for a great work to rescue and save Israel from foreign oppression. It may be that at times you feel insignificant in your church or community. It may be that you feel useless and overwhelmed by all that needs to be done and feel that you can contribute nothing. It may be that you wonder whether God has any work for you to do in His kingdom and you marvel at those who seem to be so wonderfully used. Do take heart from the story of Gideon. Do be faithful in what little you can do and make sure that you do everything for the glory of God and not for some sort of personal glory. The Lord can use you in His service and bring a great blessing to your life.

The Lord made it abundantly clear to Gideon that he was the man and God confirms it by saying, *"Surely I will be with thee, and thou shalt smite the Midianites as one man"* (Judg. 6:16). This was God's promise of victory to Gideon and eventually Gideon acted upon that promise and a great victory was achieved. However, there were many twists and turns before the plot unfolded and the Midianites' seven years of oppressive rule was broken. It is fascinating to read what happened and we look forward to the uncovering of the story next time, but for now we leave Gideon being convinced by God that he is called to this great task of being a warrior judge who will lead Israel to victory.

"God has no problems, only plans."
Corrie ten Boom

CHAPTER 20

THE FAITH OF GIDEON

PART 2

"We should never tire of the thought of God's power."

Donald Grey Barnhouse

And what shall I more say? for the time would fail me to tell of Gedeon, and of Barak, and of Samson, and of Jephthae; of David also, and Samuel, and of the prophets. Hebrews 11:32

And he said unto him, If now I have found grace in thy sight, then shew me a sign that thou talkest with me. Depart not hence, I pray thee, until I come unto thee, and bring forth my present, and set it before thee. And he said, I will tarry until thou come again. And Gideon went in, and made ready a kid, and unleavened cakes of an ephah of flour: the flesh he put in a basket, and he put the broth in a pot, and brought it out unto him under the oak, and presented it. And the angel of God said unto him, Take the flesh and the unleavened cakes, and lay them upon this rock, and pour out the broth. And he did so. Then the angel of the LORD put forth the end of the staff that was in his hand, and touched the flesh and the unleavened cakes; and there rose up fire out of the rock, and consumed the flesh and the unleavened cakes. Then the angel of the LORD departed out of his sight. And when Gideon perceived that he was an angel of the LORD, Gideon said, Alas, O Lord GOD! for because I have seen an angel of the LORD face to face. And the LORD said unto him, Peace be unto thee; fear not: thou shalt

*not die. Then Gideon built an altar there unto the
Lord, and called it Jehovahshalom: unto this day it
is yet in Ophrah of the Abiezrites. And it came to
pass the same night, that the Lord said unto him,
Take thy father's young bullock, even the second
bullock of seven years old, and throw down the altar
of Baal that thy father hath, and cut down the grove
that is by it: And build an altar unto the Lord thy
God upon the top of this rock, in the ordered place,
and take the second bullock, and offer a burnt sacrifice with the wood of the grove which thou shalt cut
down. Then Gideon took ten men of his servants,
and did as the Lord had said unto him: and so it
was, because he feared his father's household, and
the men of the city, that he could not do it by day,
that he did it by night. And when the men of the city
arose early in the morning, behold, the altar of Baal
was cast down, and the grove was cut down that was
by it, and the second bullock was offered upon the
altar that was built. And they said one to another,
Who hath done this thing? And when they enquired
and asked, they said, Gideon the son of Joash hath
done this thing. Then the men of the city said unto
Joash, Bring out thy son, that he may die: because
he hath cast down the altar of Baal, and because he
hath cut down the grove that was by it. And Joash
said unto all that stood against him, Will ye plead
for Baal? will ye save him? he that will plead for
him, let him be put to death whilst it is yet morning:
if he be a god, let him plead for himself, because one
hath cast down his altar. Therefore on that day he
called him Jerubbaal, saying, Let Baal plead against
him, because he hath thrown down his altar. Then
all the Midianites and the Amalekites and the children of the east were gathered together, and went
over, and pitched in the valley of Jezreel. But the
Spirit of the Lord came upon Gideon, and he blew a*

trumpet; and Abiezer was gathered after him. And he sent messengers throughout all Manasseh; who also was gathered after him: and he sent messengers unto Asher, and unto Zebulun, and unto Naphtali; and they came up to meet them. And Gideon said unto God, If thou wilt save Israel by mine hand, as thou hast said, Behold, I will put a fleece of wool in the floor; and if the dew be on the fleece only, and it be dry upon all the earth beside, then shall I know that thou wilt save Israel by mine hand, as thou hast said. And it was so: for he rose up early on the morrow, and thrust the fleece together, and wringed the dew out of the fleece, a bowl full of water. And Gideon said unto God, Let not thine anger be hot against me, and I will speak but this once: let me prove, I pray thee, but this once with the fleece; let it now be dry only upon the fleece, and upon all the ground let there be dew. And God did so that night: for it was dry upon the fleece only, and there was dew on all the ground. Judges 6:17-40

The great Midianite nation and its allies the Amalekites and eastern peoples had invaded the nation of Israel and oppressed them in the most awful manner. They stole the crops and food sources from Israel and many of the people of Israel hid themselves in the caves and dens of the mountains. The people were under severe oppression and they cried out to God and the Lord visited a man from the Israelite tribe of Manasseh. That man's name was Gideon, who was otherwise known as Jerubbaal and he was called by God to be the next deliverer of the nation. This was the person called to be the latest in the line of warrior-judges who would deliver the people of God from the violent oppression of invading Midianites. The Lord's call to Gideon was clear and unmistakable. God had called him personally and had promised him victory, through divine presence and help. The Lord said, *"Surely I will be with thee, and thou shalt smite the Midianites as one man"* (Judg. 6:16). It was a wonderful promise, but Gideon was so intimidated and lacked any real confidence that he needed constant affirmation of the call of God.

THE CONFIRMATION OF GIDEON'S CALL

The Lord very graciously and with wonderful patience recognised the weakness of His servant Gideon and four times He confirmed the words He had spoken with powerful and faith-inspiring signs. These led to Gideon being eventually totally assured of God's help and so he was enabled by God to gain a very great victory over the enemy. Four signs helped him gain the confidence necessary to lead the armies of Israel and bring about a wonderful victory.

THE SIGN OF FIRE
JUDGES 6:16-24

Immediately after God had called him Gideon actually requested that the Lord give him a sign to show that it was truly God speaking to him. He said, *"...shew me a sign that thou talkest with me"* (Judg. 6:17). He requested that the Lord wait while he went and prepared an offering and the Lord said, *"I will tarry until thou come again"* (Judg. 6:18). So Gideon went away and prepared a broth of goat's meat and some unleavened bread. This would not have been easy as food was in such short supply in Israel and it would certainly have meant great personal sacrifice for Gideon and his family.

However the food was brought back to the Lord, was laid out on a rock and the angel of the Lord touched the food with the tip of His staff and instantly fire flared from the rock and the food was consumed in the flames. At that point the angel of the Lord disappeared. He left as quickly as He had come. It must have been an awesome and life-changing experience for Gideon and he began to realize the enormity of the encounter and he exclaimed, *"Alas, O LORD God! for because I have seen an angel of the LORD face to face"* (Judg. 6:22). He must have at that stage felt as though he was going to die and the Lord had to assure him that he would not die but live. In fact the Lord says, *"Peace be unto thee; fear not: thou shalt not die"* (Judg. 6:23). This to our minds is very obvious, but to Gideon it was not so clear. To us it is very evident that the Lord would not have promised him victory and then allowed him to die before that victory was complete. The promise had to be fulfilled but for Gideon he must have been in a state of awed disorientation and he needed the confirming words of God.

In response to the Lord's words of reassurance he built an altar to the Lord in Ophrah. This altar was built in the area of land that had been given to the family of the Abiezrites to whom, of course, Gideon belonged. The altar was of a permanent character and the writer of the book of Judges who clearly lived long after the time of Gideon mentions the fact that it was still standing as he wrote the book. The altar was called *"Jehovah-shalom"* (Judg. 6:24) and that means "The LORD is Peace". This clearly reflected the relief that Gideon felt. His own heart was at peace and it also reflected the fact that Israel would soon be able to live in peace and tranquillity when the Midianite oppression upon them would be broken.

This also reminds us that today we can find peace, a wonderful peace that transcends all understanding when we draw close to the Lord in obedience and fellowship. Christ is our peace and He has brought peace with God through dying on the cross for our sins and also gives the peace of God to our hearts and lives by His Holy Spirit. Prayer is the key that enables us to find the peace of God in our hearts. I trust that we know *"Jehovah-shalom"*, "the LORD is Peace".

So Gideon was blessed with a glorious sign of fire, which indicated the presence of God.

THE SIGN OF PROTECTION
JUDGES 6:25-32

Before Gideon could deliver the nation of Israel from Midianite oppression he had a more pressing assignment from the Lord. That task was to destroy idolatry at home and the Lord commanded him to do three things.

1. He was to sacrifice a bull to the Lord upon a properly prepared altar. The bull was to be taken from his father's herd and was to be seven years old.

2. He was to tear down and destroy the altar that had been erected to the Canaan idol of Baal.

3. He was to cut down the Asherah pole, which was the symbol of the idol known as the goddess Asherah. The wood from the pole was to be used upon the altar of the Lord to burn the bull as an offering to God.

This was a test of Gideon's obedience to God. This was no easy task that had been given but it was the beginning of the uprooting of idol worship in Israel as Gideon obeyed the Lord. Gideon was well aware that his family and the people of the town were deeply attached to their idols. He knew that there would be reaction and maybe violent reaction when the deed was done. So with ten of his servants he went at night and did as the Lord commanded him. Here he was living up to his name because Gideon means "a hewing down" or "a cutting off". This was what he effectively did in his own town. He cut off idolatry amongst his family and neighbours. It was a brave and courageous action to take and even though he did it under cover of darkness it showed his willingness to obey God.

The next day the people awoke to the shock of seeing their altar to Baal destroyed, their Asherah pole cut down and burnt and an altar of worship to God in their place. They were clearly furious and made detailed enquiries but it soon became evident who the culprit was and they gathered around the home of Gideon and called upon his father Joash to deliver Gideon up for punishment. The people were hostile and were calling for the death penalty to be imposed upon Gideon. They made the demand, *"Bring out thy son, that he may die…"* (Judg. 6:30). Here we see the strength of Gideon's father, Joash. He stood up to the crowd and refused to let them kill his son. In fact he clearly took his son's side and demanded to know how these people could defend the idol Baal. In fact he stated the obvious that if Baal were really and truly a god then he could defend himself. If Baal were so powerful would he really need people to defend him? The answer, of course, was "No" and it very effectively showed the impotence of Baal and the futility of worshipping such an idol. Joash seemed to calm the crowd and they renamed Gideon and gave him the name of "Jerub-Baal". The meaning of this new name was "let Baal contend" and was therefore a constant reminder to the people of the uselessness of worshipping and serving idols made by the hand of man.

So God saved Gideon from being killed by the mob and this seemed to have given him standing in the community. He now had credibility and from that base he was able to bring together the army of Israel and eventually defeat the Midianites and give Israel peace and security.

THE SIGN OF CERTAINTY
JUDGES 6:36-40

Gideon experienced the Spirit of the Lord coming upon him following his victory in removing idolatry from his home. This led him to blow the trumpet and the Abiezrites joined together to follow him. Messengers were then sent throughout the rest of the tribe of Manasseh and also into Asher, Zebulun and Naphtali and men came to Gideon and formed the basis for his army that would eventually defeat the Midianites. However, Gideon still needed reassurance from the Lord.

This time he used the famous fleece test. He said to God, *"If thou wilt save Israel by mine hand, as thou hast said"* (Judg. 6:36) then do something for me. What Gideon went on to ask was for something that was very specific. In the end it involved two tests.

Firstly, he placed a wool fleece on the ground and it would stay there overnight. If in the morning the wool was wet but the ground was dry then it would confirm God's promise to Gideon. Amazingly in the morning the ground was absolutely bone dry but Gideon was able to wring out a whole bowlful of water from the fleece. That was a most remarkable miracle and should have utterly convinced Gideon.

However, he still needed a second confirming sign. He asked the Lord not to be angry and made one more request. This time if the ground was wet with dew and the fleece was dry then he would be absolutely sure. So again the fleece was left out overnight and the next day Gideon awoke to find the ground soaking wet with dew but the fleece was absolutely dry. God had done exactly as Gideon had asked and that must have given him great resolution to continue in his call to overthrow the might of Midian and give Israel freedom.

Clearly Gideon could be absolutely certain that the Lord was with him and he would win a very great battle. We may, as it were, put out our fleeces to try and determine the mind of God for us, but we must remember that we have great advantages that were not available to Gideon. We have the full canon of God's Word that enables us to see the mind of God in history and to know His will for the present. We also have the indwelling Holy Spirit that is continually in us as Christian believers. The Spirit came upon Gideon at certain times but was never a continuing, indwelling presence in Old Testament saints. So we have wonderful advantages and privileges and so have no excuse for failing to know the mind of God and the will of the Lord for our lives as Christians.

So Gideon through the fleece tests was given assurance by our gracious Lord that he would be given the victory.

THE SIGN OF THE DREAM
JUDGES 7:9-14

Again Gideon showed fear and uncertainty and this time just before he was due to attack the Midianite army. The Lord seems to have constantly recognised the weakness in his servant Gideon. So in addition to promising victory the Lord also encouraged Gideon to go near to the camp of Midian. The idea was that under cover of darkness Gideon and his servant Purah were to work their way to the outskirts of the enemy camp. They would be close enough to hear conversations between the Midianite soldiers.

So the two of them travelled to the camp and were just in time to hear two Midianites talking together. One of them announced that he had dreamed and that in his dream he had seen, *"a cake of barley bread tumbled into the host of Midian, and came unto a tent, and smote it that it fell, and overturned it, that the tent lay along"* (Judg. 7:13). It was a simple enough dream and could have been laughed off, but the man's friend gave an interpretation. This might seem surprising to us but in those days dreams may have been more significant to people than they are today. The friend said, *"This is nothing else save the sword of Gideon the son of Joash, a man of Israel: for into his hand hath God delivered Midian, and all the host"* (Judg. 7:14). Here was a Midianite predicting the demise of his own army and Gideon and his servant overheard the man. It is remarkable what God is able to do and we can imagine the surge of excitement that Gideon felt when he heard such words.

This proved to be the concluding confirmation of victory. This was the final incentive that Gideon needed to get on with the battle and lead Israel to triumph over her enemies. It must have been a great moment when Gideon heard the dream and its interpretation. It caused Gideon to worship the Lord and we can imagine him expressing praise and gratitude to his God. God had confirmed and given assurance of victory before they had even engaged in battle. It was remarkable confirmation for Gideon and for Israel.

So we see that God in a wonderfully gracious, patient and loving manner gave Gideon many signs and assurances that confirmed to him the call upon his life. Gideon in the end had no choice but to accept the fact that God had called him to lead the nation of Israel to victory over the Midianites and its allied forces from the East.

God is still the same gracious and loving God and as we trust Him and seek His will He will make His desire known and it will be plain and clear for us. We may not have the same confirming signs as Gideon received but the Lord will make very clear to us where our life's work will be and how we can utilize our gifts for His glory. May the Lord richly bless you.

"Faith saves us but assurance satisfies us."

C. H. Spurgeon

CHAPTER 21

THE FAITH OF GIDEON

PART 3

"Let us be as watchful after the victory as before the battle."

Andrew Bonar

And what shall I more say? for the time would fail me to tell of Gedeon, and of Barak, and of Samson, and of Jephthae; of David also, and Samuel, and of the prophets. Hebrews 11:32

Then Jerubbaal, who is Gideon, and all the people that were with him, rose up early, and pitched beside the well of Harod: so that the host of the Midianites were on the north side of them, by the hill of Moreh, in the valley. And the LORD said unto Gideon, The people that are with thee are too many for me to give the Midianites into their hands, lest Israel vaunt themselves against me, saying, Mine own hand hath saved me. Now therefore go to, proclaim in the ears of the people, saying, Whosoever is fearful and afraid, let him return and depart early from mount Gilead. And there returned of the people twenty and two thousand; and there remained ten thousand. And the LORD said unto Gideon, The people are yet too many; bring them down unto the water, and I will try them for thee there: and it shall be, that of whom I say unto thee, This shall go with thee, the same shall go with thee; and of whomsoever I say unto thee, This shall not go with thee, the same shall not go. So he brought down the people unto the water: and the LORD said unto Gideon, *Every one that lappeth of the water with his tongue, as a dog lappeth, him shalt thou set by himself; likewise every one that boweth down upon his knees to drink. And the number of them that lapped, putting their hand to their mouth, were three hundred men: but all the rest of the people bowed down upon their knees to drink water. And the* LORD *said unto Gideon, By the three hundred men that lapped will I save you, and deliver the Midianites into thine hand: and let all the other people go every man unto his place. So the people took victuals in their hand, and their trumpets: and he sent all the rest of Israel every man unto his tent, and retained those three hundred men: and the host of Midian was beneath him in the valley. And it came to pass the same night, that the* LORD *said unto him, Arise, get thee down unto the host; for I have delivered it into thine hand. But if thou fear to go down, go thou with Phurah thy servant down to the host: And thou shalt hear what they say; and afterward shall thine hands be strengthened to go down unto the host. Then went he down with Phurah his servant unto the outside of the armed men that were in the host. And the Midianites and the Amalekites and all the children of the east lay along in the valley like grasshoppers for multitude; and their camels were without number, as the sand by the sea side for multitude. And when Gideon was come, behold, there was a man that told a dream unto his fellow, and said, Behold, I dreamed a dream, and, lo, a cake of barley bread tumbled into the host of Midian, and came unto a tent, and smote it that it fell, and overturned it, that the tent lay along. And his fellow answered and said, This is nothing else save the sword of Gideon the son of Joash, a man of Israel: for into his hand hath God delivered Midian, and all the host. And it was so, when Gideon heard the telling of the dream, and the interpretation thereof, that he worshipped, and returned into the host of Israel, and said, Arise; for the* L<small>ORD</small> *hath delivered into your hand the host of Midian. And he divided the three hundred men into three companies, and he put a trumpet in every man's hand, with empty pitchers, and lamps within the pitchers. And he said unto them, Look on me, and do likewise: and, behold, when I come to the outside of the camp, it shall be that, as I do, so shall ye do. When I blow with a trumpet, I and all that are with me, then blow ye the trumpets also on every side of all the camp, and say, The sword of the* L<small>ORD</small>, *and of Gideon. So Gideon, and the hundred men that were with him, came unto the outside of the camp in the beginning of the middle watch; and they had but newly set the watch: and they blew the trumpets, and brake the pitchers that were in their hands. And the three companies blew the trumpets, and brake the pitchers, and held the lamps in their left hands, and the trumpets in their right hands to blow withal: and they cried, The sword of the* L<small>ORD</small>, *and of Gideon. And they stood every man in his place round about the camp; and all the host ran, and cried, and fled. And the three hundred blew the trumpets, and the* L<small>ORD</small> *set every man's sword against his fellow, even throughout all the host: and the host fled to Bethshittah in Zererath, and to the border of Abelmeholah, unto Tabbath. And the men of Israel gathered themselves together out of Naphtali, and out of Asher, and out of all Manasseh, and pursued after the Midianites. And Gideon sent messengers throughout all mount Ephraim, saying, Come down against the Midianites, and take before them the waters unto Bethbarah and Jordan. Then all the men of Ephraim gathered themselves together, and took the waters unto Bethbarah and Jordan. And they took two princes of the Midianites, Oreb and*

Zeeb; and they slew Oreb upon the rock Oreb, and
Zeeb they slew at the winepress of Zeeb, and pursued
Midian, and brought the heads of Oreb and Zeeb to
Gideon on the other side Jordan. And the men of
Ephraim said unto him, Why hast thou served us
thus, that thou calledst us not, when thou wentest to
fight with the Midianites? And they did chide with
him sharply. And he said unto them, What have I
done now in comparison of you? Is not the gleaning
of the grapes of Ephraim better than the vintage of
Abiezer? God hath delivered into your hands the
princes of Midian, Oreb and Zeeb: and what was I
able to do in comparison of you? Then their anger
was abated toward him, when he had said that. And
Gideon came to Jordan, and passed over, he, and the
three hundred men that were with him, faint, yet
pursuing them. And he said unto the men of Succoth,
Give, I pray you, loaves of bread unto the people that
follow me; for they be faint, and I am pursuing after
Zebah and Zalmunna, kings of Midian. And the
princes of Succoth said, Are the hands of Zebah and
Zalmunna now in thine hand, that we should give
bread unto thine army? And Gideon said, Therefore
when the LORD hath delivered Zebah and Zalmunna
into mine hand, then I will tear your flesh with the
thorns of the wilderness and with briers. And he
went up thence to Penuel, and spake unto them likewise: and the men of Penuel answered him as the
men of Succoth had answered him. And he spake also
unto the men of Penuel, saying, When I come again
in peace, I will break down this tower. Now Zebah
and Zalmunna were in Karkor, and their hosts with
them, about fifteen thousand men, all that were left of
all the hosts of the children of the east: for there fell an
hundred and twenty thousand men that drew sword.
And Gideon went up by the way of them that dwelt
in tents on the east of Nobah and Jogbehah, and

smote the host; for the host was secure. And when Zebah and Zalmunna fled, he pursued after them, and took the two kings of Midian, Zebah and Zalmunna, and discomfited all the host. And Gideon the son of Joash returned from battle before the sun was up, And caught a young man of the men of Succoth, and enquired of him: and he described unto him the princes of Succoth, and the elders thereof, even threescore and seventeen men. And he came unto the men of Succoth, and said, Behold Zebah and Zalmunna, with whom ye did upbraid me, saying, Are the hands of Zebah and Zalmunna now in thine hand, that we should give bread unto thy men that are weary? And he took the elders of the city, and thorns of the wilderness and briers, and with them he taught the men of Succoth. And he beat down the tower of Penuel, and slew the men of the city. Then said he unto Zebah and Zalmunna, What manner of men were they whom ye slew at Tabor? And they answered, As thou art, so were they; each one resembled the children of a king. And he said, They were my brethren, even the sons of my mother: as the Lord liveth, if ye had saved them alive, I would not slay you. And he said unto Jether his firstborn, Up, and slay them. But the youth drew not his sword: for he feared, because he was yet a youth. Then Zebah and Zalmunna said, Rise thou, and fall upon us: for as the man is, so is his strength. And Gideon arose, and slew Zebah and Zalmunna, and took away the ornaments that were on their camels' necks. Then the men of Israel said unto Gideon, Rule thou over us, both thou, and thy son, and thy son's son also: for thou hast delivered us from the hand of Midian. And Gideon said unto them, I will not rule over you, neither shall my son rule over you: the Lord shall rule over you. And Gideon said unto them, I would desire a request of you, that ye would give me every man

the earrings of his prey. (For they had golden ear-
rings, because they were Ishmaelites.) And they
answered, We will willingly give them. And they
spread a garment, and did cast therein every man the
earrings of his prey. And the weight of the golden
earrings that he requested was a thousand and seven
hundred shekels of gold; beside ornaments, and col-
lars, and purple raiment that was on the kings of
Midian, and beside the chains that were about their
camels' necks. And Gideon made an ephod thereof,
and put it in his city, even in Ophrah: and all Israel
went thither a whoring after it: which thing became
a snare unto Gideon, and to his house. Thus was
Midian subdued before the children of Israel, so that
they lifted up their heads no more. And the country
was in quietness forty years in the days of Gideon.
And Jerubbaal the son of Joash went and dwelt in his
own house. And Gideon had threescore and ten sons
of his body begotten: for he had many wives. And his
concubine that was in Shechem, she also bare him a
son, whose name he called Abimelech. And Gideon
the son of Joash died in a good old age, and was bur-
ied in the sepulchre of Joash his father, in Ophrah of
the Abiezrites. Judges 7:1-8:32

The forces of Midian had oppressed the Israelites for seven years and terribly exploited them. It was a dreadful time for God's chosen people, but the Lord had the man in place who would be their deliverer. His name was Gideon and he was from the Israelite tribe of Manasseh. The Lord had clearly called Gideon to his great task of saving Israel and had confirmed that call with very definite signs. In response Gideon had blown a trumpet and had drawn together an army made up of men from his own tribe of Manasseh, together with those of Asher, Zebulun and Naphtali. This was essentially a confederation of troops from the northern tribes of Israel.

Gideon led his men towards the Midianites and they camped to the south of that great army. However Gideon's army was made up of merely thirty-two thousand soldiers. By modern standards such a force would be small and even by the standards of the day it was not big and certainly not in contrast with the overwhelming forces of Midian and the confederate forces to which they were joined. It would seem absurd that such a small force could defeat the might of Midian. Yet Gideon was in touch with Almighty God and with God nothing is impossible.

SMALL IS BEAUTIFUL

Even though Gideon had such a small army it was still too big for the Lord to use. Indeed the Lord said, *"The people that are with thee are too many for me to give the Midianites into their hands"* (Judg. 7:2). The Lord was very conscious that Israel was prone to self-congratulations and would claim that the victory over the Midianites was due to their own strength. So there had to be a pruning of numbers. The army had to be smaller, reduced in size so that victory could only be through God's great and awesome power.

THE FIRST REDUCTION
JUDGES 7:2-3

The Lord gave anyone who was afraid the opportunity for returning home. The Lord was not going to allow any weak-willed or trembling soldiers to undermine the possibility of victory. So if anyone was too frightened to go forward to battle they were allowed to return home. In total twenty-two thousand left Mount Gilead and retreated to the comfort and safety of their families and homes. This left just ten thousand to face the might of the Midianite army and yet even that number was too much for the Lord.

THE SECOND REDUCTION
JUDGES 7:4-8

This time there was a little test for the remaining men. As they drank water from the river the men who scooped the water to their mouths and lapped it from their hands were chosen, while the others who put their mouths right down to the water were able to return home. This time nine thousand and seven hundred men returned home and left a mere three hundred with Gideon and that small group would face the awesome might of the Midianite army.

The question could be asked as the apostle Andrew asked in the New Testament. *"What are they among so many?"* (John 6:9). In human terms it would be impossible for such a small group to defeat the great army of Midian, but God specializes in doing impossible things.

We remember that five loaves and two small fishes were used by the Lord to feed five thousand people. Also that one hundred and twenty early Christians were used by God to bring about the greatest spiritual revolution in history, as they turned the world upside down. So God would do great things with the small force at Gideon's disposal. This vindicates the words of a later prophet, namely Zechariah who wrote, *"Not by might, nor by power, but by my spirit, saith the LORD of hosts"* (Zech. 4:6).

THE VICTORY

Gideon had a simple strategy for defeating the Midianites. He divided his men into three companies and each man was given a trumpet and an earthen jar with a burning torch inside. The three companies parted and set up positions around the great camp of Midian. Then in the middle of the night, just after a change of guard, when those same guards would be at their most nervous there would be concerted action. Each man would blow his trumpet and smash his earthen jar. Then they would all cry together, *"The sword of the LORD, and of Gideon"* (Judg. 7:20). The result of that action was a spectacular victory.

The Midianites in confusion attacked each other and fled and many of these were pursued by other Israelites who were called out from the tribe of Naphtali, Asher and Manasseh. Also soldiers from the tribe of Ephraim were called to man the fords of the river Jordan and they killed many Midianites. They even killed two Midianite leaders. The first was Oreb and he was killed at the rock that was afterwards known as "the rock of Oreb", while the second was Zeeb and he was killed at the winepress that was afterwards known as "the winepress of Zeeb". It was a glorious victory and Gideon and his three hundred men pursued the final remnants of the Midianite army.

That remnant was under the leadership of two kings Zebah and Zalmunna and they had fifteen thousand men with them. Gideon and his men overtook them and routed them in an ambush when they were least expecting to be attacked and they captured the two kings of Midian. Altogether one hundred and twenty thousand swordsmen of Midian had been killed, as well as the fifteen thousand of the remnant that had tried to run away. It had been a great deliverance for Israel and Gideon was confirmed as a brilliant military leader. Yet there were further problems to face.

THE MEN OF EPHRAIM
JUDGES 8:1-3

The men of the tribe of Ephraim sharply criticized Gideon for not calling them to the initial battle. Perhaps they felt that he was gaining all the glory and they should have some share in it. Gideon needed a great deal of tact and considerable diplomacy to deal with the situation and prevent the dispute turning into a civil war in Israel. His words were soothing words as he said, *"What have I done now in comparison of you? Is not the gleaning of the grapes of Ephraim better than the vintage of Abiezer? God hath delivered into your hands the princes of Midian, Oreb and Zeeb: and what was I able to do in comparison of you?"* (Judg. 8:2-3). His words were effective and the resentment of the men of Ephraim subsided. Yet there is a lesson for all of us and we must be very careful that we do not seek personal glory as the men of Ephraim. In Christian work it is not the limelight which is important but a faithfulness to do the will of God.

THE PEOPLE OF SUCCOTH
JUDGES 8:4-7; 13-16

As Gideon and his three hundred men pursued the remnants of the Midianite army who were under the leadership of Zebah and Zalmunna they came to the city of Succoth. Gideon and his men were worn out and hungry and they asked the city officials for provisions, but sadly they were refused. The city leaders somewhat arrogantly proclaimed that the enemies were not in their hands and why should they therefore give such supplies. It seemed they despised Gideon's weakness, not realizing that God was with him and when he returned triumphantly it was a very different story. Those same officials were punished by Gideon and were whipped with desert thorns and briers.

THE PEOPLE OF PENIEL
JUDGES 8:8-9; 17

Again on his way to victory over the Midianites and having been denied provisions at Succoth they came to the city of Peniel. Again he asked for help and food for his journey only to be denied in a similar way to that of Succoth. Retribution came when he returned and the tower of Peniel was pulled down and destroyed and the men of the city were killed as punishment.

In both these instances of Succoth and Peniel we are reminded of the Lord Jesus. He came the first time to earth in weakness and humility and died for our sins on the cross. Many people derided Him and still do to this day not realizing that in a coming day He will return in power and glory. He came the first time as Saviour, but will return the second time as Judge. We certainly need to take warning.

THE DEATHS OF ZEBAH AND ZALMUNNA
JUDGES 8:18-21

Gideon and his men secured a great and notable victory over Midian and captured the two kings: Zebah and Zalmunna. He then proceeded to question those two monarchs and specifically asked them about some men whom the Midianites had killed in Tabor. Their answer was very clear and they said that the men had looked like Gideon and each one had the bearing of a prince. Gideon and the men who were killed had a regal quality, a princely bearing. Instantly Gideon knew that those men were his brothers, the sons of his own mother. Indeed if the Midianites had spared their lives, then he would have spared the lives of Zebah and Zalmunna. So he ordered their execution and called upon his oldest son Jether to perform the deed. However Jether was only a boy and had never used a sword and so was too afraid to kill the two kings. Indeed the kings themselves urged Gideon to perform the deed himself and they must have felt that it was more dignified to die at the hands of a victorious warrior than at the hand of an untrained youth.

So Gideon carried out the execution and removed ornaments from the necks of their camels. Those ornaments were no doubt a sign that Gideon was victorious but they became a problem to him later and undermined some of the good work he had done. If all this seems a bit gruesome and upsets our twenty-first century Western sensitivities then we must remember that it was a more violent age in Gideon's day and it was necessary to utterly destroy the enemy to prevent it regrouping and conquering the nation of Israel again.

GIDEON'S EPHOD
JUDGES 8:22-27

It would seem that the people of Israel were so relieved that they had been delivered from the bondage of Midianite oppression that they were quite prepared to let Gideon become their king. Indeed they wanted him to start a dynasty with his sons and grandchildren ruling the nation in succession. However Gideon refused such an honour and rightly pointed the nation to God and said, *"I will not rule over you, neither shall my son rule over you: the* LORD *shall rule over you"* (Judg. 8:23). It was so necessary for the people of Israel to remember that God had secured their victory and deliverance and it was to the Lord that they should show their allegiance.

Yet just at the high point in Gideon's experience came the greatest problem in his life. He made one simple request for a gold earring from each one who had taken plunder from the Midianites. The Israelites gave willingly and they accumulated seventeen hundred shekels of gold or about forty-three pounds. This was Gideon's own possession, his reward for leading the nation to victory. He also had the ornaments, pendants, purple garments from the kings of Midian and the chains of gold that were on the necks of their camels. Gideon was a rich man and he fashioned the gold into an ephod. It is not clear what is meant by an ephod in this instance. An ephod was usually a priestly garment and that is what it may have been, simply an elaborate and ornate garment. It may have been some kind of statue or charm and seems to have been used for divination purposes.

Gideon set up the ephod in his hometown of Ophrah and it caused Israel to sin against the Lord. They came and worshipped that ephod and this violated the commandments of the Lord. Indeed the whole thing was a spiritual snare to Gideon and his family. It essentially turned Gideon and the whole of Israel away from wholeheartedly serving the Lord.

It is a warning to us that at the point of greatest spiritual blessing and victory we are at our most vulnerable. It is then that we can fall and allow sin to enter our lives. It is then we can fail and be weak in our service for God. So we are warned.

GIDEON'S FAMILY
JUDGES 8:28-32

Gideon and his small army of soldiers had subdued the great Midianite hordes. Yet the victory was not through their own skill and strength but by the great resources that the Lord had supplied. The result was that the Midianites never again raised their heads to invade Israel and were never again a serious threat to the people. The land of Israel had peace and tranquillity for the rest of Gideon's lifetime, namely forty years. Gideon seems to have gone back to domestic life rather than take on any national leadership, though undoubtedly he was venerated for the rest of his days.

He had many wives and had seventy sons. Certainly he lived the life of an affluent leader and his life style reminds us of the monarch of Israel, namely Solomon who had many wives and many children. He also had one son, named Abimelech who was born not from one of Gideon's wives but from a concubine he had in the town of Shechem. Later that son by a concubine was to cause grave problems for Israel and especially for the legitimate family of Gideon.

However Gideon lived to a good old age and was buried in the tomb of his father Joash in the town of Ophrah, which belonged to the clan of the Abiezrites. For his great victory he has an honoured place in the history of Israel and his faith is highlighted in Hebrews chapter eleven. For as the writer mentions many people from the Old Testament who achieved so much for God by faith he comes to verse thirty-two and says, *"And what more shall I say about Gideon?"*. He was a man who through faith in God achieved so much, may we follow in his faithful footsteps.

*"Be careful that victories do not carry
the seeds of future defeats."*
Ralph W. Sockman

CHAPTER 22

THE FAITH OF BARAK

"The intrigue of this story is its focus on two women, Deborah and Jael, who overshadow the actual 'deliverer,' Barak."

Fee & Stuart

And what shall I more say? for the time would fail me to tell of Gedeon, and of Barak, and of Samson, and of Jephthae; of David also, and Samuel, and of the prophets. **Hebrews 11:32**

And the children of Israel again did evil in the sight of the LORD, when Ehud was dead. And the LORD sold them into the hand of Jabin king of Canaan, that reigned in Hazor; the captain of whose host was Sisera, which dwelt in Harosheth of the Gentiles. And the children of Israel cried unto the LORD: for he had nine hundred chariots of iron; and twenty years he mightily oppressed the children of Israel. And Deborah, a prophetess, the wife of Lapidoth, she judged Israel at that time. And she dwelt under the palm tree of Deborah between Ramah and Bethel in mount Ephraim: and the children of Israel came up to her for judgment. And she sent and called Barak the son of Abinoam out of Kedeshnaphtali, and said unto him, Hath not the LORD God of Israel commanded, saying, Go and draw toward mount Tabor, and take with thee ten thousand men of the children of Naphtali and of the children of Zebulun? And I will draw unto thee to the river Kishon Sisera, the captain of Jabin's army, with his chariots and his multitude; and I will deliver him into thine hand. And Barak said unto her, If thou wilt go with me, then I will go: but if thou wilt not go with me, then

I will not go. And she said, I will surely go with thee: notwithstanding the journey that thou takest shall not be for thine honour; for the LORD shall sell Sisera into the hand of a woman. And Deborah arose, and went with Barak to Kedesh. And Barak called Zebulun and Naphtali to Kedesh; and he went up with ten thousand men at his feet: and Deborah went up with him. Now Heber the Kenite, which was of the children of Hobab the father in law of Moses, had severed himself from the Kenites, and pitched his tent unto the plain of Zaanaim, which is by Kedesh. And they shewed Sisera that Barak the son of Abinoam was gone up to mount Tabor. And Sisera gathered together all his chariots, even nine hundred chariots of iron, and all the people that were with him, from Harosheth of the Gentiles unto the river of Kishon. And Deborah said unto Barak, Up; for this is the day in which the LORD hath delivered Sisera into thine hand: is not the LORD gone out before thee? So Barak went down from mount Tabor, and ten thousand men after him. And the LORD discomfited Sisera, and all his chariots, and all his host, with the edge of the sword before Barak; so that Sisera lighted down off his chariot, and fled away on his feet. But Barak pursued after the chariots, and after the host, unto Harosheth of the Gentiles: and all the host of Sisera fell upon the edge of the sword; and there was not a man left. Howbeit Sisera fled away on his feet to the tent of Jael the wife of Heber the Kenite: for there was peace between Jabin the king of Hazor and the house of Heber the Kenite. And Jael went out to meet Sisera, and said unto him, Turn in, my lord, turn in to me; fear not. And when he had turned in unto her into the tent, she covered him with a mantle. And he said unto her, Give me, I pray thee, a little water to drink; for I am thirsty. And she opened a bottle of milk, and gave him drink, and covered him. Again he said unto her, Stand in the door of the tent, and it shall be, when any man doth come and enquire of thee, and say, Is there any man here? that thou shalt say, No. Then Jael Heber's wife took a nail of the tent, and took an hammer in her hand, and went softly unto him, and smote the nail into his temples, and fastened it into the ground: for he was fast asleep and weary. So he died. And, behold, as Barak pursued Sisera, Jael came out to meet him, and said unto him, Come, and I will shew thee the man whom thou seekest. And when he came into her tent, behold, Sisera lay dead, and the nail was in his temples. So God subdued on that day Jabin the king of Canaan before the children of Israel. And the hand of the children of Israel prospered, and pre-vailed against Jabin the king of Canaan, until they had destroyed Jabin king of Canaan.   Judges 4

The time of the judges was a difficult and dangerous per-iod in the history of the nation of Israel. The Israelites seemed to so easily slip into idolatrous ways and turn their backs upon the Lord and for that they suffered successive invasions by hostile foreign powers. These invasions were the disci-pline of the Lord upon Israel and it led to the nation realizing into what depths of sin it had fallen and then consequently repenting of its sinfulness. There was then a national cry for deliverance and God sent them a warrior-judge who led the attack on the occupying army and delivered Israel from oppression and they were granted freedom. Eventually the cycle would restart and the process would proceed again.

The first two major judges were Othniel and Ehud. Othniel had dealt with the forces from the northeast from Aram in Mesopotamia. Ehud had broken the oppression of invad-ing forces from the east namely the Moabites who were in confederation with Ammon and Amalek. Shamgar is briefly described in Judges 3:31 as someone who saved Israel by strik-ing down six hundred Philistines who must have invaded from the west. We now come to the third major judge and his name was Barak. In many ways a woman who was a prophetess overshadowed him and her name was Deborah. She must be given credit for the victory that Barak achieved and she was certainly the inspiration behind the nation's achievement. In some ways she must be considered a judge in her own right and could be described as a prophetess-judge.

There are two unique features in the account of the victory of Barak. Firstly, the enemy commander was killed in an unusual way by the hand of a woman. Secondly, there is a glorious song of praise to God in Judges chapter five. Indeed it has been described as "the greatest and grandest battle-song in the world". It was the song of Deborah sung in triumph following Israel's victory over her enemies. It ends in wonderful praise to God, *"So let all thine enemies perish, O LORD: but let them that love him be as the sun when he goeth forth in his might"*(Judg. 5:31).

THE ENEMY OF ISRAEL

This time the invading enemy seemed to come from within the borders of Israel, because we read *"And the LORD sold them into the hand of Jabin king of Canaan, that reigned in Hazor; the captain of whose host was Sisera, which dwelt in Harosheth of the Gentiles"* (Judg. 4:2). Canaan was the name of the land into which Israel had invaded and this king of Canaan had his headquarters in the northern city of Hazor. This city had in fact been overrun and burnt with fire during the days of Joshua (Josh. 11) but had obviously been rebuilt and occupied by forces that eventually became hostile to Israel. It was from this stronghold that Jabin launched his invasion of Israel and oversaw the oppression of Israel from that capital city.

His field commander, the chief officer of his armed forces was a man named Sisera. He was quartered in Harosheth Haggoyim that is believed to be not too far from Mount Carmel and was nearer the coast. This man commanded a powerful force that included nine hundred chariots and these chariots are specifically called *"chariots of iron"* (Judg. 4:3). This mounted mobile force certainly gave the Canaanite army a decided advantage in the conditions of the age and we presume that Israel was overwhelmed merely at the sight of such a powerful force. For twenty years, and they must have seemed like very long years, Israel was oppressed by this Canaanite rule. In fact the description is that the Israelites were *"mightily oppressed"* (Judg. 4:3). Details are not actually given but we can imagine how national life in Israel was reduced to servitude under the iron grip of these Canaanite masters.

THE LEADERS OF ISRAEL

The key leader at this time in Israel was a woman named Deborah. This is really the first time in human history that a woman had risen to national prominence as a leader. She is described in a number of ways.

A Prophetess: this means that she had particular knowledge and insight given to her by God. She was God's chosen vessel for instilling His word to the people of Israel at that time.

The wife of Lappidoth: we certainly do not know too much about this man or what his occupation might have been. He is mentioned in Scripture only once and is famous simply for being the husband of an outstanding woman of God, whose work helped to save the nation of Israel.

She was leading Israel at that time: this essentially meant that she "judged" Israel. She held court in the tribal area of Ephraim between the towns of Ramah and Bethel and she sat under a palm tree. The tree was known as *"the palm tree of Deborah"* and *"the children of Israel came up to her for judgment"* (Judg. 4:5). She was obviously the spiritual and judicial heart of the nation and clearly knew the Lord's leading upon her life.

Deborah's name means "bee" and she certainly seems to have worked hard and lived up to being "as busy as a bee". However, she also had the ability to sting like a bee and made her point of view effectively heard. She was a mighty influence for spiritual good to the nation of Israel in her time.

It is of interest to wonder why there was a woman leader in Israel at that time. It may be that no man was willing to assume such a public responsibility under the Canaanite regime that then existed. It may be that the Canaanites would have not allowed a man to assume such a position of responsibility as they might have suspected that such a man would have used the law courts to organize a rebellion against the oppressive Canaanites.

There was one male leader who eventually with Deborah's help led Israel to victory over Canaan. His name was Barak and he came from the north of the country, the very part of Israel that had taken the brunt of the invading force. Barak was from the Israelite tribe of Naphtali, which represented the furthest northward extent of Israel in the time of the Judges. Naphtali occupied the western shores of the Sea of Galilee and then stretched northward. The tribal area of Naphtali included the very city of Hazor where Jabin had his headquarters, so Naphtali in particular had felt weakened and very demoralized by the invasion from the north.

The name Barak means "lightening" and he eventually became a destructive force to the Canaanites. He came from the town of Kadesh, which is to the north of Hazor and is described as the son of Abinoam. Deborah sent for him because he must have been a leading man in Naphtali and to him she gave a message from the Lord.

THE DELIVERANCE OF ISRAEL

Barak arrived at Deborah's court and he was given the message from God. It was a simple and straightforward message: *"Go and draw toward mount Tabor, and take with thee ten thousand men of the children of Naphtali and of the children of Zebulun? And I will draw unto thee to the river Kishon Sisera, the captain of Jabin's army, with his chariots and his multitude; and I will deliver him into thine hand"* (Judg. 4:6-7). Here was a clear and definitive word from God. It contained both a command and a promise.

THE FAITH OF BARAK

The **command** was to gather an army of ten thousand troops from two of the tribes of Israel. Those tribes were Naphtali which was Barak's home tribe and Zebulun which was the tribe that bordered onto Naphtali. These two tribes who had borne the brunt of Canaanite invasion were to join forces and make their way to Mount Tabor. Mount Tabor was the meeting place for three of the tribes of Israel: Zebulun, Naphtali and Issachar. Thus Mount Tabor was the assembling point for this northern Israelite army.

The **promise** was that Sisera would be lured to the River Kishon that flowed into the Mediterranean Sea through what we call today the city of Haifa. The river flows below Mount Carmel. There in that river valley God promised that He would deliver this great army into the hands of Barak and his men.

All Barak had to do was to accept God's Word and act upon it but instead he imposed a condition. He categorically refused to go to battle and fulfil God's commandment unless Deborah accompanied him. Barak was unable to simply obey God and take His Word at face value. It may be that twenty years of Canaanite oppression had robbed him of his spiritual faculties and perhaps it all seemed too impossible to contemplate. He made his service to the Lord conditional and as a result he lost the honour which would have been his, had he wholeheartedly served God. Deborah agreed to go with him but does mildly rebuke him with these words, *"I will surely go with thee: notwithstanding the journey that thou takest shall not be for thine honour; for the* Lord *shall sell Sisera into the hand of a woman"* (Judg. 4:9).

So Barak gathered his army on Mount Tabor and word soon reached Sisera and so he mustered his mobile forces of nine hundred chariots in the Kishon River valley. Water does not flow continually through that valley, only in seasons of rainfall. At this point Deborah again gives a message from the Lord to Barak, *"Up; for this is the day in which the* Lord *hath delivered Sisera into thine hand: is not the* Lord *gone out before thee?"* (Judg. 4:14). That is exactly what Barak did and Israel routed the Canaanites who were forced to abandon their chariots. Clearly what happened was that the Lord sent a flash flood that swept down the valley and made it impossible for the chariots to function in battle. This is eulogized in Deborah's song, *"The river of Kishon swept them away, that ancient river, the river Kishon"* (Judg. 5:21).

The Lord gave Barak a great victory and what chariots did escape from the flood were pursued and destroyed along with the rest of the Canaanite army. It was a very great victory. What had seemed an impossibility after twenty years of cruel oppression had become a wonderful reality of freedom as the Lord broke the yoke of Canaanite power. It is a bit like the wonderful feeling of freedom when the Lord breaks the power of sin in a person's life as they believe on the Lord Jesus Christ. The risen Christ is the only one who can bring true spiritual freedom and it is so important that we trust Him with all of our hearts.

THE DEATH OF SISERA

The commander of the Canaanite army had not been killed by Barak's forces but managed to escape on foot and seemed to be making his way not to his camp near the coast but to Kadesh where his king was headquartered. No doubt he reasoned that there were still troops at Kadesh which he might be able to use to counter attack the forces of Israel.

It was a long hike and he came upon a tented encampment that belonged to a group of people known as the Kenites. They were not Israelites but had close association with the people of God. It was from this particular Semitic tribe that Moses, the greatest Israelite leader had taken his wife and so they were very closely allied to Israel. Heber had descended from Hobab who had been a brother in law to Moses and he headed this group of Kenites. They were encamped at a place called Zaanannim by *"the great tree"* (Judg. 4:11, NIV). Heber's wife was a lady called Jael and it was to her tent that Sisera arrived.

THE FAITH OF BARAK

He was exhausted and must have been relieved to be at the tent of the Kenites. Firstly they were not Israelites and so were not part of the enemy who were pursuing him. Secondly there seemed to have been friendly relations between King Jabin and the clan of the Kenites. Presumably they had received special treatment from the Canaanites and had not experienced the same level of cruel oppression that had been the lot of Israel.

All seemed to go well for Sisera as he arrived at the tent of Jael. She welcomed him into the cool comfort of the tent and gave him a bed with a covering to lie down and rest. She also opened a skin of milk and gave him something to quench his thirst. She also seemed to agree to stand at the door of the tent and to protect him by saying to anyone who enquired that he was not inside. So Sisera fell into an exhausted sleep and must have felt content and secure but his fate was already sealed. Jael took a tent peg and hammered it through his temple killing him instantly. The putting up of tents was woman's work in those days so Jael was undoubtedly skilled in the use of a hammer to secure tent pegs. Her skills were put to use to destroy the tormentor of Israel and led to increasing strength for the nation. When Barak arrived in hot pursuit of Sisera he is shown the man in Jael's tent and the deed had been already done. A woman had killed the great commander of Canaan and so no counter attack could even be contemplated.

Deborah speaks so highly of Jael, "*Blessed above women shall Jael the wife of Heber the Kenite be, blessed shall she be above women in the tent. He asked water, and she gave him milk; she brought forth butter in a lordly dish. She put her hand to the nail, and her right hand to the workmen's hammer; and with the hammer she smote Sisera, she smote off his head, when she had pierced and stricken through his temples. At her feet he bowed, he fell, he lay down: at her feet he bowed, he fell: where he bowed, there he fell down dead*" (Judg. 5:24-27). So Jael is highlighted as the one who had the honour of destroying the scourge of Israel.

God had delivered Israel and from the day of Sisera's defeat it was the beginning of the end of Jabin's power. Gradually Israel grew stronger and stronger until eventually they destroyed Jabin altogether. So after twenty dreadful years under the Canaanites Israel was free. God had delivered them under the leadership of Barak and through the influence of the remarkable lady Deborah. I trust that we also know God's glorious deliverance over a more insidious enemy that is known as sin. We can be delivered, forgiven and granted eternal life through Jesus Christ our Lord.

"God raised up Deborah as a prophetess, Jael as a heroine, and Barak as a deliverer, and proved to Israel that God is not impressed by iron chariots."

John Phillips

CHAPTER 23

THE FAITH OF SAMSON

"Samson never called the armies of Israel together; he asked for no assistance."

Herbert Lockyer

And what shall I more say? for the time would fail me to tell of Gedeon, and of Barak, and of Samson, and of Jephthae; of David also, and Samuel, and of the prophets. Hebrews 11:32

And the children of Israel did evil again in the sight of the LORD; and the LORD delivered them into the hand of the Philistines forty years. And there was a certain man of Zorah, of the family of the Danites, whose name was Manoah; and his wife was barren, and bare not. And the angel of the LORD appeared unto the woman, and said unto her, Behold now, thou art barren, and bearest not: but thou shalt conceive, and bear a son. Now therefore beware, I pray thee, and drink not wine nor strong drink, and eat not any unclean thing: For, lo, thou shalt conceive, and bear a son; and no razor shall come on his head: for the child shall be a Nazarite unto God from the womb: and he shall begin to deliver Israel out of the hand of the Philistines. Then the woman came and told her husband, saying, A man of God came unto me, and his countenance was like the countenance of an angel of God, very terrible: but I asked him not whence he was, neither told he me his name. Judges 13:1-6

And the woman bare a son, and called his name Samson: and the child grew, and the LORD blessed him. And the Spirit of the LORD *began to move him at times in the camp of Dan between Zorah and Eshtaol.*   Judges 13:24-25

And Samson went down to Timnath, and saw a woman in Timnath of the daughters of the Philistines. And he came up, and told his father and his mother, and said, I have seen a woman in Timnath of the daughters of the Philistines: now therefore get her for me to wife. Then his father and his mother said unto him, Is there never a woman among the daughters of thy brethren, or among all my people, that thou goest to take a wife of the uncircumcised Philistines? And Samson said unto his father, Get her for me; for she pleaseth me well. But his father and his mother knew not that it was of the LORD, *that he sought an occasion against the Philistines: for at that time the Philistines had dominion over Israel. Then went Samson down, and his father and his mother, to Timnath, and came to the vineyards of Timnath: and, behold, a young lion roared against him. And the Spirit of the* LORD *came mightily upon him, and he rent him as he would have rent a kid, and he had nothing in his hand: but he told not his father or his mother what he had done. And he went down, and talked with the woman; and she pleased Samson well.*
                    Judges 14:1-7

And Samson said unto them, I will now put forth a riddle unto you: if ye can certainly declare it me within the seven days of the feast, and find it out, then I will give you thirty sheets and thirty change of garments: But if ye cannot declare it me, then shall ye give me thirty sheets and thirty change of garments. And they said unto him, Put forth thy riddle, that we may hear it. And he said unto them, Out of the eater came forth meat, and out of the strong came forth sweetness. And they could not in three days expound the riddle.   Judges 14:12-14

And she wept before him the seven days, while their feast lasted: and it came to pass on the seventh day, that he told her, because she lay sore upon him: and she told the riddle to the children of her people. And the men of the city said unto him on the seventh day before the sun went down, What is sweeter than honey? And what is stronger than a lion? and he said unto them, If ye had not plowed with my heifer, ye had not found out my riddle. And the Spirit of the LORD came upon him, and he went down to Ashkelon, and slew thirty men of them, and took their spoil, and gave change of garments unto them which expounded the riddle. And his anger was kindled, and he went up to his father's house. But Samson's wife was given to his companion, whom he had used as his friend.   Judges 14:17-20

But it came to pass within a while after, in the time of wheat harvest, that Samson visited his wife with a kid; and he said, I will go in to my wife into the chamber. But her father would not suffer him to go in. And her father said, I verily thought that thou hadst utterly hated her; therefore I gave her to thy companion: is not her younger sister fairer than she? take her, I pray thee, instead of her. And Samson said concerning them, Now shall I be more blameless than the Philistines, though I do them a displeasure. And Samson went and caught three hundred foxes, and took firebrands, and turned tail to tail, and put a firebrand in the midst between two tails. And when he had set the brands on fire, he let them go into the standing corn of the Philistines, and burnt up both the shocks, and also the standing corn, with the vineyards and olives. Judges 15:1-5

Then three thousand men of Judah went to the top of the rock Etam, and said to Samson, Knowest thou not that the Philistines are rulers over us? what is this that thou hast done unto us? And he said unto them, As they did unto me, so have I done unto them. And they said unto him, We are come down to bind thee, that we may deliver thee into the hand of the Philistines. And Samson said unto them, Swear unto me, that ye will not fall upon me yourselves. And they spake unto him, saying, No; but we will bind thee fast, and deliver thee into their hand: but surely we will not kill thee. And they bound him with two new cords, and brought him up from the rock. And when he came unto Lehi, the Philistines shouted against him: and the Spirit of the LORD *came mightily upon him, and the cords that were upon his arms became as flax that was burnt with fire, and his bands loosed from off his hands. And he found a new jawbone of an ass, and put forth his hand, and took it, and slew a thousand men therewith. And Samson said, With the jawbone of an ass, heaps upon heaps, with the jaw of an ass have I slain a thousand men. And it came to pass, when he had made an end of speaking, that he cast away the jawbone out of his hand, and called that place Ramathlehi.* Judges 15:11-17

Then went Samson to Gaza, and saw there an harlot, and went in unto her. And it was told the Gazites, saying, Samson is come hither. And they compassed him in, and laid wait for him all night in the gate of the city, and were quiet all the night, saying, In the morning, when it is day, we shall kill him. And Samson lay till midnight, and arose at midnight, and took the doors of the gate of the city, and the two posts, and went away with them, bar and all, and put them upon his shoulders, and carried them up to the top of an hill that is before Hebron. And it came to pass afterward, that he loved a woman in the valley of Sorek, whose name was Delilah. And the lords of the Philistines came up unto her, and said unto her, Entice him, and see wherein his great strength lieth, and by what means we may prevail against him, that we may bind him to afflict him; and we will give thee every one of us eleven hundred pieces of silver.

Judges 16:1-5

That he told her all his heart, and said unto her, There hath not come a razor upon mine head; for I have been a Nazarite unto God from my mother's womb: if I be shaven, then my strength will go from me, and I shall become weak, and be like any other man. And when Delilah saw that he had told her all his heart, she sent and called for the lords of the Philistines, saying, Come up this once, for he hath shewed me all his heart. Then the lords of the Philistines came up unto her, and brought money in their hand. And she made him sleep upon her knees; and she called for a man, and she caused him to shave off the seven locks of his head; and she began to afflict him, and his strength went from him. And she said, The Philistines be upon thee, Samson. And he awoke out of his sleep, and said, I will go out as at other times before, and shake myself. And he wist not that the LORD was departed from him. But the Philistines took him, and put out his eyes, and brought him down to Gaza, and bound him with fetters of brass; and he did grind in the prison house. Howbeit the hair of his head began to grow again after he was shaven. Judges 16:17-22

And Samson took hold of the two middle pillars upon which the house stood, and on which it was borne up, of the one with his right hand, and of the other with his left. And Samson said, Let me die with the Philistines. And he bowed himself with all his might;

> *and the house fell upon the lords, and upon all the*
> *people that were therein. So the dead which he slew*
> *at his death were more than they which he slew in his*
> *life. Then his brethren and all the house of his father*
> *came down, and took him, and brought him up, and*
> *buried him between Zorah and Eshtaol in the bury-*
> *ingplace of Manoah his father. And he judged Israel*
> *twenty years.* Judges 16:29-31

We have now arrived at the last of the judges as mentioned in the book of Judges. This man is the best known of them all and his name was Samson. He was noted for his great physical strength and God gives him a major place in the history of Israel. This is evident when we realize that much more space is devoted to Samson in the book of Judges than to any of the other judges. His story stretches from chapters 13-16. Also he is mentioned amongst the spiritually great people of God in this tremendous list in Hebrews 11, where it says in verse 32, *"And what shall I more say? for the time would fail me to tell of Gedeon, and of Barak, and of Samson…"* So God certainly considered this man a man of faith. That does not mean that he never failed God but that ultimately faith triumphed and overcame his failures.

It is interesting to note that it is recorded four times that the Spirit of God moved Samson:

"And the Spirit of the LORD began to move him at times in the camp of Dan between Zorah and Eshtaol…" (Judg. 13:25). This was the first stirrings of God upon him.

"And the Spirit of the LORD came mightily upon him…" (Judg. 14:6). This enabled him to kill a lion.

"And the Spirit of the LORD came upon him…" (Judg. 14:19). This enabled him to kill thirty men of the Philistines in Ashkelon.

"…the Spirit of the LORD came mightily upon him…" (Judg. 15:14). This gave him the strength to break out of cords that bound him and to then kill one thousand Philistines with the jawbone of a donkey.

THE FAITH OF SAMSON

It was the Spirit of the Lord that was the secret of his great strength, for when the Lord left him (Judg. 16:20) his powerful physique had dissipated.

God's judgment upon Israel for its sinfulness had allowed two invasions, one from the east and one from the west. The Ammonites invaded from the east and Israel dealt with them under the leadership of Jephthah. The Philistines invaded from the west and they held onto the coastal plain that bordered the Mediterranean Sea. They did not control the mountainous regions of Israel but at times were strong enough to invade and control large areas of Israel. Essentially they inhabited five fortified cities, Gaza, Ashkelon, Gath (where later Goliath would come), Ashdod and Ekron. They were certainly a powerful people and the name Palestine derives from them.

Interestingly Samson was not called by God to totally subdue and destroy the Philistines. His work was to begin that process as is stated in Judges 13:5, *"he shall begin to deliver Israel out of the hand of the Philistines."* God stated this before he was born and the process Samson started was later completed by King David when the upper hand was truly gained over the Philistines and they were incorporated into Israel. Yet at this time in the period of the judges the Philistines ruled Israel for forty years. This appears to have been a partial invasion of southwest Israel, with influence spreading over a larger territory. Into this situation was born Israel's deliverer, the man who dominates the book of Judges, Samson.

The name "Samson" appears to derive from the word that means "Sun". It may refer to the fact that the barren parents, who were given this special child, felt as though a ray of sunshine and light had been brought into their lives. It may also indicate the idea that as the sun is a powerful energy source, so Samson would have great energy and strength. He would be a powerful ruler of Israel.

HIS LIFE WAS PROPHESIED

Samson came from the Israelite tribe of Dan. It must be remembered that Dan had been given their allotted section of land in the west central area of Israel near the coast. However at an early date they experienced real resistance from the Philistines and under great pressure part of the tribe migrated northward and settled in the extreme north of the country. There they named a city after their founding father, 'Dan' who had been one of the twelve sons of Jacob. That city was the northern extremity of Israel.

Samson's parents had not been part of those who had migrated north. They still lived in the original tribal area of Dan, in a town called Zorah. Samson's father was named Manoah, but we have no record of his mother's name. Initially they were childless as it says, *"a wife who was sterile and remained childless"*(Judg. 13:2). It was this couple who were chosen by God to bear Samson. They received the news through a theophany, which is a pre-incarnational appearance of Christ. Firstly he spoke to the woman, then to her husband, then He received their sacrifice and finally ascended back into heaven. It was a stunning and terrifying experience for this couple but it also gave them excited expectation.

Just in passing we can note that this couple had the sort of marriage that worked. They were able to communicate and share with each other. The wife shared all that had been revealed to her with her husband. They were true marriage partners.

The instructions of the Lord were as follows,

- During the pregnancy she was not to drink *"wine nor strong drink"* (Judg. 13:7).
- During pregnancy she was not to eat any food that was considered ceremonially unclean (Judg. 13:7).
- The boy's hair must never be cut (Judg. 13:5)
- The boy was to be *"a Nazarite unto God from the womb"* (Judg. 13:5).

THE FAITH OF SAMSON

To understand the term "Nazarite" we need to read Numbers 6. A Nazarite has nothing to do with the town of Nazareth. An inhabitant of that town was a "Nazarene". The word "Nazarite" means "to separate, consecrate or abstain". It was essentially when a person separated himself from others to be fully consecrated to God. At such a moment a vow was taken and it may have been for a short period of time for a specific issue or it might have been for life as in the case of Samson. The rules for a Nazarite were threefold,

- Abstinence from wine and anything to do with the vine.
- Hair was to be uncut
- There was to be no contact with death or corpses.

So a Nazarite was known by his abstinence and uncut hair.

The birth of Samson and his future life were prophesied and marked out by the statements of God. Like Isaac before and John the Baptist later Samson had angelic announcements of his birth. Yet we also see something greater, we see the true mighty One, our Lord and Saviour Jesus Christ. He was prophesied, angels announced His birth and He was separated totally to His Father's will and His life's pathway was marked out in detail until its fulfilment at Calvary's cross. So in Samson the historical character we have a picture of the prophesied Christ.

HIS LIFE WAS POWERFUL

Samson was noted above all else for his miraculous, God-given strength. It certainly came from God because in most instances when he demonstrated his strength it was in connection with the Spirit of God. We remember the instances.

He killed a young lion (Judg. 14:5-6). This was no old, decrepit lion but a young, virile lion bent upon destruction. Samson killed it with his bare hands. It must be remembered that lions were numerous in Palestine in those days. Sometime later a swarm of bees lived in the carcass of that lion and produced honey. From this fact Samson made up a riddle for the Philistine guests at his wedding to work out. The riddle was

"Out of the eater came something to eat, And out of the strong came something sweet" (Judg. 14:14, NIV). The men were unable to work out the riddle but gave the answer by threatening Samson's wife and making her tell them the answer. So they won what was essentially a bet. Samson then had to give each of those thirty guests some garments.

He killed thirty men of Ashkelon and took their clothes (14:19) and so obtained the robes that he needed to give to the thirty men who had discovered the riddle.

In chapter 15 Samson went to visit his wife but found that she had been given to someone else. In an act of revenge Samson caught three hundred foxes and tied them tail to tail in pairs. He then fastened a lighted torch to their tails and let them loose in the cornfields of the Philistines. Thus their crops were destroyed. The Philistines extracted revenge by killing Samson's wife and her family and invading the tribal area of Judah in Israel.

To appease the Philistines the Israelites took Samson, tied him with new cords and delivered him as a prisoner to the Philistines. The Philistine triumph at his capture was short-lived because under the Spirit of the Lord he broke out of the cords and killed one thousand Philistines with the jawbone of a donkey (Judg. 15:9-17). Once again Samson's great strength had saved him but he was now public enemy number one to the Philistines who were still dominant over Israel. However for twenty years Samson was the judge and leader of Israel.

In chapter 16 Samson was in Gaza at the home of a woman and the Philistines thought they would trap him by locking the gates of the city. However, Samson simply lifted the gate off its hinges and carried it from the city thirty-eight miles to the east and dumped it near Hebron.

Finally, his strength was demonstrated when he was with Delilah. When tied with seven fresh thongs or bowstrings he simply snapped them, and he did the same when tied with new ropes. When his hair was weaved into the fabric on the loom he simply lifted the weaving machine by his hair.

THE FAITH OF SAMSON

He was a man of immense strength and physical power. Yet it was a strength which was dependent upon obedience to the Lord. No razor was to touch his hair and when he disobeyed he became powerless, weak and like other men. In a similar way our spiritual strength depends upon our obedience to Christ, not in any matter of haircuts but in surrender to the will of the Lord for our lives.

HIS LIFE WAS PROFLIGATE

Essentially Samson had many failures in his life. His most glaring weakness was his passion for women who had immoral lifestyles. His failures are clearly recorded for us so that we might be warned and avoid similar defeats in our own lives.

HE LACKED TRUE RESPECT FOR HIS PARENTS

He wanted to marry a Philistine woman and that was despite the protests of his parents. His actions broke the commandments of God and violated their sensibilities. However he was insistent that he have his way and nothing and no one was going to stop him acting selfishly. It is important that as Christians we act and react in a God glorifying way. Our motives should never be selfish and we should have deep respect for others especially our parents, church leaders and those in authority.

HE BROKE HIS NAZARITE VOW

Firstly he came into contact with a dead body, namely the lion he had killed when he drew honey out of the corpse. Secondly, he allowed Delilah to cut his hair. Both were strictly forbidden under the Nazarite vow.

HE ASSOCIATED WITH WRONG WOMEN

Samson trod the downward path in his association with women. Altogether he had three women.

A Philistine Woman of Timnath: here we see *"the lust of the eyes"* (1 John 2:16) in action because as he looked at her she pleased him deeply. The wrong here was that God had expressly forbidden his people to marry the heathen, because He knew how those wives would encourage Israel into idol worship.

A Prostitute in Gaza: again this was a city of the Philistines and here we can note that Samson partook of *"the lust of the flesh"* (1 John 2:16). Prostitution was strictly forbidden in Israel and any who practiced it were put to death. So Samson indulged his passion with a heathen woman who constantly broke the laws of God. There needs to be discipline in sexual activities. It should not be conducted in an irresponsible way and marriage is the God-given place for intimate relationships. This is a basic biblical truth but needs to be constantly re-emphasized.

A Philistine Named Delilah: here we see Samson engaging in *"the pride of life"* (1 John 2:16). He boasted to her and told her his secrets. Here was the final means of his downfall. She worked closely with the Philistine authorities and was paid 1,100 shekels of silver for betraying Samson and finding out the secret of his strength. So with his hair shaved he was captured, blinded and set to work by the Philistines grinding corn. Sin and disobedience always bring their reward. The man had failed God and his Achilles' heel, his weakness for women rendered him powerless and useless. The deliverer of Israel was captured by the enemies of his nation.

However the story ends on a note of some victory. Samson had time to ponder and contemplate in the prison as he ground out the corn. He had time to confess his sin and repent of it. It also gave time for his hair to grow again. He became a man of prayer and God answered his prayer. He was taken to a heathen temple where the Philistines were celebrating and he was the centre of their mocking laughter. The rulers of the Philistines were present and on the roof were about three thousand men and women watching. Samson cried to

God for one last moment of power to avenge the Philistines for putting out his eyes. He heaved at the supporting pillars of the temple and the edifice crashed down. He was killed along with many of the hated Philistines. He killed more in his death than he had in his life of warfare with the Philistines.

His relatives came and took his body and buried it in his father's tomb. Samson has been given a name with the spiritually great people of God. Ultimately his faith triumphed over his failures. So we take encouragement when we fail. We do not need to remain failed but can be renewed by the power of God to successfully serve our Lord and Saviour Jesus Christ.

"The complex story of Samson teaches us the evils of mixed...marriages, the laxity of sexual relations and of playing with temptation."
Herbert Lockyer

CHAPTER 24

THE FAITH OF JEPHTHAH

"The man who made a vow."

Herbert Lockyer

And what shall I more say? for the time would fail me to tell of Gedeon, and of Barak, and of Samson, and of Jephthae; of David also, and Samuel, and of the prophets. Hebrews 11:32

And the children of Israel did evil again in the sight of the LORD, *and served Baalim, and Ashtaroth, and the gods of Syria, and the gods of Zidon, and the gods of Moab, and the gods of the children of Ammon, and the gods of the Philistines, and forsook the* LORD, *and served not him. And the anger of the* LORD *was hot against Israel, and he sold them into the hands of the Philistines, and into the hands of the children of Ammon. And that year they vexed and oppressed the children of Israel: eighteen years, all the children of Israel that were on the other side Jordan in the land of the Amorites, which is in Gilead. Moreover the children of Ammon passed over Jordan to fight also against Judah, and against Benjamin, and against the house of Ephraim; so that Israel was sore distressed.* Judges 10:6-9

Now Jephthah the Gileadite was a mighty man of valour, and he was the son of an harlot: and Gilead begat Jephthah. And Gilead's wife bare him sons; and his wife's sons grew up, and they thrust out Jephthah, and said unto him, Thou shalt not inherit in our father's house; for thou art the son of a strange woman. Then Jephthah fled from his brethren, and dwelt in the land of Tob: and there were gathered vain men to Jephthah, and went out with him. And it came to pass in process of time, that the children of Ammon made war against Israel. Judges 11:1-4

Then Jephthah went with the elders of Gilead, and the people made him head and captain over them: and Jephthah uttered all his words before the Lord in Mizpeh. And Jephthah sent messengers unto the king of the children of Ammon, saying, What hast thou to do with me, that thou art come against me to fight in my land? And the king of the children of Ammon answered unto the messengers of Jephthah, Because Israel took away my land, when they came up out of Egypt, from Arnon even unto Jabbok, and unto Jordan: now therefore restore those lands again peaceably. And Jephthah sent messengers again unto the king of the children of Ammon: And said unto him, Thus saith Jephthah, Israel took not away the land of Moab, nor the land of the children of Ammon. Judges 11:11-15

Then the Spirit of the Lord came upon Jephthah, and he passed over Gilead, and Manasseh, and passed over Mizpeh of Gilead, and from Mizpeh of Gilead he passed over unto the children of Ammon. And Jephthah vowed a vow unto the Lord, and said, If thou shalt without fail deliver the children of Ammon into mine hands, Then it shall be, that whatsoever cometh forth of the doors of my house to meet me, when I return in peace from the children of Ammon, shall surely be the Lord's, and I will offer it up for a burnt offering. So Jephthah passed over unto the children of Ammon to fight against them; and the Lord delivered them into his hands. And he smote them from Aroer, even till thou come to Minnith, even twenty cities, and unto the plain of the vineyards, with a very great slaughter. Thus the children of Ammon were subdued before the children of Israel. And Jephthah came to Mizpeh unto his house, and, behold, his daughter came out to meet him with timbrels and with dances: and she was his only child; beside her he had neither son nor daughter. And it came to pass, when he saw her, that he rent his clothes, and said, Alas, my daughter! thou hast brought me very low, and thou art one of them that trouble me: for I have opened my mouth unto the LORD, and I cannot go back. Judges 11:29-35

And the men of Ephraim gathered themselves together, and went northward, and said unto Jephthah, Wherefore passedst thou over to fight against the children of Ammon, and didst not call us to go with thee? we will burn thine house upon thee with fire....And Jephthah judged Israel six years. Then died Jephthah the Gileadite, and was buried in one of the cities of Gilead. Judges 12:1, 7

As we read the book of Judges we come to a fascinating character whose name was Jephthah and he is the latest character to be listed in Hebrews 11. He was one of the six major judges who saved Israel from foreign oppression. There is a specific reference to the Holy Spirit in relation to Jephthah, as we read, *"Then the Spirit of the LORD came upon Jephthah"* (Judg. 11:29). This work of the Spirit is only mentioned in relation to three other judges, Othniel, Gideon and Samson. So Jephthah stands with that unique band of warrior judges who specifically knew the power of God's Holy Spirit.

Jephthah is highlighted as a man of faith in the New Testament, as in Hebrews 11:32 it says, *"And what shall I more say? for the time would fail me to tell of Gedeon, and of Barak, and of Samson, and of Jephthae…"* Also in the Old Testament the great prophet Samuel mentioned Jephthah and noted him as an example of God's faithful dealings with the nation of Israel (1 Sam. 12:11).

The name Jephthah means "to open or to set free" and that was exactly what his life's work turned out to be. He set Israel free from the domination and exploitation of a nation known as the Ammonites.

POLITICAL BACKGROUND

Again the root cause of Israel's problems was her sins. We read, *"And the children of Israel did evil again in the sight of the* LORD*...forsook the* LORD*, and served not him"* (Judg. 10:6). Instead they served idols namely, Baal and Ashtoreth who were idols of the original Canaanite inhabitants. They also served the idols of Aram and Sidon from the north, the gods of Moab and Ammon from the east and those of the Philistines from the west. Israelite society had become saturated with idol worship and with all its associated depraved, immoral practices.

It would seem that Israel was more concerned about the visible than the invisible, the material rather than the spiritual. They failed to worship the true and only God, failed to seek His guidance and to do His will. It is a warning to us not to focus upon the wrong priorities. The values of the material, the tangible and the visible are not eternal. Knowing God personally through Jesus Christ is the most lasting and enduring reality we can ever know.

The result for Israel was that God allowed two invasions. The first was from the west (by sea) and was the nation of the Philistines. A later judge named Samson dealt with that nation. The second invasion came from the east (from the deserts) and was the Ammonite nation. They over-ran the three tribes to the east of Jordan and occupied and controlled the area for eighteen years. They also made forays across the River Jordan and attacked the Israelite tribes of Judah, Benjamin and Ephraim. They *"vexed and oppressed"* Israel (Judg. 10:8) and *"Israel was sore distressed"* (Judg. 10:9).

The result was that Israel turned back to Lord and cried out to Him for deliverance. God reminded them of the way He had delivered them in the past and urged them to go back to their idols for deliverance. Clearly the Lord was highlighting the futility of worshipping dumb statues. Yet Israel truly repented of their sins, got rid of their foreign idols and set about raising an army to fight the Ammonites. Their problem was that they had no leader and therefore no one to take the initiative in battle. This was where Jephthah came into the picture.

JEPHTHAH'S BACKGROUND

The Bible is nothing if not graphic and it does not hide from unpalatable facts. Jephthah was a man of Gilead, which was an area on the East Bank of Jordan in the tribal area of Manasseh. His father, named Gilead had an affair with a prostitute and the result was the birth of Jephthah. Prostitutes were banned in Israel and no Israelite lady was allowed to be a prostitute (Deut. 23:17). So either God's laws were being ignored or the woman in question was not an Israelite but a Canaanite and so that made Jephthah a man of mixed racial descent. This may have contributed to the antagonism that his brothers felt towards him. They were children born inside their father's marriage relationship and they rejected Jephthah and refused to let him have any part in their family's inheritance.

So Jephthah fled from his siblings and lived in the land of Tob. The location of this land is still being debated but was probably just outside the borders of Israel. In that land Jephthah became the leader of a band of adventurers, who were no doubt a rough crowd of tough men and to have commanded their respect would have meant that he had very real leadership qualities.

Years later the elders of Gilead sent for him and asked him to become their leader. The elders may have included some of Jephthah's own family, the very ones who had previously rejected him. They desperately needed his leadership and military skill and practically begged him to be their leader and assured him that after victory over the Ammonites they would make him their permanent leader. So he was made *"head and captain"* (Judg. 11:11). This presumably means that he had absolute power both as head of the civilian government and as commander of the military, namely the army of Israel. So from an outcast he became leader, from exclusion he received exaltation.

We notice that Israel, who had rejected God, called upon Him for help in their hour of need. They had also rejected Jephthah but turned to him in their time of distress. We need to acknowledge the authority of the Lord in our lives today and not wait for the crisis that can invariably drive us to cry out for His help. Let God be our God today.

JEPHTHAH'S WAR

HE TRIED TO AVOID WAR

Jephthah was clearly and obviously a man of God. He had a clear understanding of both Scripture and history and he used that knowledge to try and avoid war with the Ammonites. He used words before taking military action.

The king of Ammon made the astounding claim that a piece of land between the rivers Jabbok and Arnon had been illegally taken from the Ammonites by the Israelites hundreds of years before under the leadership of Joshua. Jephthah makes it abundantly clear that this was just an excuse for invasion and exposes it for the worthless and shallow idea it is. In his response he makes two appeals.

He appealed to Scripture and particularly to Numbers chapters 20 and 21. It was clear from the account in that passage that at no time had Israel taken the land in question from the Ammonites. It had been taken after battle with the Amorites under Sihon their king. At all times Israel had been scrupulous in their observation of the territorial integrity of other nations including Edom and Moab and had only fought against Sihon when he had mustered his forces to attack Israel. So at no time had the piece of land ever belonged to Ammon.

He appealed to History. At no time in the whole of the three hundred-year period of time from the occupation of the land by Israel had the Ammonites ever made claim to that particular stretch of land. They had never thought of it as their own and had never made any efforts to recover it in the past. It was a put-up job, an excuse for invasion and all attempts at negotiations by Jephthah were rejected by the Ammonites. So there was nothing left but war.

JEPHTHAH'S TRIUMPH

Jephthah led Israel to victory, recovered twenty cities and totally subdued the Ammonites. It was a great triumph and the eighteen years of Ammonite oppression was over. Israel was free. It was a time for great celebration, rejoicing and gladness. It was a time for singing and praising God and that was how the people of Israel responded. However the celebrations turned to ashes and were ruined very quickly by two factors.

THE FOOLISHNESS OF JEPHTHAH

This wonderful man of God was seeped in Scripture and the history of Israel. He had urged his family to seek and fear God. He knew the experience of the Holy Spirit coming upon him. Yet he could make a serious mistake and that is a great warning for every Christian. It is all too easy to go wrong and make a grave mistake like Jephthah.

The simple fact was that before he went into battle he made a vow in the presence of the Lord. It was totally unnecessary to do such a thing. It turned out to be an act of great foolishness and was obviously against the will of God. He said to the Lord, *"If thou shalt without fail deliver the children of Ammon into mine hands, Then it shall be, that whatsoever cometh forth of the doors of my house to meet me, when I return in peace from the children of Ammon, shall surely be the Lord's, and I will offer it up for a burnt offering"* (Judg. 11:30-31). I just wonder who he thought would emerge first but the tragedy was that it was his only daughter. She came out dancing at the victory to the sound of the tambourines and she was not only his only daughter but also his only child. Jephthah's distress was overwhelming and he had to explain to her that he had made a vow that he could not break.

In response his daughter asked for two months to go into the mountains with her friends and weep for the fact that she would never marry and would die a virgin having never experienced the blessing of motherhood. Now what happened after those two months is a matter of some debate. There tend to be two schools of thought.

That she was actually sacrificed and put to death in accordance with the vow. F. F. Brice points out that verse 39 seems to be conclusive on this point where it says *"who did with her according to his vow"*.

That Jephthah paid a sum of money instead of the sacrifice but that she remained celibate for the rest of her life. R. A. Torrey takes this line and points out that we are nowhere told specifically that she was put to death. Also it could be argued that human sacrifices were forbidden in Israel and therefore it was unlikely that Jephthah fulfilled his vow. However if he was half Canaanitish he may have had fewer scruples on this point than his fellow Israelites.

Whatever happened nowhere did God ever give approval to Jephthah's vow and subsequent action. May God keep us from making foolish and rash promises. We are called to simply and faithfully obey Him. We must know the Lord's will and do it. What damage we can do by hasty words. How we can destroy the joy and gladness of others by wounding, insensitive and wrongful use of words. We are warned by Jephthah's experience and the writer James in the New Testament also gives real advice on the right use of the tongue.

So Jephthah's foolishness turned the celebrations for victory into a time of mourning and loss. His foolishness was commemorated every year as the young women of Israel went out for four days to remember the daughter of Jephthah. However there was a second factor that took the gloss off this great victory.

THE PERVERSENESS OF EPHRAIM

The men of the Israelite tribe of Ephraim took great offence at the fact that they had not been included in the army that had defeated the Ammonites. They took issue with Jephthah who pointed out that they had been called but had failed to respond. He and his men had therefore risked their lives to deliver Gilead, the Lord had given victory and now Ephraim had arrived spoiling for a fight.

The Ephraimites were not appeased and added insult to injury by casting slurs upon the racial purity of the people of Gilead. So a civil war took place and Jephthah and his men defeated the forces of the Ephraimites. Jephthah's men captured the fords of the River Jordan and any man who tried to cross was given a linguistic test. They had to say the word, "Shibboleth" and if they failed and could only say "Sibboleth" then they were clearly men of Ephraim and so were captured and put to death. Sadly forty-two thousand men of Ephraim were killed through battle and at the fords. It was a tragic day for the tribe Ephraim and the nation of Israel as a whole.

So after the wonder of victory and the great triumph over the Ammonites came the discord of division and disloyalty amongst the people of God. It is often true that after a time of wonderful spiritual blessing we as Christians are at our most vulnerable. We must be particularly careful and prayerful whenever things go well because it is at the moment of supreme victory and blessing that we are most prone to fall into temptation and sin against the Lord. We need to constantly be in touch with the Lord through prayer and through His Word so that we can find His glorious resources to enable us to be faithful in all we do.

Jephthah ruled Israel for just six years, then he died and was buried in the city of Gilead. His whole life had been preparation for one great victory and then just six short years of leading the nation. Later the prophet Haggai spent a lifetime preparing for a public ministry of just three months and twenty-four days. The great Welsh revivalist preacher, Evan

Roberts spent his life in preparation for a short period of just a few weeks and months when revival came to Wales. He was hardly ever heard of again because his work for God was essentially completed.

We must remember that our lives are constantly in preparation maybe for an important ministry here on earth. It might be only a matter of months or just a few years where we achieve something significant and lasting for the Lord's glory. However ultimately our lives are one great preparation for eternity where we can serve the Lord forever.

"Jephthah...who suffered iniquitous disability...
was a great man."

G. Campbell Morgan

CHAPTER 25

THE FAITH OF DAVID
PART 1

"Although young, his faith was strong and he was deeply convinced that God was wonderfully sufficient."

Raymond Brown

And what shall I more say? for the time would fail me to tell of Gedeon, and of Barak, and of Samson, and of Jephthae; of David also, and Samuel, and of the prophets.   Hebrews 11:32

Now the Philistines gathered together their armies to battle, and were gathered together at Shochoh, which belongeth to Judah, and pitched between Shochoh and Azekah, in Ephesdammim. And Saul and the men of Israel were gathered together, and pitched by the valley of Elah, and set the battle in array against the Philistines. And the Philistines stood on a mountain on the one side, and Israel stood on a mountain on the other side: and there was a valley between them. And there went out a champion out of the camp of the Philistines, named Goliath, of Gath, whose height was six cubits and a span. And he had an helmet of brass upon his head, and he was armed with a coat of mail; and the weight of the coat was five thousand shekels of brass. And he had greaves of brass upon his legs, and a target of brass between his shoulders. And the staff of his spear was like a weaver's beam; and his spear's head weighed six hundred shekels of iron: and one bearing a shield went before him. And he stood and cried unto the armies of Israel, and said unto them, Why are ye come out to set your battle in array? am not I a Philistine, and ye servants to Saul? choose you a man for you, and let him come down to me. If he be able to fight with me, and to kill me, then will we be your servants: but if I prevail against him, and kill him, then shall ye be our servants, and serve us. And the Philistine said, I defy the armies of Israel this day; give me a man, that we may fight together. When Saul and all Israel heard those words of the Philistine, they were dismayed, and greatly afraid. Now David was the son of that Ephrathite of Bethlehemjudah, whose name was Jesse; and he had eight sons: and the man went among men for an old man in the days of Saul. And the three eldest sons of Jesse went and followed Saul to the battle: and the names of his three sons that went to the battle were Eliab the firstborn, and next unto him Abinadab, and the third Shammah. And David was the youngest: and the three eldest followed Saul. But David went and returned from Saul to feed his father's sheep at Bethlehem. And the Philistine drew near morning and evening, and presented himself forty days. And Jesse said unto David his son, Take now for thy brethren an ephah of this parched corn, and these ten loaves, and run to the camp of thy brethren; And carry these ten cheeses unto the captain of their thousand, and look how thy brethren fare, and take their pledge. Now Saul, and they, and all the men of Israel, were in the valley of Elah, fighting with the Philistines. And David rose up early in the morning, and left the sheep with a keeper, and took, and went, as Jesse had commanded him; and he came to the trench, as the host was going forth to the fight, and shouted for the battle. For Israel and the Philistines had put the battle in array, army against army. And David left his carriage in the hand of the keeper of the carriage, and ran into the army, and came and saluted his brethren. And as he talked with them, behold, there came up the champion, the

Philistine of Gath, Goliath by name, out of the armies of the Philistines, and spake according to the same words: and David heard them. And all the men of Israel, when they saw the man, fled from him, and were sore afraid. And the men of Israel said, Have ye seen this man that is come up? surely to defy Israel is he come up: and it shall be, that the man who killeth him, the king will enrich him with great riches, and will give him his daughter, and make his father's house free in Israel. And David spake to the men that stood by him, saying, What shall be done to the man that killeth this Philistine, and taketh away the reproach from Israel? for who is this uncircumcised Philistine, that he should defy the armies of the living God? And the people answered him after this manner, saying, So shall it be done to the man that killeth him. And Eliab his eldest brother heard when he spake unto the men; and Eliab's anger was kindled against David, and he said, Why camest thou down hither? and with whom hast thou left those few sheep in the wilderness? I know thy pride, and the naughtiness of thine heart; for thou art come down that thou mightest see the battle. And David said, What have I now done? Is there not a cause? And he turned from him toward another, and spake after the same manner: and the people answered him again after the former manner. And when the words were heard which David spake, they rehearsed them before Saul: and he sent for him. And David said to Saul, Let no man's heart fail because of him; thy servant will go and fight with this Philistine. And Saul said to David, Thou art not able to go against this Philistine to fight with him: for thou art but a youth, and he a man of war from his youth. And David said unto Saul, Thy servant kept his father's sheep, and there came a lion, and a bear, and took a lamb out of the flock: And I went out after him, and smote him, and delivered it out of his mouth: and when he arose against me, I caught him by his beard, and smote him, and slew him. Thy servant slew both the lion and the bear: and this uncircumcised Philistine shall be as one of them, seeing he hath defied the armies of the living God. David said moreover, The LORD that delivered me out of the paw of the lion, and out of the paw of the bear, he will deliver me out of the hand of this Philistine. And Saul said unto David, Go, and the LORD be with thee. And Saul armed David with his armour, and he put an helmet of brass upon his head; also he armed him with a coat of mail. And David girded his sword upon his armour, and he assayed to go; for he had not proved it. And David said unto Saul, I cannot go with these; for I have not proved them. And David put them off him. And he took his staff in his hand, and chose him five smooth stones out of the brook, and put them in a shepherd's bag which he had, even in a scrip; and his sling was in his hand: and he drew near to the Philistine. And the Philistine came on and drew near unto David; and the man that bare the shield went before him. And when the Philistine looked about, and saw David, he disdained him: for he was but a youth, and ruddy, and of a fair countenance. And the Philistine said unto David, Am I a dog, that thou comest to me with staves? And the Philistine cursed David by his gods. And the Philistine said to David, Come to me, and I will give thy flesh unto the fowls of the air, and to the beasts of the field. Then said David to the Philistine, Thou comest to me with a sword, and with a spear, and with a shield: but I come to thee in the name of the LORD of hosts, the God of the armies of Israel, whom thou hast defied. This day will the LORD deliver thee into mine hand; and I will smite thee, and take thine head from thee; and I will give the carcases of the host of the Philistines this day unto the fowls of the air, and to the wild beasts of the earth; that all the earth may know that there is a God in Israel. And all this assembly shall know that the LORD saveth not with sword and spear: for the battle is the LORD's, and he will give you into our hands. And it came to pass, when the Philistine arose, and came, and drew nigh to meet David, that David hastened, and ran toward the army to meet the Philistine. And David put his hand in his bag, and took thence a stone, and slang it, and smote the Philistine in his forehead, that the stone sunk into his forehead; and he fell upon his face to the earth. So David prevailed over the Philistine with a sling and with a stone, and smote the Philistine, and slew him; but there was no sword in the hand of David. Therefore David ran, and stood upon the Philistine, and took his sword, and drew it out of the sheath thereof, and slew him, and cut off his head therewith. And when the Philistines saw their champion was dead, they fled. And the men of Israel and of Judah arose, and shouted, and pursued the Philistines, until thou come to the valley, and to the gates of Ekron. And the wounded of the Philistines fell down by the way to Shaaraim, even unto Gath, and unto Ekron. And the children of Israel returned from chasing after the Philistines, and they spoiled their tents. And David took the head of the Philistine, and brought it to Jerusalem; but he put his armour in his tent. And when Saul saw David go forth against the Philistine, he said unto Abner, the captain of the host, Abner, whose son is this youth? And Abner said, As thy soul liveth, O king, I cannot tell. And the king said, Enquire thou whose son the stripling is. And as David returned from the slaughter of the Philistine, Abner took him, and brought him before Saul with the head of the Philistine in his hand. And Saul said to him, Whose son art thou, thou young

> *man? And David answered, I am the son of thy ser-*
> *vant Jesse the Bethlehemite.*   1 Samuel 17

In the list of Old Testament saints that are mentioned in Hebrews 11 we have come to the penultimate. His name is David and he is the only one mentioned in the list who was a king. He was monarch in Israel, over whom he reigned for forty years and his name means "beloved". Even today he is revered in modern Israel and this is three thousand years after his time as king. There is no doubt that he was a very great monarch and was one of the greatest national leaders that this world has ever seen. Herbert Lockyer writes, "Volumes have been written on the trials and triumphs of David, a mountain peak among Bible characters, who was carefully chosen as Israel's second king by God Himself."

David was an outstanding musician, a hymn writer who wrote nearly half the psalms, a wise and just ruler of his people, a man devoted to God and a great and powerful warrior, who led his army to many notable victories. It was David who extended the rule of Israel to its furthest extent ever in its history. He ruled from the river Euphrates in the north to the Sinai Desert in the south and from the Mediterranean Sea in the west to the deserts of Arabia in the east. He subdued the surrounding nations and made them vassal states that paid tribute into the Israelite treasury in Jerusalem. He was a powerful man but also a man of deep spiritual perception who meditated in the presence of Almighty God. His reign became one of splendour and majestic power, which was continued and consolidated by his son Solomon. For the eighty years of their combined reigns Israel was at its most influential and at the height of its wealth and authority.

David's place in Scripture is due to the fact that he loved, served and trusted God. His life story is outlined for us in 1 Samuel 16-1 Kings 2 and again in 1 Chronicles 11-29. His was a life full of incident, with many setbacks and failures but he came through them all with triumphant and vibrant faith. He is mentioned in over 25 books of the Bible and is quoted by the Lord Jesus in His ministry and by the apostle Paul in his writings in the New Testament.

Yet the first few years of David's life were not in the public eye and at that time it would have seemed very unlikely that he would have risen to such prominence. However from obscurity God brought him to the place of public triumph.

THE SHEPHERD LAD IN BETHLEHEM

David was the eighth son of Jesse who was an inhabitant of the town of Bethlehem. Jesse does not appear to have been a man of significant rank and the town was hardly one of the greatest in Israel. Being the youngest son David was not given any public notice and he was not thought of in an important light. He was simply trained to tend his father's sheep on the slopes and lonely places of southern Judah. However that simple job gave him the basis for his life's work. It was while tending the sheep that he came to know God and it was there that he learned to trust and depend upon the Almighty.

The work of caring for sheep required devotion and care for the flock and also courage and faith to defend the flock from attack. He did his job extremely well and became a shield and a protection to those sheep as there were serious dangers for sheep in those days. At different times David faced both a lion and a bear as they came to attack the flock. On both occasions he killed the predators and saved the flock from destruction. He did the work of shepherding with faithfulness and devotion but was only considered the child of the family and therefore one of no significance or consequence.

Yet it was from this background that God called David to his life's work of ruling over the nation of Israel and which ultimately enabled him to make his mark upon history. In 1 Samuel 16 King Saul was ruler in Israel but God was displeased with him and so sent the prophet Samuel to Bethlehem. There the prophet met with Jesse and in turn seven of Jesse's sons were brought before the prophet. Each one may have had a fine bearing but God was not so interested in how they looked on the outside but He looked at their hearts.

Finally, David the youngest boy was sent for and he came before the prophet and God clearly told Samuel that this was the one to become ruler of Israel. There and then Samuel anointed the head of David with oil and this signified that he had been chosen by God to be king in Israel but it would be many years before he was actually crowned king and recognised as sovereign by the people.

The prophet Asaph wrote a psalm and in it he mentioned this great change from insignificance to divine appointment as king. He wrote, *"He chose David also his servant, and took him from the sheepfolds: From following the ewes great with young he brought him to feed Jacob his people, and Israel his inheritance. So he fed them according to the integrity of his heart; and guided them by the skilfulness of his hands"* (Ps. 78:70-72). So from the sheepfolds he was called by God, anointed by Samuel and destined to replace Saul as king of Israel.

In this call of David we see three great principles at work. The first is that those who are faithful to God in small things can be given responsibility for greater things. David cared for the sheep with integrity and faithfulness and so he was given responsibility for the flock of God, namely the nation of Israel. Are we faithful in small things such as maintaining our daily quiet time of Bible reading and prayer? Are we faithful in our attendance and commitment to our local church? Are we faithful in our responsibilities to family, home and work? Are we faithful in our witness and testimony to Jesus Christ? David clearly could be relied upon to do the minor things and so God gave him great responsibility. The Lord Jesus put it this way, *"He that is faithful in that which is least is faithful also in much: and he that is unjust in the least is unjust also in much"* (Luke 16:10). Let us learn to be trustworthy with the minor issues of life and only then can we ever expect responsibility for more important matters.

Secondly, we see in the experience of David the principle which is enunciated by the apostle Paul, *"…God hath chosen the weak things of the world to confound the things which are mighty"* (1 Cor. 1:27). David as the youngest son, who simply attended to his father's few sheep on the hills of Bethlehem would have been considered of little consequence. He was not a great warrior or a rich person. He was not a great scholar or a powerful man. Yet God looked upon his heart and saw integrity and devotion. He saw faith and love and so called him to become the most powerful man in the land. God is always much more interested in our availability than in our ability. He sees what the human eye cannot see and calls some of the most unlikely people to serve him in a great and full capacity. One of my heroes as I am sure some of you know is William Carey an insignificant shoemaker from Northampton who was a part time Baptist minister. He was called by God to take the gospel to India and he devoted his life to that work and was mightily used by God on the sub-continent. He helped to change the social and spiritual atmosphere of the country, becoming one of the greatest linguistic missionaries who have ever lived and the father of the modern missionary movement. So we see that God can take weak things to confound the mighty and foolish things to confound the wise.

Thirdly, we must remember that God is sovereign. He chose David and called David specifically and personally to be king of Israel. No doubt God saw a responsive heart in the shepherd boy of Bethlehem but it was God's sovereign choice to move him from tending sheep to caring for the flock of Israel. There may have been others in the land that could have done the job but God chose David. God's sovereignty does not remove our responsibility to utilize our gifts and fulfil our God-given responsibilities.

FUGITIVE ON THE RUN

The first part of David's life was to be a shepherd boy and it ended with two great events. Firstly he was anointed by Samuel to be king of Israel and secondly he killed Goliath and released Israel from the oppressive rule of the Philistines. David became a captain in the army of King Saul and was so successful that the women welcomed the victorious army with music, dancing and singing. They sang, *"Saul hath slain his thousands, and David his ten thousands"* (1 Sam. 18:7). This produced the most intense and terrible jealousy in the heart of Saul and finally his black moods caused him to seek the death of David. David managed to escape the immediate danger posed by the king but ended up for five years on the run, just one step away from death or capture from Saul and his army.

David received great help from Ahimelech the priest, from Samuel the prophet, from a group of prophets and even from the enemies of Israel the Philistines who for a time gave him protection. David was eventually joined by four hundred people made up of his own family and all discontents of the time. He was their leader and they had to live carefully as Saul with his army pursued them. It was a dangerous time for David as he was being hunted by a cruel and hostile king, yet God cared for him and protected him and helped him out of every danger. Indeed there were occasions when David had King Saul at his mercy and could have killed him. His followers even encouraged him to destroy his enemy. David, however, was a man of very great integrity and huge compassion. He realized that Saul had originally been anointed as King of Israel and so he refused to raise his hand against the anointed of the Lord and that despite the fact that the King had slipped from his position of trust in God. I am sure also that David remembered the commandment of the Lord, *"Thou shalt not kill"* (Ex. 20:13). David fully and totally trusted God to bring about the fulfilment of His will and would not use human means to hurry the process along.

This turned out to be David's training ground for the high office he would eventually hold. It was there he truly learned to trust God and to pray. It seems to have been at that period in his life that he learned many great lessons from the Lord. We must never forget that the difficulties and problems of life are not there to destroy us but are put there by the Lord to improve us and make our character more like that of our blessed Lord and Saviour Jesus Christ.

So the second period of David's life was to be a fugitive on the run from an avenging king of Israel.

THE KING OF ISRAEL

Eventually the day came when Saul and his son Jonathan were killed on the slopes of Mount Gilboa and David's enemy was dead. David then began his long and distinguished reign that was to last for forty years. Initially he did not rule over the whole of Israel but only over the southern part, namely the tribal area of Judah and there he ruled from his capital city of Hebron. The rest of Israel was ruled by a weak and ineffectual descendant of Saul named Ishbosheth. That king was kept in power through the efforts of his army commander named Abner. When Abner fell out with the king it heralded the end of the dynasty of Saul as Ishbosheth was murdered by two conspirators who felt they were doing David a favour. Such treachery was not rewarded but punished when David heard what they had done.

So David was crowned King of Israel and was acclaimed by the whole of the nation and reigned for a further thirty-three years. It was a spectacular reign but was not without its problems and some of them were of David's own making. Yet there were significant achievements.

Firstly, he conquered the citadel of Jerusalem. It had seemed an impregnable fortress and the defenders thought they were completely safe from David's besieging army. Yet David and his army did capture the city and it became the capital city of the nation. David made it even more impregnable by constructing stronger walls and made it the place to which the nation looked for guidance and leadership.

Secondly, he was a victorious warrior. He became a man of war and a great leader of his army. He was a successful general and the nations around Israel were all defeated in turn and became subservient to the people of Israel. David was the greatest force in the politics and military activities of the Middle East in 1000 B.C. So he secured and extended the frontiers of the nation and took them to their greatest extent ever in their history. He was universally recognised as a great soldier and a very courageous leader of his armed forces.

He showed very great spiritual perception and had a deep appreciation of God and this is revealed in the beauty and praise that are expressed in the psalms he wrote. For a man of such intense action who saw wars in many theatres of conflict he had a very sensitive and spiritually attuned aspect to his character and personality. It would be hard to imagine many people who showed such contrasting sides to their lives and in David we see the rich combination of action and contemplation, busyness and meditation. Here was a man who communed very deeply with God and also took an active role in the service of God. He was a man of action and a man of prayer; a man who did things and a man who worshipped God.

He also was a very wise and caring ruler in Israel. The people had a wonderful monarch who deeply cared for their needs and who exercised deep compassion in his judgments upon his subjects. This is not to say that David was perfect and as we read his life's story we find that he had many defects. For example he became proud and chose to number the people as a reflection of his own glory and this angered God and brought judgment upon the nation. He failed to deal with his corrupt and deceitful general and commander of the army Joab and this led to serious repercussions. Also he failed to exercise discipline and limitations upon his children and their behaviour. This also produces serious problems for him in later life. He committed the terrible sin of adultery with Bathsheba and arranged for her husband to be killed. Certainly the Bible does not gloss over the sins of David. However, David repented and genuinely repented of his sins as Psalm 51 makes clear and he re-established fellowship with God and was known as the "man after God's own heart". He has a deeply revered place in the history of Israel and in the pages of Holy Scripture. We have a lot to learn from David.

"David was concerned about the honour of God's Name."
Raymond Brown

CHAPTER 26

THE FAITH OF DAVID
PART 2

"David the sweeter singer of Israel."

David was a man of many parts and is still revered today as the greatest leader that the nation of Israel have ever had as their king. He was a great, powerful, wise, God honouring, just and careful ruler of the nation. The people of Israel loved him as their king and were blessed as a people because he was their monarch. He had been specially and specifically chosen by God to be leader of Israel. Yet he was a man of deep sensitivity and real awareness of God.

MUSICIAN AND SONGWRITER

David was famous for playing the harp and on more than one occasion he was called upon to play for the king. This was not at a party or a reception but at times of turbulence in the king's emotional life. King Saul was given to bouts of deep melancholy and seemed to have experienced times of deep and dark depression and it was at such times that David played for the king and it helped bring him out of his depression. David's playing had a soothing and therapeutic effect upon the king.

Also David wrote some of the greatest songs the world has ever known. He wrote nearly half of the psalms recorded in the Old Testament, including "the pearl of the psalms" namely Psalm 23 which begins, *"The LORD is my shepherd"*. David's song writing was a very rich blessing to Israel and he was known as the "sweet singer in Israel."

DANCER AND ACTOR

David led Israel in praising and thanking God by dancing at the head of the procession as the ark of the covenant of God was brought up to the city of Jerusalem. Israel followed his lead and danced before the Lord as part of their expression of praise to God. In our Western world we are reluctant to get out of our seats at church and dance before the Lord and I share that reluctance. However, I have seen African churches where members do get up and dance during the hymn singing. There was nothing unseemly about their activities and it seemed to be a cultural expression of worship to God.

Also David was a convincing actor. At one time he took refuge in the Philistine city of Gath when he was escaping from the evil intentions of King Saul. However he soon realized that he was viewed with suspicion by the Philistines and so he feigned madness and acted as someone who was totally insane. His "performance" was so convincing that he was encouraged to leave and so he escaped from the Philistines.

WARRIOR AND KING

Clearly he was a very skilful army commander and led Israel to many great and notable victories. He brought Israel to the most powerful position it has ever occupied both politically and militarily in its history. During David's time the nation was the dominant force in the whole of the Middle East. He was also a wise and compassionate leader in Israel and cared deeply about the nation over which he ruled. He was wise in the exercise of justice and led Israel in worship to God. He maintained the spiritual integrity of Israel.

FAITHFUL TO GOD

His faithfulness to God was absolute and he totally trusted in the God of Israel. We see this clearly expressed in his encounter with Goliath in 1 Samuel 17. In that chapter David achieved three notable and wonderful victories.

1. Victory over the Tongue (1 Sam. 17:22-30): David had learned a valuable lesson and it was that there are times to speak and times to keep silent. It is a lesson that we all need to learn and yet so often we are very slow to appreciate this truth.

David had been sent by his father Jesse to the Israelite army to take some supplies for his brothers who were serving as soldiers under King Saul. The army was set in battle array across a valley from the Philistine army. To David's amazement every day a Philistine voice roared out across the valley issuing a challenge to any Israelite to do battle with him. It was the giant Goliath and he mocked Israel, taunted their God and caused the most awful dread and fear amongst the soldiers of Israel. They all cowered and were utterly frightened.

David could hardly believe that no one would go out and fight the giant. No one was prepared to trust God and deal with this terrible problem that induced weakness and demoralization amongst the forces of Israel. This really showed that Israel had no godly leader at that time and there was no faith in God and His Almighty power. The nation demonstrated the truth that unbelief leads to fear.

David realized that the conflict was really between two faiths, between two deities the god Dagan of the Philistines and God, Jehovah of the Israelites. David knew there was only one true God and was prepared to fight the giant but his radiant faith was deeply offensive to his older brother Eliab. Eliab may have been big and strong but he had a heart of fear and so he mocked David by saying with anger, *"Why camest thou down hither? and with whom hast thou left those few sheep in the wilderness? I know thy pride, and the naughtiness of thine heart; for thou art come down that thou mightest see the battle"* (1 Sam. 17:28). Yet he did not know David's heart and was very quick to point the finger at him because he must have been very aware of the failings in his own heart and life.

When we realize our own failings then so often we want to highlight other people's sins so that our sins will not be exposed. The problem was the pride in the heart of Eliab and not any pride in David's. David gave a very mild reply and then simply turned away to talk with others. He had the wisdom and the personal strength to control his tongue and that was remarkable for such a young man. He did not reply to his brother's false accusations with anger or the natural inclination to justify himself or to accuse his brother of failure and sin. He did not argue, he did not return a hasty word and did not try to defend himself.

We can take a leaf out of David's book and remember that the old wartime slogan was "Careless talk costs lives". Certainly the failure to control the tongue from gossip, anger, criticism and antagonism had caused many people to be dreadfully wounded in their spirits. The hasty word may have deeply discouraged them and it can take a very long time to recover from wounding words. One of the hardest things to control is our tongues. The Apostle James in his epistle in the New Testament talks of the person who can control his tongue as being perfect. Also he says that the tongue is a little member but full of deadly poison. However, David had won a great victory over his tongue and he could control his emotions because he loved the Lord and lived close to His God.

2. Victory over the Flesh (1 Sam. 17:31-39): having gained victory over the use of his tongue and controlled his speech in the face of severe provocation then another temptation emerged. It is so often the case that when we are triumphant in one area of life that Satan sees to it that we are quickly confronted with a different kind of temptation.

David's desire to confront the giant was conveyed to the King of Israel and David was ushered into the royal presence. There he pronounced, *"Let no man's heart fail because of him; thy servant will go and fight with this Philistine"* (1 Sam. 17:32). Very quickly it was pointed out to David that he was just a boy and soldiering had been a way of life for Goliath for many years. He was a mighty man utterly familiar with the ways of combat. The implication was that David would have no chance against such a formidable foe. Yet David pointed out that he was not going to fight the giant in his own strength or with his own experience but with the Lord's power. He recalled that he had saved his father's sheep from a bear and a lion and it was God who had helped him then and it would be God who would help him fight the Philistine enemy.

THE FAITH OF DAVID: PART 2

The result was that Saul said to David, *"Go, and the LORD be with thee"* (1 Sam. 17:37). He then gave David his own suit of armour, including helmet and sword and it must have been a moment of glory when David was clothed in the king's armour. Had anyone ever worn that armour besides the king and the answer is that probably no one except Saul had put that armour on. So it must have been tempting for David to go out in front of the whole Israelite army and show that he was specially clothed in the king's armour. The difficulty was that David could hardly move while carrying such a weight because he was not used to it and so he took it all off and went out with only his shepherd's staff, sling and five smooth stones.

Clearly it was not possible for him to meet and confront the giant with man made weapons and armour. He had to follow the directives of the Lord for victory. Today we need to remember that lesson. Ultimately our weapons are not organization, efficiency, business-like methods, buildings, buses or equipment and none of these things are bad in themselves, indeed they are very good. However they will never move the spiritual giants that mock at our efforts today. Our weapons are spiritual and involve:

i.   **Prayer**: that is earnest, desperate and heartfelt.

ii. **Faith**: that believes that God is able to do impossible things.

iii. **Bible**: that is read, believed, obeyed and proclaimed.

iv. **Witness**: that is fearless and Spirit led.

v.   **Worship**: that is for the glory of God and the fullness of Christ.

So David conquered the temptation to wear the King's armour and military equipment. Instead he went out utterly trusting in God.

3. Victory over the Giant (1 Sam. 17:40-54): this was a glorious victory as the giant was felled and the people of Israel rejoiced. Yet we see a number of aspects in David's approach.

Firstly, he recalled the past. The God who had helped him to gain past victories over the lion and the bear would also help him win the fight with the giant. The blessings of the past gave him confidence in the present and he had faith to believe that God would work as He had done in the past. Our church building is called "Ebenezer" and it means "Hitherto has the Lord helped us" and it is a constant reminder that the Lord has helped us mightily in the past and it continually gives us confidence that He will bless us in the present. His character has not changed and like David of old we can have the same total confidence in the all sufficiency of God.

Secondly, David did take some practical measures. He did his utmost to be prepared for the coming fight. He took his staff, which was undoubtedly the same staff with which he had killed the bear and the lion. He also took five smooth stones out of the stream and also held onto his sling. Here we see the practical and the spiritual going together. David relied on the Lord but also took what might have been needed. I have been blessed over the years with people near me who are wonderfully practical. They may not be so gifted for a public speaking role but their support and help has been utterly invaluable and has freed me to do my spiritual ministry. We must do practical things and take wise steps under the hand of God to prepare for the future.

Thirdly, he relied upon the Lord's greatness and power. He was willing to use the shepherd skills which he possessed but he was not willing to rely upon them. He recognised that the battle was the Lord's. In preaching and teaching ministry the preacher must do everything in his power to be thoroughly prepared for delivering the message. He must do the research, prepare the outline, write up the sermon but he is utterly conscience that of themselves they are inadequate. The spiritual battle of convincing men of the truth, convicting them of sin and seeing them converted to Christ is the Lord's and ultimately it is the work of His Holy Spirit in the lives of people to whom we minister.

Fourthly, his motive and driving concern was that God's name might be honoured. He was determined to win because he wanted all those assembled that day to know that the true God did not save with spears and swords but with His own mighty arm.

We can well imagine the scene that day when an insignificant youth emerges from the army of Israel to fight against the giant champion of the Philistines. Maybe some could not bear to look because they felt that David's life would be snuffed out with one blow from the giant's sword. Indeed Goliath himself was totally incensed that they should send out this boy rather than a true fighting soldier. He uttered terrible curses as David came towards him and really felt insulted by the people of Israel. David affirmed to the giant that God would grant a victory and that was a tremendous statement of faith. David had total confidence in the greatness of the true God. He ran towards Goliath and let go with one sling shot. The stone struck the Philistine on the forehead and sank into his skull and he fell face downwards and died. So without use of sword or spear David had killed the champion of the Philistines. It was a great and momentous victory not only for David but for all of Israel in their on-going struggle with the forces of the Philistines.

We all have giants to face and fight. There are giants in our personal or family lives such as illness, depression, redundancy, retirement, higher education, new jobs and failures of all kinds. These have to be faced up to with faith and courage and so often they seem intractable but we must reach for God with His wisdom, love and power and enable Him to help us through the problems that loom so large. We must face the giants at work, in our church, in our society and a whole host of other areas of life. We must take up the weapons that the Lord has given us and spend time in His presence in prayer until we know what His will is and how we can fulfil it.

We read in Acts 13:36 that David served his generation and that must be true for us. We have only one generation to serve and that is the one we live in today. Let us help to bring about a spiritual revolution in our generation by effectively bringing the gospel to those who need to hear it today. Maybe we have slipped, sin has engulfed us and the first love has been lost, we thus need to rededicate our lives to the Lord in confession and repentance and then we can live for His glory and see the giants of our times slain and victory achieved.

"A victory inside of us is ten thousand times more glorious than any victory can be outside of us."
Henry Ward Beecher

CHAPTER 27

THE FAITH OF DAVID
PART 3

"Those sins that seem most sweet in life will prove most bitter in death."

Thomas Brooks

And what shall I more say? for the time would fail me to tell of Gedeon, and of Barak, and of Samson, and of Jephthae; of David also, and Samuel, and of the prophets. **Hebrews 11:32**

And the LORD sent Nathan unto David. And he came unto him, and said unto him, There were two men in one city; the one rich, and the other poor. The rich man had exceeding many flocks and herds: But the poor man had nothing, save one little ewe lamb, which he had bought and nourished up: and it grew up together with him, and with his children; it did eat of his own meat, and drank of his own cup, and lay in his bosom, and was unto him as a daughter. And there came a traveller unto the rich man, and he spared to take of his own flock and of his own herd, to dress for the wayfaring man that was come unto him; but took the poor man's lamb, and dressed it for the man that was come to him. And David's anger was greatly kindled against the man; and he said to Nathan, As the LORD liveth, the man that hath done this thing shall surely die: And he shall restore the lamb fourfold, because he did this thing, and because he had no pity. And Nathan said to David, Thou art the man. Thus saith the LORD God of Israel, I anointed thee king over Israel, and I delivered thee out of the hand of Saul. **2 Samuel 12:1-7**

King David was a wonderful man of God but certainly he was not perfect. Like us all he was a sinful person and at times failed to act in righteousness. His sins came back to haunt him and his relationship with a beautiful woman called Bathsheba reveals the truth of Numbers 32:23: *"...and be sure your sin will find you out."* David found those words to be true and it is a profound lesson to learn that we cannot sin with impunity; we cannot get away with sinning. There is always a price to pay when we break the laws of God.

David was blessed with exceptional gifts as a warrior, a hymn writer, a wise judge and had reached the pinnacle in Israelite society as monarch, who ruled the country with absolute power. Yet he broke the commandments of God and though he tried to hide his sin and keep it secret it was eventually exposed by the prophet Nathan. He came to David and told him a simple parable of a rich man who had many sheep and his neighbour who was poor and had only one sheep and that had been reared by hand and was loved by his family. The rich man had visitors and rather than use any of his own sheep for dinner he took the single sheep from the poor man. David was incensed by such bad behaviour and demanded to know the identity of the rich man so he could be punished. Imagine David embarrassment when Nathan said, *"You are the man!"* (2 Sam. 12:7, NKJV). David who had many wives had chosen to steal the wife of one of his most faithful soldiers.

So David's sin was known to the court and his immediate circle. Then the whole nation got to hear of it and eventually the whole world came to know of David's sin. This makes the Word of God so credible and creditable because it does not gloss over the sins of the servants of God but exposes, highlights and draws attention to them. In 2 Samuel 11 David's temptation follows the classical pattern.

THE CAUSE OF SIN: WHY DID IT HAPPEN?

The king's fall into sin was the result of being in the wrong place. He should have been with his army which was fighting a war. His men were engaged in battles with Israel's enemies the Ammonites. They were laying siege to the city of Rabbah and we read, *"But David tarried still at Jerusalem"* (2 Sam. 11:1). He was not fulfilling his responsibilities as leader of his people. In the past he had always been with them and had prayed for God's guidance in battle and for divine help for victory. Now he had not gone with the army and had stayed at home. Why did he do this?

1. Possibly he did not want to face the rigours of campaign with its travel, noise, dust and heat. He now preferred the comforts and luxuries of life in the palace at Jerusalem and so he took the soft option. He wanted to rest while others did the work. He stayed in bed while his troops slept on the hard ground. He relaxed in the shade, while his men fought in the hot sun. He felt protected and away from danger in the palace while his men risked their lives on the battlefield. So by not assuming his rightful place at the head of his army and getting involved in the battle he became prey to temptation.

   Every Christian is called to battle in prayer, in Bible study, in evangelism, in church work, in ministry, in holy living and when we decide to take it easy we become prone to temptation. We must be in the place and involved in our God given calling and take every opportunity to fulfil His will for our lives.

2. Possibly because David had achieved so much that he was now self-assured and even self-confident. He had become proud, arrogant and conceited and felt no need to join his troops. He would not condescend to join them and simply put Joab, his general in charge and sent the army off to battle. There is no suggestion that David prayed about the situation or asked God for direction. It seemed that he felt that he was the power and the sole authority in Israel. He was trying to manage without God and that is always a dangerous situation to be in. When we feel self-assured and think that we have no need to consult God and seek His divine

help, wisdom and guidance then we are very prone to making mistakes, taking wrong decisions and ending up in the mess of sin. This may not only have ruinous effect upon us but also upon the lives of other people. So we are warned by the example of David.

THE COURSE OF SIN: HOW DID IT HAPPEN?

We fully realize that the course of sin is always downward and if not arrested it will eventually lead down into the darkness and torment of hell. The first thing was that **David looked: He saw**. His sin was initially triggered by allowing his eyes to focus upon something forbidden. This was Eve's problem in the Garden of Eden. She saw that the fruit was good to look at and it was the first step towards the fall of mankind into sin. The apostle John calls it the *"lust of the eyes"* (1 John 2:16).

There are times when we cannot help what we see and that is not the problem. It is the times we can help what we see and choose to focus our attention upon certain films, television programmes, newspapers and magazines. We can actually be active in allowing our eyes to look lustfully. The problem is compounded if we feast our eyes upon things that we should avoid seeing. We may not be able to avoid the glance but the prolonged look must be utterly avoided.

David looked out from the palace roof and saw a beautiful woman bathing. Her name was Bathsheba and she was the wife of one of David's most loyal soldiers named Uriah. Uriah was away at the battle serving king and country, while David looked lustfully upon his wife.

The look fed the lust in David's heart and mind and so the next step in his downward progression is recorded. **David sent** for her. Presumably she had little choice in going because when the king sent for a subject to appear at the court it was essentially a royal command. So she arrived at the palace and was guided into the presence of the king.

The third stage was that **David seduced** her and so violated God's Law by breaking the seventh commandment:

"Thou shalt not commit adultery" (Ex. 20:14). Thus the lust of the eye had led to the lust of the flesh. So David in his passion for this woman had neglected the clear statements and commandments of the Lord to Israel. He was someone who loved God and the laws of God and knew all about the holiness of God and yet he broke at least two of the commandments. Besides breaking the seventh he also broke the tenth commandment which states. *"Thou shalt not covet…thy neighbour's wife"* (Ex. 20:17). It was to turn out to be a dreadful night of sin for David and sin is very serious in the eyes of God.

Today we live in a world that ignores God and thinks nothing of breaking His laws. Yet every thought, word and action is taken into account and will be revealed at the Day of Judgment. David had caused a great deal of ruin.

Firstly, he had come between a man and his wife in an act of adultery. Secondly he had ruined his testimony in the eyes of his close servants who knew what he had done. Thirdly he had ruined his relationship with God who was disappointed, grieved, hurt and angry by David's actions of selfish thoughtlessness. Finally, he carried scars from this sinful relationship and eventually he became heavily burdened by his guilt and sense of failure.

THE CONSEQUENCES OF SIN:
WHAT WERE THE RESULTS?

There are always consequences arising from sinful behaviour and those consequences will be negative and painful. They certainly were for King David. The first point to make is that the secret sin committed in the dark of night-time became an open and revealed sin when it was found that Bathsheba was pregnant. We read, *"And the woman conceived, and sent and told David, and said, I am with child"* (2 Sam. 11:5). The sin could not be hidden indefinitely. Today we see the breakdown of morality in our society and despite sex education in schools, which at times is of the most graphic nature, we are still witnessing teenage pregnancies, so called unwanted pregnancies, enormous numbers of abortions taking place and all sorts of family and personal dislocation as the result of sinful practices.

At this stage David showed no signs of repentance or regret or maybe he was too proud to do anything honourable at this point in time. His reaction is to compound his sinfulness by recalling Uriah from the battlefield. Once recalled David used every kind of strategy to make Uriah sleep with his wife and then any subsequent birth could be claimed as being fathered by Uriah. The strategy failed because of the integrity and upright heart of Uriah. He refused the comforts of his own home and of his own bed when he knew that his fellow soldiers were roughing it at the battle front. He refused to stay in his house when he knew that the army were in tents. He refused to take it easy and enjoy home comforts when his colleagues had to endure the harsh conditions of the army camp. So David's strategy failed because he was dealing with a good man, who was a loyal soldier and devoted subject of David.

So David sent Uriah back to the battle front with a letter for the commander Joab. The letter was a sealed message and sealed the death of Uriah. It urged Joab to put Uriah in the place of the heaviest fighting and then cause all the other Israelite soldiers to retreat. Uriah would then be killed and David would be free to marry Bathsheba the widow. Joab who was one of the great commanders of Israel but also one of the most deceitful and scheming of men followed David's orders to the letter and the result was that Uriah was killed. The man of integrity, loyalty and devotion was in effect killed by David, who had now also broken the sixth commandment, *"Thou shalt not kill"* (Ex. 20:13). The man whom David had cheated was now a murder victim of the king. This was the lowest point morally in David's life and he had committed crimes that would haunt him for the rest of his days.

We need to learn a lesson that to break the commandments of God can lead to the compounding of sinfulness in our lives as we break more laws to cover up the ones we initially broke.

After a suitable period of time to mourn the loss of her husband David called Bathsheba to the palace. There he married her and she joined his harem of wives. The result was that she produced a son for the king but we read, *"the thing that David had done displeased the LORD"* (2 Sam. 11:27). These were ominous words and eventually led to God dealing very severely with David His servant. There were painful experiences resulting from his sin for David.

Firstly, the son of Bathsheba developed a serious illness and despite all David's fasting and prayers the child was not spared. The child died seven days after it had contracted the illness and was taken straight into heaven. Indeed David said, *"I shall go to him, but he shall not return to me"* (2 Sam. 12:23). There was deep heartache for David and that must have reminded him of his sin.

Secondly God promised through his servant Nathan that calamity would come upon David from one of his own household. Eventually David's son Absalom led an armed insurrection against David and forced a hurried retreat by David across the River Jordan. David quickly left Jerusalem with his personal body guard, loyal servants and parts of his army. He was once again on the fugitive trail with his own son wanting him dead. Absalom reigned in Jerusalem but it would not be for long. Eventually the battle took place and David was victorious with Absalom slain by Joab. David wept for his son and for the carnage that had taken place in the civil war. Israel had suffered because David had sinned.

David's heart is revealed in Psalm 51 where in deep contrition and real repentance he pours out his heart to God. He fully and completely confesses his sins and casts himself upon God for forgiveness. He cried out for cleansing by saying, *"Purge me with hyssop, and I shall be clean: wash me, and I shall be whiter than snow"* (Ps. 51:7). He truly wanted to be cleansed from sin and forgiven by God. He also seeks a pure heart and says, *"Create in me a clean heart, O God; and renew a right spirit within me"* (Ps. 51:10). He also knew that it was not the externals of religious ritual and activity that God sought from His people but true hearts. So he says, *"The sacrifices of God are a broken spirit: a broken and a contrite heart, O God, thou wilt not despise"* (Ps. 51:17).

David's heart was utterly contrite and he reached out for God and for His forgiveness. Amazingly he receives that blessing and God gives him a place amongst the spiritually great people of God. He never committed such sins again and he was in communion with God for the rest of his days.

If David could fail then it must be obvious that any one can fail. We all face temptations and at times it is a desperate battle to resist them. We need to focus upon two things if we are to resist the temptation to sin.

Firstly, we need to be living in the fullness of the Spirit and thus in deep communion with God. We are reminded of a commandment in Ephesians 5:18 and that is that we should be filled with the Spirit. The marks of the fullness of the Spirit in the believer are laid out in that chapter but the filling is not once and for all. It must be a continuous, daily filling that enables us to know the power of God's Spirit in every area of our lives, especially in the face of temptation. Therefore we must do nothing that will grieve or quench the work of the Spirit in our lives.

Secondly, we need to have our minds filled with the Word of God. We remember that the Lord Jesus was full of the Word of God and when He was tempted by Satan in the wilderness He answered those temptations with the words of Holy Scripture. The Word of God was His defence in the face of temptation and it can be ours if we are willing to read, meditate, study and learn the Holy Bible. Also Psalm 119:11 says, *"Thy word have I hid in mine heart, that I might not sin against thee."* The Word of God stored up in our minds gives us great defence against the temptations we face every day.

Yet when we fail then we should confess our sins to the Lord and truly repent of them. We must seek His forgiveness and He then renews us for service and we can take up the reins of our ministry again with renewed confidence and to very rich blessing. So we learn so much from David's failure.

"Sin has two great powers; it reigns and it ruins."
John Blanchard

CHAPTER 28

THE FAITH OF DAVID
PART 4

"A friend is one who comes in when the world goes out."

Anonymous

And what shall I more say? for the time would fail me to tell of Gedeon, and of Barak, and of Samson, and of Jephthae; of David also, and Samuel, and of the prophets. Hebrews 11:32

And it came to pass, when he had made an end of speaking unto Saul, that the soul of Jonathan was knit with the soul of David, and Jonathan loved him as his own soul. And Saul took him that day, and would let him go no more home to his father's house. Then Jonathan and David made a covenant, because he loved him as his own soul. And Jonathan stripped himself of the robe that was upon him, and gave it to David, and his garments, even to his sword, and to his bow, and to his girdle. 1 Samuel 18:1-4

And Saul spake to Jonathan his son, and to all his servants, that they should kill David. But Jonathan Saul's son delighted much in David: and Jonathan told David, saying, Saul my father seeketh to kill thee: now therefore, I pray thee, take heed to thyself until the morning, and abide in a secret place, and hide thyself: And I will go out and stand beside my father in the field where thou art, and I will commune with my father of thee; and what I see, that I will tell thee. And Jonathan spake good of David unto Saul his father, and said unto him, Let not the king sin against his servant, against David; because he hath not sinned against thee, and because his

249

*works have been to thee-ward very good: For he
did put his life in his hand, and slew the Philistine,
and the LORD wrought a great salvation for all
Israel: thou sawest it, and didst rejoice: wherefore
then wilt thou sin against innocent blood, to slay
David without a cause? And Saul hearkened unto
the voice of Jonathan: and Saul sware, As the LORD
liveth, he shall not be slain. And Jonathan called
David, and Jonathan shewed him all those things.
And Jonathan brought David to Saul, and he was
in his presence, as in times past.* 1 Samuel 19:1-7

William Penn once wrote, "A true friend unbosoms
freely, advises justly, assists readily, adventures boldly, takes
all patiently, defends courageously and continues a friend
unchangeable." That statement may be couched in old fashioned English but it truly summarizes real friendship and that
was the experience between David and Jonathan. Their relationship was one of genuine friendship and very real loyalty.
It is a beautiful story of devotion despite the difficulty of circumstances and the pressure of events. It is delightful to read
this story but in our much more debased Western society the
suggestion has been made that their relationship was corrupt,
degrading and immoral. The Bible gives no credence to such
an outlook because this was a true, God-honouring friendship.

Jonathan was a prince in Israel being son of the first
king whose name was Saul. David was a very great soldier
in the king's army and was married to the king's daughter
whose name was Michal. Somehow the two men found a
deep and abiding friendship which had an enriching effect
upon them both. Someone has said that "a man is not the
whole himself; his friends are half of him." In other words
friends help to make us what we are. Bad friends can ruin
our lives, while good friends can enrich us. Jonathan was
an outstanding friend to David. The prince befriended the
former shepherd boy. The heir to the throne of Israel was
loyal to David despite the fact that David was growing in

popularity to such an extent that it would eventually ruin Jonathan's chances of becoming king.

JONATHAN ADMIRED DAVID

That admiration was never diverted despite the fact that Saul was angry with David, was jealous of David, wanted to kill David and in fact ordered Jonathan to kill David. We read in 1 Samuel 19:1, *"Saul spake to Jonathan his son, and to all his servants, that they should kill David."* Yet despite such orders Jonathan still admired David and was absolutely loyal in defending him, even in the presence of his father the king. Four characteristics of David stand out and were admired by Jonathan and would obviously have brought delight to the heart of God.

Loyalty: Jonathan described David to his father in these terms, *"his servant...David"* (1 Sam. 19:4). Saul was issuing orders to kill one of his own servants and a faithful servant who had been totally loyal. This servant had shown no pretensions to the throne, had been involved in no palace intrigues and had never been involved in any method to usurp the throne. Jonathan clearly admired this quality of loyalty in David and was willing to risk his own life to save David on a number of occasions.

Every Christian should show this characteristic of loyalty to our Saviour, Jesus Christ so that we always do His will. Also we should show loyalty to the truth of the gospel by obeying it and proclaiming it. We should also be loyal to our local church and all the members with whom we are joined in the body of Christ.

Is loyalty one of our characteristics?

Innocence: again Jonathan highlighted this quality to Saul his father and said, *"he hath not sinned against thee"* (1 Sam. 19:4). Jonathan recognised the quality of purity in the life of David and obviously admired that quality. Indeed the pure life of David acted as a rebuke to King Saul and like so many wilful sinners when confronted with a pure life he reacted with violence and without true cause. This was later seen when violence was inflicted upon the holy Son of God and He was crucified upon the cross. The same was done to Stephen, whose holy life infuriated his enemies and he was stoned to death by a violent mob.

Yet we must always maintain our innocence even in the face of adverse reactions from those who do not want to obey Christ. We as Christians are called to live good, holy and upright lives, not to get praise from people but simply out of true obedience to our Lord and Saviour Jesus Christ.

Is innocence one of our characteristics?

Service: this was another characteristic that Jonathan highlighted to his father and he said, *"his works have been to thee-ward very good"* (1 Sam. 19:4). It would seem that every-one in the court of King Saul and maybe in the wider circle of the nation of Israel were aware of David's devoted service to king and country. Jonathan admired this great quality in his friend David. Yet David's final payment for such service was to be hunted with the intention of being killed by the very king he had served so faithfully.

Thankfully our God does not react like King Saul. Our God is gracious with our failures and rich in reward for what we do in true service. Our service must take many forms such as the personal devotions of prayer and praise, the ministry of encouragement to others and the work of evangelism and of doing good. Some of the people we serve might not express gratitude and like King Saul they might turn against us but ultimately we serve the Lord and He is well pleased with our true sacrifice of service.

Is service one of our characteristics?

Courage: is also highlighted by Jonathan to the king in the following words, *"For he did put his life in his hand, and slew the Philistine, and the LORD wrought a great salvation for all Israel: thou sawest it, and didst rejoice: wherefore then wilt thou sin against inno-cent blood, to slay David without a cause?"* (1 Sam. 19:5). Clearly

Jonathan admired David's courage. Jonathan himself was a brave soldier and had killed many enemies of Israel, but it would seem that he recognized unusual bravery in David and surely that was God-given. He would have remembered how the Israelite army had trembled at the threats of Goliath and yet David had stepped out saying, *"for the battle is the LORD's, and he will give you into our hands"* (1 Sam. 17:47). Jonathan could vividly recall the fall of Goliath and the great victory Israel had over the Philistines which was all due to David's bravery.

Are we courageous or timid Christians? We need a holy boldness to declare the gospel of Jesus Christ at work, in school or college, at home or in the community. It is the truth and it is the answer to the deepest needs that people have, namely the need for their sins to be forgiven. Therefore we must take every opportunity to proclaim it to people we meet.

Is courage one of our characteristics?

So Jonathan spoke up for his friend in front of the king and highlighted the great qualities of David. The result was that the king changed his mind and said, *"As the LORD liveth, he shall not be slain"* (1 Sam. 19:6). Here Jonathan was clearly seen as the peacemaker as he spoke up for his friend and outlined the four qualities that stood out in David. Yet the peace was short lived and Saul later changed his mind and David had to escape and be a fugitive being hunted by the army of King Saul.

The lesson for us is very clear and it is that we must not look at each other to find fault but to find qualities that we can admire and praise. Let us highlight the blessings that others bestow upon us and always give credit to those who encourage and bless us.

So Jonathan demonstrated real admiration for his friend David.

"The only way to have a friend is to be one."
Ralph Waldo Emerson

CHAPTER 29

THE FAITH OF SAMUEL

PART 1

"Prayer is not the least we can do; it is the most."
John Blanchard

And what shall I more say? for the time would fail me to tell of Gedeon, and of Barak, and of Samson, and of Jephthae; of David also, and Samuel, and of the prophets. Hebrews 11:32

Now there was a certain man of Ramathaimzophim, of mount Ephraim, and his name was Elkanah, the son of Jeroham, the son of Elihu, the son of Tohu, the son of Zuph, an Ephrathite: And he had two wives; the name of the one was Hannah, and the name of the other Peninnah: and Peninnah had children, but Hannah had no children. And this man went up out of his city yearly to worship and to sacrifice unto the Lord *of hosts in Shiloh. And the two sons of Eli, Hophni and Phinehas, the priests of the* Lord, *were there. And when the time was that Elkanah offered, he gave to Peninnah his wife, and to all her sons and her daughters, portions: But unto Hannah he gave a worthy portion; for he loved Hannah: but the* Lord *had shut up her womb. And her adversary also provoked her sore, for to make her fret, because the* Lord *had shut up her womb. And as he did so year by year, when she went up to the house of the* Lord, *so she provoked her; therefore she wept, and did not eat. Then said Elkanah her husband to her, Hannah, why weepest thou? and why eatest thou not? and why is thy heart grieved? am not I better to thee than ten sons? So Hannah rose up after they had eaten in Shiloh, and after they had drunk. Now Eli the priest sat upon a seat by a post of the temple of the LORD. And she was in bitterness of soul, and prayed unto the LORD, and wept sore. And she vowed a vow, and said, O LORD of hosts, if thou wilt indeed look on the affliction of thine handmaid, and remember me, and not forget thine handmaid, but wilt give unto thine handmaid a man child, then I will give him unto the LORD all the days of his life, and there shall no razor come upon his head. And it came to pass, as she continued praying before the LORD, that Eli marked her mouth. Now Hannah, she spake in her heart; only her lips moved, but her voice was not heard: therefore Eli thought she had been drunken. And Eli said unto her, How long wilt thou be drunken? put away thy wine from thee. And Hannah answered and said, No, my lord, I am a woman of a sorrowful spirit: I have drunk neither wine nor strong drink, but have poured out my soul before the LORD. Count not thine handmaid for a daughter of Belial: for out of the abundance of my complaint and grief have I spoken hitherto. Then Eli answered and said, Go in peace: and the God of Israel grant thee thy petition that thou hast asked of him. And she said, Let thine handmaid find grace in thy sight. So the woman went her way, and did eat, and her countenance was no more sad. And they rose up in the morning early, and worshipped before the LORD, and returned, and came to their house to Ramah: and Elkanah knew Hannah his wife; and the LORD remembered her. Wherefore it came to pass, when the time was come about after Hannah had conceived, that she bare a son, and called his name Samuel, saying, Because I have asked him of the LORD.* 1 Samuel 1:1-20

In our studies of the outstanding Old Testament characters mentioned in this glorious chapter of Hebrews 11 we have come to the last name in that list. It is the man who was both a judge and a prophet and who gives his name to two books of the Old Testament and that is Samuel. Samuel was a mighty man of God and was a dominant force for spiritual good to his generation and he left a wonderful legacy of faithfulness to the Lord and devotion to God. He was good for the nation of Israel and they greatly benefited from his leadership and example.

Samuel lived in what could be described as very turbulent times in the history of Israel. It was a time of profound and deep-seated change in the life of the nation. It was very much a transition period for the people of God. Israel under the leadership of Joshua had invaded the land of Canaan and had occupied and settled into the Promised Land. That had happened four hundred years before the birth of Samuel and so by his time the people were the people of the land and had become accustomed to life in Palestine. Their borders stretched from the city of Dan in the north to the city of Beersheba in the south and from the Mediterranean Sea in the west to the land of Arabia on the eastern side of the River Jordan.

It had not been an easy four hundred years, but the troubles for Israel were largely of their own making. Time and again they rebelled against the Lord and turned their back upon Him. They worshipped idols and bowed down to them and even indulged in the sinful and evil practices associated with idolatry that were the hallmark of depravity in a pagan society. The result was that God punished His people and He exercised that judgment through invading armies that cruelly oppressed the people of God. Some of the invasions lasted for years and the yoke of indignity and oppression was deeply felt by the people of Israel. Eventually they learned their lesson and turned back to God in repentance and then cried out to Him for deliverance. The result was that God sent the people a deliverer, who was known as a judge and he raised an army that won victories over the invaders and drove them from the land of Israel. Usually the people followed the Lord with faithfulness for the rest of the life of the victorious judge, but when he died the sad fact was that the cycle started again.

Some of the judges are mentioned in Hebrews 11 such as Barak, Gideon, Jephthah and Samson.

Samuel lived at the end of the period of the judges and it was a difficult time for the nation. In many ways Israel was not a united people. They were twelve tribes who tended to be a loose confederation with each other but often acted alone and even against each other. Their commonality consisted of an identical history, identical forefathers and a common religious life that was centred upon worship to God in the tabernacle that was pitched in the town of Shiloh. Yet by the time Samuel was born many things had gone wrong in Israel and certain changes were being implemented.

1. A strong enemy was becoming entrenched in the coastal region near the Mediterranean Sea. This was the seafaring nation of the Philistines who had become a major thorn in the side of Israel because as a nation they occupied the coastal plain in five strongly fortified cities. Samson had won some notable victories over this powerful and hostile people but their final subjugation would only come under the leadership of King David.

2. The time of the judges was coming to a close and the people were clamouring for a new system of government. They wanted a king to rule over them and so in Samuel's lifetime came the rise of the monarchy in Israel that would centralize power and give a genuine focus for national unity. That unity would not last for long but while it lasted it was a powerful and potent force for national self-determination.

3. Samuel was the last of the judges and essentially the first of the prophets. This was because God was starting to speak to the people through prophets and this would lead to the great prophetic tradition that would emerge in Israel. That tradition would include the great prophets of Elijah, Elisha, Jonah, Isaiah and many more right up to the last of the prophets namely John the Baptist. So Samuel was "the last and the greatest of the judges and the first of the prophets" (Martin). Acts 3:24 makes this point very clear, *"Yea, and all the prophets from*

Samuel and those that follow after…" and makes it quite clear that Samuel was the fountainhead of Israelite prophetic tradition. Also he was considered one of the most outstanding prophets and spiritual leaders that Israel ever experienced. This is seen in the words that God spoke through Jeremiah, *"Then said the Lord unto me, Though Moses and Samuel stood before me…"* (Jer. 15:1). Clearly the idea is that these were the two outstanding characters from the earlier history of Israel. Moses represented the law, while Samuel represented the prophets. So Samuel was without a doubt a great man of God. So his life and work can be summarized as "The earliest of the great Hebrew prophets after Moses and the last of the judges" (Davis).

SAMUEL AND PRAYER

Samuel has been described as "the man who had God's ear" (Herbert Lockyer). God listened to Samuel and answered his prayers in remarkable and wonderful ways. Prayer was the central aspect in the life of Samuel and it was prayer that was the major factor in making and sustaining Samuel as the great leader of Israel that he became. We will focus upon three aspects of prayer in the life and times of the prophet Samuel.

HE WAS BORN AS A RESULT OF PRAYER

Samuel was the son of godly parents who were faithful in their attendance at Shiloh to worship God. His father's name was Elkanah and he had two wives, the first was named Penninah and she had many children, while his second wife was named Hannah and she was childless. Yet it was this childless wife that became the mother of Samuel. Elkanah was a member of the tribe of Levi, which was the priestly tribe in Israel and he lived with his family in the tribal area of Ephraim, because Levi had no tribal territory of their own. He was a godly man who, with his family went up to Shiloh every year to offer sacrifices to God. Yet he seemed to have no idea of the tensions in his family.

The tension was between his two wives. Penninah was an adversary to Hannah and provoked her and made her fret about the fact that she had no children. It seemed as if the pressure upon Hannah was compounded each year when they went up to Shiloh to worship God. Penninah seems to have gloried in the fact that she had children and mocked Hannah who was childless. In those days it was a deep source of shame to be barren. Hannah felt the provocation very deeply and was badly wounded in her spirit and so she went into the presence of God to pray. As she prayed her heart was filled with bitterness, her eyes were stung by tears of weeping and she prayed to God and before the Lord she made a vow.

Her vow was as follows, *"O Lord of hosts, if thou wilt indeed look on the affliction of thine handmaid, and remember me, and not forget thine handmaid, but wilt give unto thine handmaid a man child, then I will give him unto the Lord all the days of his life, and there shall no razor come upon his head"* (1 Sam. 1:11). It was a cry of anguish wrung from a deeply troubled heart but the words were not uttered out loud. Her mouth moved but no sound was heard and the priest who was named Eli observed her. He had never seen anything like this behaviour and his reaction was to assume that she was drunk and so he started to rebuke her and condemned her for taking too much wine. However, with gracious humbleness Hannah explained that she was not drunk but was pouring out her soul to the Lord. Clearly her sincerity impinged upon Eli and he immediately changed his tune and blessed her and prayed that God would grant her request.

That cry from a desperate, passionate heart was the sort of prayer to which God would listen. God does not want the tepid, insipid, caricature of prayer but wants our prayer to be deeply felt burdens. It is not eloquence but sincerity and passion that the Lord looks for in us as we pray. It is prayer from the heart and that was Hannah's prayer and God answered her prayer in wonderful way.

God gave her a son and that son was named Samuel. The name "Samuel" has various meanings. It could mean "heard" and that is in line with the fact that God heard Hannah's prayer. It could mean "asked of God" because he was the direct result of her request to God for a son. It could mean "offering of God" because Hannah gave that little boy back to the Lord as a living offering. It could mean "appointed by God" and certainly Samuel was appointed by God for powerful and strong leadership in Israel. Hannah subsequently had three further sons and two daughters but we do not know their names. They were totally eclipsed by the greatness of Samuel.

Samuel was given to the Lord and grew up with the High Priest, Eli and lived with him and there Samuel served the Lord in the tabernacle that was sited in Shiloh. Every year Hannah faithfully visited her son with new clothes and also monitored his development. During those formative years Samuel became a faithful servant of God and that was despite the fact that the two sons of Eli were evil and broke God's laws. They abused both the people who came to worship and the sacrifices they offered and Eli seems to have been powerless to prevent them abusing their position. Eventually God sent a message to Eli through the young boy Samuel. Josephus the ancient historian suggests that Samuel was just twelve years of age when he heard God's message and then related it to Eli the next day. The message was sad news and was a deep grief to Samuel and it was that Eli's sons would die and that soon afterwards so would Eli himself.

Samuel's influence became extensive and people from all parts of the country heard about him and recognised him as a prophet of God. We read, *"And all Israel from Dan even to Beersheba knew that Samuel was established to be a prophet of the* Lord*"* (1 Sam. 3:20). Also we read, *"And the child Samuel grew on, and was in favour both with the* Lord*, and also with men"* (1 Sam. 2:26). Thus Samuel developed into a real man of God and was clearly set apart to be God's chosen leader in Israel. Thus the man who was born as the result of passionate prayer became the prepared leader and prophet to the people of God.

HE WON MILITARY VICTORIES
THROUGH PRAYER

"Samuel had been born in answer to prayer and his name constantly reminded him of the power of prayer and of the necessity of maintaining holy intimacy with God. Samuel deemed it a sin not to pray for others" (Herbert Lockyer). The message he had from God that he relayed to Eli came true. The sons of Eli were killed in battle against the Philistines and the Ark of the Covenant was captured. When Eli heard the terrible news he fell back and broke his neck and he died at the age of ninety-eight. Eli had been a sort of priest and judge in Israel for forty years but he ended his days in desperate unhappiness. However the Ark of the Covenant was returned to Israel by a miracle of God and then under the leadership of Samuel Israel inflicted defeat upon their enemies.

Samuel gathered the armies of Israel and called the nation to repentance. They fasted and sacrificed to the Lord but the Philistines heard of Israel's gathering and mustered their forces to go to battle with Israel. Yet *"Samuel cried unto the Lord for Israel; and the Lord heard him"* (1 Sam. 7:9). God sent terrifying thunder amongst the Philistine army that sent the soldiers into a blind panic. At this Israel took advantage to attack and inflicted heavy losses upon the Philistines. Never again did that nation invade Israel in the days of Samuel. As long as he was at the helm of national leadership the Philistines did not invade.

The place of victory was commemorated as "Ebenezer" and that means "Thus far has the Lord helped us". It was a monument to the fact that Israel's victory was due to God's greatness and that help had come through the prayers of Israel's leader, Samuel. He knew the power of prayer and God was moved to act in direct response to the prayers of His servant. Do we find our prayer actually moving the hand of God to act?

SAMUEL WAS IN CONSTANT PRAYER

We read, *"Moreover as for me, God forbid that I should sin against the Lord in ceasing to pray for you..."* (1 Sam. 12:23).

THE FAITH OF SAMUEL: PART 1

Even though Israel had moved away from total trust in God Samuel continued to pray for the nation and refused to give up his responsibility on behalf of the people. Samuel took the need for intercession very seriously and is one of the great prayer warriors of Holy Scripture. He is an outstanding example of someone who believed in prayer, practiced prayer and saw God answer his prayers in many wonderful ways.

Prayer was an integral part of the life of Samuel and it was the essential secret to his success as a leader. It was the foundation of his very being and it should be the same for all who are followers of the Saviour. Prayer should be a major focus in life of every Christian and to neglect prayer is one of the gravest problems in a believer's life. Prayer is not limelight work and is not an easy work to undertake. Yet it is the most powerful activity which any Christian can perform for God. It is activity that touches God and which brings great spiritual influence into our lives and circumstances and into the lives of those around us. P. T. Forsyth has written, "All sin can be traced to prayerlessness" and I am sure that he is right. It is obvious that when we keep close to the Lord in prayer and communion then sin is kept at bay. When we neglect that vital relationship then sin seems to become dominant in our lives and our work for God becomes weak and ineffective. May we be enabled by the Spirit of God to keep close to the Lord and in regular touch and contact with Him. There we will be protected from sin and be given power to serve Him in fullness.

Certainly this was the experience of Samuel who was genuinely a man of prayer and that was demonstrated in the power he exercised for the good of the nation of Israel. The connection between genuine prayer and real spiritual power is demonstrated time and again in Holy Scripture and can be our experience today as those who follow the Lord Jesus Christ.

"Abandon the secret chamber and the spiritual life will decay."
Isaac Watts

CHAPTER 30

THE FAITH OF SAMUEL
PART 2

*"Samuel had to reprove the king as well as the people...
His faithfulness to God's word might easily
have cost him his life..."*

Raymond Brown

*And what shall I more say? for the time would fail
me to tell of Gedeon, and of Barak, and of Samson,
and of Jephthae; of David also, and Samuel, and of
the prophets.*   Hebrews 11:32

*Then Samuel took a vial of oil, and poured it upon
his head, and kissed him, and said, Is it not because
the LORD hath anointed thee to be captain over his
inheritance? When thou art departed from me to
day, then thou shalt find two men by Rachel's sepulchre in the border of Benjamin at Zelzah; and they
will say unto thee, The asses which thou wentest to
seek are found: and, lo, thy father hath left the care of
the asses, and sorroweth for you, saying, What shall
I do for my son? Then shalt thou go on forward from
thence, and thou shalt come to the plain of Tabor, and
there shall meet thee three men going up to God to
Bethel, one carrying three kids, and another carrying three loaves of bread, and another carrying a
bottle of wine: And they will salute thee, and give
thee two loaves of bread; which thou shalt receive
of their hands. After that thou shalt come to the hill
of God, where is the garrison of the Philistines: and
it shall come to pass, when thou art come thither to*

the city, that thou shalt meet a company of prophets coming down from the high place with a psaltery, and a tabret, and a pipe, and a harp, before them; and they shall prophesy: And the Spirit of the LORD will come upon thee, and thou shalt prophesy with them, and shalt be turned into another man. And let it be, when these signs are come unto thee, that thou do as occasion serve thee; for God is with thee. And thou shalt go down before me to Gilgal; and, behold, I will come down unto thee, to offer burnt offerings, and to sacrifice sacrifices of peace offerings: seven days shalt thou tarry, till I come to thee, and shew thee what thou shalt do. And it was so, that when he had turned his back to go from Samuel, God gave him another heart: and all those signs came to pass that day. And when they came thither to the hill, behold, a company of prophets met him; and the Spirit of God came upon him, and he prophesied among them. And it came to pass, when all that knew him beforetime saw that, behold, he prophesied among the prophets, then the people said one to another, What is this that is come unto the son of Kish? Is Saul also among the prophets? And one of the same place answered and said, But who is their father? Therefore it became a proverb, Is Saul also among the prophets? And when he had made an end of prophesying, he came to the high place. And Saul's uncle said unto him and to his servant, Whither went ye? And he said, To seek the asses: and when we saw that they were no where, we came to Samuel. And Saul's uncle said, Tell me, I pray thee, what Samuel said unto you. And Saul said unto his uncle, He told us plainly that the asses were found. But of the matter of the kingdom, whereof Samuel spake, he told him not. And Samuel called the people together unto the LORD to Mizpeh; And said unto the children of Israel, Thus saith the LORD God of Israel, I brought up Israel out of Egypt, and delivered you out of the hand of the Egyptians, and out of the hand of all kingdoms, and of them that oppressed you: And ye have this day rejected your God, who himself saved you out of all your adversities and your tribulations; and ye have said unto him, Nay, but set a king over us. Now therefore present yourselves before the LORD by your tribes, and by your thousands. And when Samuel had caused all the tribes of Israel to come near, the tribe of Benjamin was taken. When he had caused the tribe of Benjamin to come near by their families, the family of Matri was taken, and Saul the son of Kish was taken: and when they sought him, he could not be found. Therefore they enquired of the LORD further, if the man should yet come thither. And the LORD answered, Behold he hath hid himself among the stuff. And they ran and fetched him thence: and when he stood among the people, he was higher than any of the people from his shoulders and upward. And Samuel said to all the people, See ye him whom the LORD hath chosen, that there is none like him among all the people? And all the people shouted, and said, God save the king.

1 Samuel 10:1-24

Samuel is the last of the famous and spiritual great Old Testament saints to be mentioned in this wonderful chapter of Hebrews 11. He was the last of the judges and in his lifetime he saw the end of that era known to us as that of the judges in the nation of Israel. He saw the rise of the monarchy and the centralizing of power in the throne of the king. He was also the first of the prophets and became the fountainhead of a prophet tradition whereby God communicated to His people by means of specially raised up men who were supernaturally given the truth by God and were given courage to proclaim that truth to the nation of Israel.

Samuel is remembered as a man of prayer. His birth was as the result of his mother's sincere and passionate prayer to God for a son. He won military victories over Israel's enemies as the result of spending time in prayer with God. Also he seemed to live in an atmosphere of prayerfulness. He was constantly in prayer and fulfilled the New Testament injunction to *"pray without ceasing"* (1 Thess. 5:17). Samuel was a man of prayer but that was the springboard for action. He was a man of action.

SAMUEL WAS A NAZARITE

Before his birth his mother Hannah had promised God that *"I will give him unto the LORD all the days of his life, and there shall no razor come upon his head"* (1 Sam. 1:11). This was the Nazarite vow for her son and it essentially meant that he was to be separated from other people and was to be fully consecrated to God. The rules of a Nazarite were outlined in Numbers 6 and were threefold,

i. Abstinence from wine and anything to do with the vine.
ii. Hair was to be uncut.
iii. There was to be no contact with death or corpses.

So a Nazarite was known by his abstinence and uncut hair. Samson had been a Nazarite and had led Israel to some great and notable military victories but there were times when he violated his Nazarite vows, there were no such lapses recorded in the life of Samuel.

SAMUEL AND POWER

Samuel rose to great prominence in the nation of Israel and he exercised considerable power over the nation. He was both a spiritual and political force amongst the people of Israel. He seemed to combine all the most powerful offices of state in his own hands. He seems to have led Israel in worship to God and so was the head of the nation's religious life. He was the person who judged disputes amongst the people and so he was head of the judicial system. He was also leader of the secular or political aspects of his people. It was as if he combined the roles of Archbishop of Canterbury, the Lord Chancellor and the Prime Minister.

HIS SPIRITUAL WORK

Samuel was God's chosen leader in Israel and he belonged to the priestly tribe of Levi. He had grown up helping the High Priest serve God in the Tabernacle that had been pitched in Shiloh. He had a great reputation, among the people, as someone who was in touch with God and who reflected the character of God. He was marked out as a man of God who took over the priestly leadership of Israel following Eli's death by establishing an altar and offering sacrifices to the Lord. Clearly he led Israel in worship.

HIS JUDICIAL WORK

Samuel established himself as a sort of circuit judge and each year he went round the circuit through the cities of Bethel, Gilgal, Mizpah and back to Ramah. In each place he set up a sort of magistrate's court and there he dispensed justice and arbitrated in disputes amongst the people. He also dispensed wisdom and the teaching of the law to the people. In some senses this was also Samuel acting as a civil administrator for the nation as he was the only national authority in the land at that time.

In old age he passed on certain responsibilities to his sons but sadly they lacked the integrity and honest character of their father. They were more interested in money than justice and so took bribes and perverted the course of justice. They had a legal system but not a justice system. They allowed the richest people who could pay the highest bribe to get their own way and so avoid the consequences of their criminal activity. They made a mockery of the good and sound legal system that Samuel had so meticulously built up.

HIS POLITICAL WORK

The moral failure of Samuel's sons, together with the obviously powerful monarchical systems of the surrounding nations caused the leaders of Israel to ask Samuel for a king.

They wanted him to select someone who could be anointed as monarch and would lead the nation with a centralized authority. The request caused deep grief to the heart of Samuel as he felt rejected and disowned. However, when he sought God in prayer the Lord answered him by telling him to give them a king. The drawbacks of having a monarch were pointed out, namely sons to be soldiers in a standing army, taxes to pay for royal upkeep and so on but the people still demanded a king. It was not simply a matter of rejecting Samuel but in some ways the nation was rejecting God. They wanted a visible, earthly symbol of their national power and greatness and that symbol was to be a king. So Samuel exercised his power and influence by becoming a kingmaker. Indeed he was used by God to anoint two men as king.

KING SAUL

The first king of Israel came from the tribe of Benjamin and his name was Saul. He was a humble man who never sought political power or national influence. Indeed he tried to hide from the responsibility of being king. Yet he was anointed with oil by the prophet Samuel and became the first monarch to reign over God's people. At first he was a good king who won some notable victories and exercised a strong but just rule over the people of Israel. Yet when he was established he became proud, arrogant and wanted to be the spiritual, as well as the secular leader of Israel. He also became a jealous, vindictive and unstable person, who certainly had some psychological and emotional problems in his personality. Eventually God rejected him from being king.

KING DAVID

As Saul became more and more unreliable and was personally disintegrating Samuel felt deeply disappointed. He was bitterly disillusioned with the one he had anointed king of Israel. Indeed Samuel grieved over the failure of the king and parted company from the one who now ruled Israel.

THE FAITH OF SAMUEL: PART 2

Samuel was so deeply troubled and worried that he seemed to become almost distraught and depressed. He worried about the present and future problems that faced his people. Yet clearly God had the next phase of Israel's development and history well in hand. God had already chosen a successor and the replacement for the throne was being prepared. That replacement turned out to be the shepherd boy of Bethlehem, David who was to become the greatest and most godly ruler the nation of Israel has ever had.

Samuel was called by God to rise out of his depression and journey to Bethlehem where he was to anoint a son of Jesse as the new king of Israel. This was not as easy as it sounds because though Samuel grieved over Saul he also feared the unstable monarch. Samuel had been the courageous leader of Israel but was now reduced to fear by an unpredictable king who would not take kindly to the prophet anointing another man as king. He would not view with favour a rival to the throne of Israel. So Samuel had to take care.

The sad fact is that when we are worried or fearful some of our best qualities leave us and we may act out of character. This was true for Samuel and the normally fearless prophet became terribly frightened but he was still in touch with God and that enabled him to do what was right and what he did would turn out to be best for the nation. The Lord in a wonderful manner quietly reassured his servant and enabled him to go to Bethlehem as part of a routine journey to offer sacrifices and bring praise and worship on behalf of the people of the town.

So Samuel conquered his despair, depression, fear and worry and journeyed to the town of Bethlehem. He met with Jesse and instructed that his son was to be brought before him. To Samuel this oldest son looked strong and kingly and he felt sure that he would be king of Israel. However the Lord said, "No." This happened to all seven sons as they in turn came before the prophet. They were strong, tall and capable but not one of them was acceptable to God. So here God teaches the prophet and therefore us two very important lessons.

DON'T BE IMPATIENT

When Eliab the first son came before the prophet it would seem that Samuel almost had the oil out to anoint him before he truly consulted God. This was true for all seven sons but God simply instructed him to wait and listen for the voice of instruction that would truly indicate who the new king would be. Samuel must have wondered when the seventh son was rejected whether the right one would ever be found.

DON'T BE MISLED

Samuel with the first sons was very impressed by their outward appearances. They gave the right impression and seemed to have the right physical qualifications for ruling over God's people. We have a tendency to judge people by outward appearances as we look at how they dress and listen to the way in which they speak, yet God has a deeper and much more exacting standard by which to measure people. It wasn't height but heart that God looked for and eventually the youngest son David was called from the fields where he tended his father's sheep. He was the one who would replace King Saul and so God said to Samuel, *"Arise, anoint him: for this is he"* (1 Sam. 16:12). God looked beyond the superficial and saw in David a heart of love, faith and devotion which was clearly missing in the other sons. Indeed God had said to Samuel when the eldest son had been brought before him, *"Look not on his countenance, or on the height of his stature; because I have refused him: for the LORD seeth not as man seeth; for man looketh on the outward appearance, but the LORD looketh on the heart"* (1 Sam. 16:7).

So we see the priorities of God are never physical or material but spiritual and eternal. The values and priorities of God are not focused on the outward appearance but are centred upon the heart. It is what we are in our character and in our personality that count with God and in David God saw *"a man after his own heart"* (1 Sam. 13:14). Here was a man who had spiritual priorities and who had real and genuine faith. Here was a man who cared for people and who wanted to bring glory to the name of God. Here was a man who was concerned for others before himself. Here was a man who had been found faithful in the fulfilment of his work as a shepherd of sheep and who would now be given responsibility to be a shepherd of the nation of Israel. He had been faithful in performing small matters and so was rewarded by God with being given responsibility for greater things.

So Samuel anointed David to be king over Israel. However it would be some time before David was ready to take on the responsibility of being king. He would have to endure many trials and hardships, many difficulties and dangers before eventually he would be crowned as King of Israel. His reign would be splendid and glorious. It would powerful and mighty. It would make Israel the foremost power in the Middle East and in his reign and that of his son Solomon the nation would reach the zenith of wealth and greatness. However the prophet Samuel would not witness any of that glory but would be translated into the glory of God's presence well before.

SAMUEL'S DEATH

We read these words, *"Now Samuel was dead, and all Israel had lamented him, and buried him in Ramah"* (1 Sam. 28:3). Samuel the last of the judges and the first of the prophets eventually left this life and entered into the next. He had led Israel with integrity and courage through one of its greatest transition periods and he left an indelible mark upon its history. Two books of the Bible are named after him, not because he wrote them but because he features so strongly in them and so we can read of his exploits to this day. However even in death there was a ministry on earth to do.

Saul in an appalling act of sinfulness and wilful disobedience went to consult a medium or a woman who dabbled with evil spirits. Such activities were expressly forbidden as practices in Israel and they had been purged from the land by King Saul but because he could hear no communication from the Lord he chose to consult a medium who lived in Endor. He went in disguise but the whole experience was terrifying both for the woman and for the king. The consultation became a conversation between Saul and the dead Samuel. The message to Saul was deeply disturbing and he was simply reminded of his sin and disobedience to God and that the kingdom would be given to David. Also Israel under Saul's leadership would be defeated by the Philistines and the Lord now refused to communicate with Saul any longer. All that Samuel said to Saul came to pass and eventually Saul was defeated and died on the battlefield and David finally became ruler of Israel.

May we like Samuel be faithful to the Lord in all things, including prayer and proclamation of the truth of the gospel. Prayer is so necessary as we talk to God about the people and proclamation is vital as we talk to the people about God.

"Remember that whilst we are worrying about our present problems God is already planning something for us about which at present we know nothing."

Raymond Brown

PAUL YOUNG

The Bitter Spirit: The Deadly Effects of Bitterness*

Bitterness is a deeply destructive emotion. It can develop in our spirits like infection in a wound. It can make us ineffective and useless for God's service and could undermine the work of our church. A bitter reaction will always undermine the integrity of the gospel because the gospel is a message that conquers bitterness.

The Lord Jesus took all our bitterness on the cross where He paid the ultimate price for sin. So in Christ we can find release from the bondage that bitterness produces. May God grant us the grace to always leave bitterness at the feet of the Saviour so that we can live life unburdened by the weight of a bitter spirit which ultimately will cause the most damage to ourselves.

To Be Like Jesus: Studies in the Fruit of the Spirit*
"But the fruit of the Spirit is love, joy, peace, patience, kindness, goodness, faithfulness, gentleness and self-control" (Gal. 5:22-23).

The New Testament places an abundance of emphasis upon Christian fruitfulness. Indeed Jesus says that we can recognize true Christians from those who are false by their fruit. He said, *"by their fruit you will recognize them"* (Matt. 7:20, NIV). So this is an important subject with strong implications for us today.

We can also say that the fruit of the Spirit was most fully and most wonderfully witnessed in the life of the Lord Jesus. He is our example of someone who truly lived the fruit of the Spirit. We are called to walk in His footsteps, to be like Him and to show the nine-fold fruit of the Spirit in our lives as Christians.

*The End of a Nation: Studies of Obadiah**

*The Friend Abraham and the Promise of God Isaac**

*Understanding the Bible**
Inspiration, Inerrancy & Interpretation

Outreach Through the Local Church
Problems and needs

*The New Age Movement: A Cunningly Devised Fable**
A detailed look at this movement

Raging Waves: Studies in the Epistle of Jude

*Cunningly Devised Fables**
A look at 13 cults and religions and an overview of
their characteristics

The Challenge of Revival
A look back at the 1904 Welsh Revival and a challenge
for us in the present

The Diary of a Prophet
Studies in the book of Haggai

A Glimmer of Light
Studies in the book of Lamentations

All books available from:
31, Fairmeadows, Maesteg, South Wales, CF34 9JL

*Books available from 🔲 **GOSPEL FOLIO PRESS**
www.gospelfolio.com • (905)-835-9166